Real World
POSTSCRIPT®

Techniques From POSTSCRIPT Professionals

▲▼ Addison-Wesley Publishing Company, Inc.   Reading, Massachusetts · Menlo Park, California · New York

Real World
POSTSCRIPT®

Techniques From POSTSCRIPT
Professionals

Edited by Stephen F. Roth

Don Mills, Ontario · Wokingham, England · Amsterdam · Bonn · Sydney · Singapore · Tokyo · Madrid · San Juan

Many of the designations used by manufacturers and sellers to distinguish their products are claimed as trademarks. Where those designations appear in this book, and Addison-Wesley was aware of a trademark claim, the designations have been printed in initial caps or all caps.

The name POSTSCRIPT® is a registered trademark of Adobe Systems Incorporated. All instances of the name POSTSCRIPT in the text are references to the POSTSCRIPT *language* as defined by Adobe Systems Incorporated, unless otherwise stated. The name POSTSCRIPT also is used as a product trademark of Adobe Systems' implementation of the POSTSCRIPT language interpreter.

Library of Congress Cataloging-in-Publication Data

Real world POSTSCRIPT.

Includes index.
1. Desktop publishing. 2. POSTSCRIPT (Computer program language) I. Roth, Stephen F., 1958–
Z286.D47R4 1988   686.2′2   88-16608
ISBN 0-201-06663-7

ISBN 0-201-06663-7
ABCDEFGHIJ-AL-898
First printing, October 1988

Contents

v

Foreword

Randy Adams
President,
Emerald City
Software

In 1985 John Warnock and Chuck Geschke gave us a clearly superior way to create graphics and text with a computer. The preeminence of the POSTSCRIPT® language is validated by the fact that hundreds of thousands of consumers have purchased laser printers with POSTSCRIPT language interpreters inside. While they may not tell you that they bought their printers because of the POSTSCRIPT interpreter, they will tell you that it was because these printers produce better graphics than anything else on the market.

While POSTSCRIPT has earned its reputation as the industry standard page description language, there are those who will tell you that it is more than that; it is a programming language that also draws. Caged inside a printer, it is hard to imagine the POSTSCRIPT interpreter as anything more than a printing engine, but this will change. Display POSTSCRIPT™ will soon unleash the interpreter from the bounds of the printer and turn it free on our screens. It will be impossible to consider POSTSCRIPT as anything less than a formal programming language.

This book represents, I believe, the first treatment of POSTSCRIPT as a formal language. The four chapters by Bill Woodruff, which form the backbone of the text, explore the intricacies of POSTSCRIPT in the context of a formal language while providing many insightful examples of highly efficient coding which you will find immediately useful. Bill's chapters set the tone for the rest of the book where you will find an incredible number of techniques and examples of real POSTSCRIPT programs that you can apply to your own work.

Secondly, and just as significantly, this is the first book about POSTSCRIPT written by people who use the POSTSCRIPT language regularly as part of their craft. Designers, illustrators, and software developers are all represented among the authors. Simon Tuckett's treatment of POSTSCRIPT as a design tool (Chapter 1) and Michael Fryd's contribution on device independence (Chapter 3) provide essential guidelines for designers and programmers alike. Jim Von Ehr, Bill Woodruff, and

Michael Mace's treatment of type (Chapters 4 through 9) provide a wealth of information on how the font mechanism works and how to go about building your own fonts. Steve Roth and Pat Wood's discussions of gray scales and color (Chapters 10 through 12) unlock the secrets of halftoning and color separations. Real POSTSCRIPT programming projects are presented in the Projects from the Pros section (Chapters 13 through 16). Since most of us learned POSTSCRIPT by looking at the programs of others, *Real World POSTSCRIPT* is a real find.

Steve Roth has done a masterful job of compiling this anthology of POSTSCRIPT gems by the experts, the people you would give your eye teeth to sit down and talk with when your program bombs and you're about to give up. As you read this book, you know that these are the words of experience, written by those who have consistently stayed up until 2 a.m. to stomp that last bug in the code. There are literally hundreds of thousands of hours of POSTSCRIPT programming experience represented on these pages, and they're sure to save you time and effort. *Real World POSTSCRIPT* is a breakthrough book, a mandatory reference for all POSTSCRIPT programmers.

Introduction

Steve Roth

In November of 1984, at the monthly meeting of The Lunch Group, an informal gathering of computer journalists and other interested parties, I first heard about POSTSCRIPT. Of course I didn't know at the time that it was called POSTSCRIPT, or what it was, really. But I listened carefully, as we all did, when hypertext visionary Ted Nelson explained to us that Apple was about to release an amazingly powerful computer-cum-laser printer built around what he called a full-blown "Forth-like" language.

We listened carefully, but with blank stares. First, why put a computer in a printer? Next, why write a whole new language and put it in there? Even those of us who were exploring inexpensive desktop alternatives to traditional typesetting were at a loss to understand exactly what all this meant.

Then came January of 1985—the LaserWriter, POSTSCRIPT, Page-Maker—the rest is history. The POSTSCRIPT language, in particular, has been the prime mover in the incredible creativity that desktop publishing has engendered. And a few pioneers were working even then to tap the full powers of POSTSCRIPT, going beyond the admittedly limited capabilities of the early crop of programs. Those people were pushing the limits of POSTSCRIPT devices even as the devices were emerging. Several of those people have come together in this book to offer their experiences, and to show how they've done what they've done.

So there are two goals for this book. First, it talks about the realities of POSTSCRIPT devices—what they actually do as opposed what POSTSCRIPT does in theory.

In talking to POSTSCRIPT users day in and day out for years, I've found that most don't know some of the basic realities of working with POSTSCRIPT devices. Users who work with gray-scale images don't know the default screen frequency and angle for the LaserWriter (even Adobe's green book errs here) or the Linotronic. And very few realize that the frequency and angle you request aren't generally what you get. Few font designers realize that there are ways to improve the quality of their typefaces at small sizes (though not, currently, with type-scaling hints as "intelligent" as Adobe's).

Second, this book shows what real people are doing with POSTSCRIPT, from designers and illustrators all the way through programmers and inveterate hackers. While POSTSCRIPT can theoretically create a character the size of Rhode Island, few people are actually doing that. This book shows how people actually use POSTSCRIPT, with (sometimes lengthy) examples of their code.

One of the big questions we asked when we conceived this book was, who should we write it for? Especially with the new crop of POSTSCRIPT tools on the market, we had to wonder whether the thousands who bought the blue and red books still wanted or needed to know about coding in POSTSCRIPT. The answer was a resounding yes, but the question remained: who is it for?

Some thought we should write it for programmers, since they are the only ones who would want such a thing in this day and age of wysiwyg. Some thought it should be for designers, since there isn't a really good book on POSTSCRIPT that designers can understand. Others thought that advanced desktop publishers—service bureau operators and the like—were the ones who really needed it, since they are the ones wrestling with multiple POSTSCRIPT-generating applications and multiple output devices.

I thought it should be for all those people, and since I'm the editor, I won.

This is a forager's book. It's a book for those who like to root around in piles of interesting stuff, absconding with the gems they uncover. I wanted there to be treasures here for every level of POSTSCRIPT user, from the designer who can't do what he wants with wysiwyg programs, to the service bureau operator whose Linotronic keeps timing out on complicated halftone pages, to the programmer who wants some neat hacks for writing fast software drivers. There is manna here for all those appetites.

You will not find the whole POSTSCRIPT language laid out on a platter for you. This book is not a comprehensive discussion of POSTSCRIPT, nor does it purport to cover every aspect equally. That's already been done. This is a smorgasbord for POSTSCRIPT users, filled with main dishes, appetizers, and tidbits. You will find POSTSCRIPT cut up into slices so it's more palatable, and in some cases it's fed to you with a silver spoon. In other cases, where the code gets really deep, you will need to tear it off the bone and chew it yourself. There's no way around it, because this is the real world.

Since each of the authors takes a different approach to POSTSCRIPT, you'll also find a lot of variance in style—in both the writing and the code itself. It was very important to me to let the authors speak in their own voices, to let their experiences of working with POSTSCRIPT come through. Though this book has been edited for accuracy and the trivialities of grammatical style, an effort was made to leave each author's work intact and complete. As a result, you may find some redundancy and some contradictions. In the real world, the experts generally disagree.

This book offers you direct, hands-on, real-world experience. The writers herein have spent thousands of hours battling and embracing POSTSCRIPT devices. It has been a pleasure and an honor to work with them, and to provide a forum for their knowledge. I hope you find their work as illuminating as I have.

Note: Throughout this book the authors refer to the three standard works on the POSTSCRIPT language written by Adobe Systems, Inc., each commonly referred to by the color of its cover. The *POSTSCRIPT Language Reference Manual* (Addison-Wesley, 1985), known as the "red book," is the standard definition of the POSTSCRIPT language. The *POSTSCRIPT Language Tutorial and Cookbook* (Addison-Wesley, 1985), known as the "blue book," is a tutorial introduction to POSTSCRIPT programs. The most recent POSTSCRIPT book from Adobe, the *POSTSCRIPT Language Program Design*, (Addison-Wesley, 1988), called the "green book," is Adobe's guide to designing efficient POSTSCRIPT programs.

About the Contributors

Steve Roth, the editor and a contributor to *Real World PostScript*, wrote the first book on microcomputers in publishing, in 1984. He spent three years as editor of *Personal Publishing* magazine and has written about computer publishing for a variety of periodicals, from *Publishers Weekly* to *MacUser*. He currently operates Open House, a book, magazine, and software publishing and production company in Seattle, Washington.

Tom Bernard is the founder of Evergreen, Colorado-based Bersearch Information Services, which offers information retrieval, computer typesetting, and custom graphic design. He has been programming since 1970 and began working in PostScript in 1985.

Henry Bortman is a staff writer for *MacUser* magazine. He was formerly the PostScript columnist for *Personal Publishing*, and has contributed to numerous computer periodicals.

Michael Fryd created the first hard-disk downloader for Linotronic PostScript Imagesetters. He operates MEFCO, Inc. in Pittsburgh, Pennsylvania.

Michael Mace is the founder of Century Software and creator of the Century line of downloadable modifications for built-in LaserWriter typefaces.

Herb Paynter is president of ImageXpress, a graphic arts software development and consulting organization. He is a consultant in graphic design and color separation to several software developers.

Tony Smith was instrumental in introducing PostScript to Australia. In January, 1986, he arranged the first gathering of PostScript afficionadoes in San Francisco, many of whom are represented in this book.

Simon Tuckett is the editor of *Graphic Perspective* and has his own graphic design company in Toronto. He writes for several magazines, and presents seminars on microcomputer design and illustration techniques.

James Von Ehr is the founder of Altsys Corp, which created Fontographer and FreeHand.

Pat Wood is editor of *The PostScript Language Journal* and the co-author of four books on UNIX and C. He is also the principal designer of a commercial color separation package.

Bill Woodruff owns DotScience, a PostScript programming house in Berkeley, California. He is one of the authors of Cricket Draw 1.1.

Part I

PostScript for Programmers and Designers

1 / PostScript as a Design Tool   *Simon Tuckett*

There are far too many things vying for our visual attention. Though it is part of every graphic designer's responsibility to address that concern on a daily basis, every person preparing material for print and subsequent viewing by the public should keep that in mind, and should address certain design principles, whether he or she is working at a drafting table, working in a wysiwyg program (that's "what you see is what you get"), or coding pages in PostScript.

Though this book has no intention of becoming a treatise on graphic design, it is imperative that all we discuss adheres to a few basic guidelines. If you can positively answer the following questions after having prepared your work, then it will have as good a chance at successfully communicating its message as anything else out there on the street.

- Is it easily readable?

- Does it have impact?

- Is it memorable enough for the viewer to retain the information it contains?

- Is it easy to comprehend?

- Does it keep the reader focused on the page?

- Does it give an image of depth?

- Does the page appear as a coherent whole (in a single page that might mean retaining identity of client) or as part of a whole (in multiple pages that might mean placing design elements strategically and repetitively aligning them to an invisible grid).

All these questions must be taken into consideration and addressed at the design stage of the project. Next comes the question of how to generate the material.

Thinking of how one will structure and organize the assembly of a page is not a very logical extension of graphic design. Until you look more closely, the two areas appear to be far apart. When you start working with PostScript, they become completely intertwined.

PostScript has the creative flexibility to achieve almost any image you can imagine in some way or another. There's no problem there. But there is a problem with the way a designer prepares material. PostScript requires a much more structured, methodical approach than many designers are willing to go for. Or does it?

Planning

Planning is the single most important element of any design project. It's not new; traditional designers have planned how they will assemble projects for years. Most often they can do it in their heads and then work at the table from there. Working in PostScript, however, requires a slightly more organized and literal tack.

Even for designers working in PostScript, ideas may come from the usual sources: sitting in a traffic jam on the freeway, walking through the park, or staring at the cereal package over breakfast. The design notes are still rendered on restaurant napkins or scrappy little bits of paper. But before heading over to the computer, it is imperative that the designer do two things. First, plan the modular elements in the design—those entirely independent portions that will appear in order from the bottom (those elements at the back) to the top (the elements that will appear at the front). This is how PostScript builds images, as I'll explain later in the chapter.

Second, designers have to think about what the piece of code they write can be used for in the future. It may not seem important at the time, but using a modular, modifiable approach to PostScript will benefit the designer/assembler enormously. What's more, it will get him or her out of a pinch or two.

WHY BOTHER?

Some designers may think that the advances in regular page layout programs and illustration packages make actively programming in PostScript a dead issue. That could be the case if you only wished to take advantage of existing programs' capabilities. The problem is that they stop far short of the output devices' capabilities.

If you want to take advantage of everything that PostScript printers can do, it's a good idea to learn PostScript. A quick wander through the next few pages will indicate that PostScript is very much an alive issue, perhaps now more than ever. It would be a lot of trouble, for instance, to create the *Graphic Perspective* logo I discuss in this chapter with any draw program.

When I start talking about clipping later on, for instance, try to figure how you'd do the same thing with Adobe Illustrator. Even Aldus FreeHand, which lets you employ clipping, can't use character paths for clipping. You can use a polygon as a cookie cutter, but you can't use type.

Aside from the sheer power to do what you want to do, the advantages of coding in PostScript fall into several categories.

Error Checking. You're printing a job and the printer returns the message "Error in PostScript; your document is okay, but cannot be printed." Now, what kind of consolation is that? If there's a problem with an Encapsulated PostScript (EPS) file you have created, you just might find out where it is and why it is happening. Without some kind of familiarity with PostScript, however, those error messages will sometimes seem like computer gobbledygook. If you know some PostScript, you can jimmy a couple of lines to make everything hunky-dory.

File Compactness. There are some things the designer needs to do that, in a regular application, require a huge file size. This is especially true when you duplicate items many times, changing and moving them slightly with each change to produce special effects. By drawing an object and using the step-and-repeat function two thousand times in some programs, you may end up with a file that is well over 400k. Disk space may not be a problem, but five- and ten-minute screen redraws—and hour-long print times—are.

It may be far more efficient to write a small 15k program in PostScript that will do the same thing, maybe four thousand times instead of 400. You end up with a better image, and though you can't see it on screen, it prints in a reasonable amount of time.

Even more likely is that you will use an illustration package to create the PostScript code of the original object, and your own PostScript code to repeat it over the page or modify it in some way.

Programmability and Control. PostScript allows you to write code that generates a line a thousandth of a point thick. Its programming capability allows you to repeat and transform that line in ways that could never be replicated at the drafting table, and only with difficulty using PostScript drawing programs.

Accuracy. Sometimes it is faster to key some coordinates into the computer than to try to find them in a drawing application. In addition, you know that no matter what else happens on the page, those coordinates will always be used for the placement of a particular graphic element.

Import Flexibility. A familiarity with PostScript allows you to hunt through a PostScript file without wrinkling your brow in consternation. You know what you are looking for, and you'll probably recognize things on the way through. This familiarity can bring on sufficient boldness to allow you to place your own code in page-making programs like PageMaker, duping the program into thinking that it has an EPS file on its hands, for example.

And that's just the start. Look on the examples here as a starting point for producing your own work. The earlier you start, the more ready you will be to track down problems, find solutions, and build on your knowledge of the language.

Working in Layers

The very first thing to understand when you start using PostScript as a design tool is that it works in layers, in a very organized fashion, from back to front. Each layer is opaque. Only selected portions of each layer are imaged. You decide what goes on each layer, and how much of each layer should actually be imaged.

As soon as you define a path (made up of lines and curves) and then do something with it, think of that as a layer. You create a circle, put a one-point line around it, and fill it with gray. That's a layer. You can put a smaller circle on top of it, with a lighter gray, and you're starting to get somewhere.

To get a clearer idea of how this works, take a look at Figure 1.1—an exploded version of the title bar for my magazine. It's a good example of how you can make use of several layers in PostScript, though

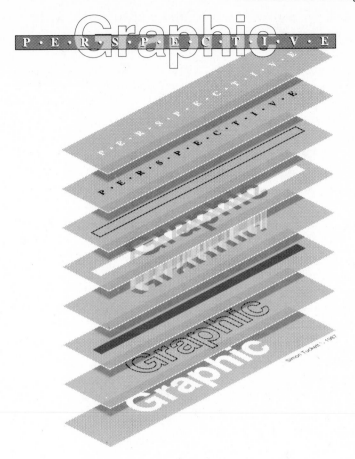

Figure 1.1 PostScript works with opaque overlays, resulting in a layered, modular approach to building an image.

Figure 1.2. The final *Graphic Perspective* logo.

I've taken a few liberties that will become clear as we walk through the construction.

The final image (Figure 1.2) is the result of eight layers lying directly on top of each other. You can see the PostScript code I used, called "Clean Code," in the section "Working in Modules" later in this chapter.

Layers 1 and 2. At the head of the file (therefore in the background) we set the word "Graphic" in white with a black outline.

Layer 3. Next (on top of that) we place a gray bar. The grey bar obscures portions of the type directly beneath it (remember, all the layers are opaque). To get a lighter version of the obscured type, giving the impression of translucence, we need to go to the next layer.

Layer 4. This is a lighter version of the type seen on the bottom layer. This time the type is not outlined to add to the translucent effect. Note how it is clipped by the previous layer.

Layer 5. This is actually the fifth layer in the illustration, but the third one to be coded. This layer merely defines an area through which the underlying layer is seen. It's called a clipping path. It specifies that only those parts of Layer 4 that fall within that rectangle will appear on the page. It's just like using a cookie cutter, or two stencils placed on top of each other.

Layer 6. We draw a black line around the gray box. If we had done it before, it would have been obscured by the "translucent" type.

Layer 7. The word "Perspective" is force-justified over a specified distance using PostScript's typesetting capabilities, set in black (to form a shadow) with bullets between each letter.

Layer 8. At the very end of the file, on the last (top) layer, the word "Perspective" is set again, but this time it is in white with an offset one point up and two points to the left as a highlight.

Now of course you could create this image in a PostScript drawing program, but here's the difference (aside from price): an EPS file of that image drawn in Adobe Illustrator occupies about 36k; a handwritten PostScript file of the the same image comes to only 3k. See what I mean about compactness? And once you get good, you might well do it faster in PostScript.

To get a similar image traditionally would cost a lot in film stripping and headaches. For one thing, it would be extremely difficult to draw the bar with a technical pen and get such sharp corners. Secondly, without film stripping it would be enormously difficult to butt the line to adhesive toned film, let alone get a clean join with the lighter portions of type cut into the bar—a join free of moiré patterns, if you please.

The only other alternative would be to airbrush the bar, risking inconsistencies in tonal depth, as well as running into a highly difficult masking session on the type. In either case, due to the halftone, you would be unable to reduce the artwork by fifty percent or any other percent, as all the dots would probably join together on the line shot. In PostScript, however, all you need to do to get a perfectly reduced image is put one line at the head of the file: .5 .5 scale.

You can look on the *Graphic Perspective* title bar as a relatively simple example of a PostScript image. Combine that with a scanned halftone, a bitmap image, and some more whiz-bang effects, and you begin to get an idea of what a normal page might be like.

Each element of the image needs to be designed at a certain level in the topography of the page. This is important for two reasons: it allows the person assembling the page to know in advance where these items should go in the file, and a page that has depth wraps around the reader—and keeps the reader looking at the page—far more than one that appears flat. Overlaying various elements is an important graphic treatment that is all too often overlooked.

Working with Elements

Now that we've seen how you work with layers in PostScript to build graphic elements, let's take a quick look at the types of elements you can have on a page.

Paths. Paths are by far the most popular type of element. They are the heart and soul of PostScript. They are simply collections of lines and curves connected to form into continuous paths. They can be closed, like circles, or open, like arcs. In each case they can be:

• Stroked (outlined) with any line weight in any color

• Filled with a tone of any color

• Clipped, which means that the path can be described as an area that exclusively receives subsequent stroking and filling—the cookie cutter again

For now we'll ignore the way PostScript devices treat type. For all intents and purposes, we can assume that it treats individual characters as single paths that can be stroked, filled, or clipped.

Images. The other kind of element is a bitmap, a collection of dots, like you get from a paint program or a scanner. A bitmap file defines whether each dot in the image is black or white, on or off.

Some bitmap files—we might call them "deep" bitmaps—specify a gray level for each dot. PostScript can use that gray level information to produce a halftone of an image.

Transformations. Having described either or both types of elements on the page, you can transform them in any of the following ways:

Positioning: using the *translate* operator

Sizing: using the *scale* operator

Rotating: using the *rotate* operator

Shearing or Skewing: using the *concat* operator

In addition, the color of the whole page can be changed by a small line of code at the head of the file that inverts the image, to produce a negative, for example.

Those are the basic visual parameters within which one is working in PostScript. It may not seem like much but it's a surprisingly flexible environment within which to work.

Working in Modules

Modularity is the other key element in preparing the PostScript material for a page. The following two pieces of code do exactly the same thing. They image the *Graphic Perspective* title bar at the top of the page:

Dirty Code

```
43 696 moveto
101.503 0 rmoveto
/Helvetica-Bold findfont 86 scalefont setfont
(Graphic)show
```

```
1 setlinewidth                    %% "PERSPECTIVE" TONAL BAR
.5 setgray
newpath
 38   730  moveto                 %% Top left corner - changeable #
 538   0  rlineto
 0  -23  rlineto
 -538   0  rlineto
closepath fill
0 setgray


 gsave                            %% CLIPPING PATH for darker type
 38   730  moveto                 %% Top left corner - changeable #
 538   0  rlineto
 0  -23  rlineto
 -538   0  rlineto
closepath clip
0.3 setgray                       %% Now set type in JustText
43 696 moveto
101.503 0 rmoveto
/Helvetica-Bold findfont 86 scalefont setfont
(Graphic)show
 grestore                         %% End of darkest type


newpath                           %% Bar outline
 38   730  moveto                 %%- changeable #
 538   0  rlineto
 0  -23  rlineto
 -538   0  rlineto
closepath stroke


newpath                           %% Info bar outline
 38   730  moveto                 %%- changeable #
0 -23 rmoveto
538   0  rlineto
 0  -25  rlineto
 -538   0  rlineto
closepath stroke


newpath
1 setlinecap
```

```
0.6 setlinewidth
0.9 setgray                          %% Lay down white topline
 39.5    729.6  moveto               %% Back to top left corner
 535    0  rlineto
stroke
0 setlinecap


gsave                                %% Perspective shadow
0.2 setgray
42 711 moveto
/Times-Bold findfont 20 scalefont setfont
15.141 0(P\267E\267R\267S\267P\267E\267C\267T\267I\267V\267E)ashow


1 setgray                            %% Now set white type in JustText
/Times-Bold findfont 20 scalefont setfont
43 712 moveto
15.141 0(P\267E\267R\267S\267P\267E\267C\267T\267I\267V\267E)ashow
grestore
```

   The first one is taken right from my archival disk, which has stored the very first issue of *Graphic Perspective*. It's from the days when we thought we were only going to be doing one issue. It is pertinent simply because the code is so bad. It was prepared with absolutely no fore-thought—just a few design sketches. The code was written simply to get the job done, with no provision for future modifications that I might want to make. Ignore what the code actually says right now and look solely at the structure of the material: few comments, no defined procedures, everything specified exactly. It works, but it's very difficult to modify, especially if you come back to it some two months later.

Clean Code

```
/DefineBar                           %% Routine to define the bar
{   newpath                          %% Clean up any previous paths
    38 730 moveto 538 0 rlineto      %% Draw a box
    0 -23 rlineto -538 0 rlineto
    closepath                        %% Closes up the box
} def


gsave                                %% Put down "Graphic"
```

```
/Helvetica-Bold findfont
86 scalefont setfont         %% Pick the font
0 setgray                    %% Set it in black
143.5 696 moveto             %% Position it
(Graphic) show               %% Place it

.5 setgray                   %% Shade for the bar
DefineBar                    %% Path for the bar
fill                         %% Fill the path

DefineBar                    %% Create a clipping path
clip                         %% Use the path to clip the following
0.3 setgray                  %% Darken the gray level a bit
143.5 696 moveto             %% Position it
(Graphic) show               %% And place it
1 setlinewidth               %% 1 point line width
0 setgray                    %% Black line
DefineBar                    %% Recreate the path
stroke                       %% Draw the outline of the box


                             %% Put in the "PERSPECTIVE"
/Times-Bold findfont
20 scalefont setfont         %% Pick the font
0 setgray                    %% First black
45 711 moveto                %% Position the letters
15.046 0
(P\267E\267R\267S\267P\267E\267C\267T\267I\267V\267E)
ashow                        %% Place them

1 setgray                    %% Then White
46 712 moveto                %% Position up and right a bit
15.046 0
(P\267E\267R\267S\267P\267E\267C\267T\267I\267V\267E)
ashow                        %% Place them


grestore                     %% We're done!
```

Now look at the second piece of code. It was written around the time we decided to do a second issue. At that point I realized that I might want to use the image in several different ways in subsequent issues. It seemed worthwhile to invest a small additional amount of time in preparing a modular piece of code that would be far easier to change and place in subsequent issues. It has never changed, except for the occasional design-pertinent modifications of tone and position. All the changeable definitions are at the head, and several mini-programs call up the outlines for the major objects. All of them have specific names for easy reference.

The actual image is set on the page at the end of the code with merely a call to the doTitleBar routine, which in itself is solely a combination of those mini-routines. Now, that may seem like an awful lot of effort just to get the image. Not only is the code more brief than in the former example, however, but once you have a small familiarity with the language, it's easy to see how many uses can be made of the material.

Naturally, if you're a first-time programmer you're far more likely to write programs in the former fashion for a while, as it is far more expedient. However, I'm going to go to considerable lengths to teach you to write programs like the latter one.

Let's look closely at the second piece of code.

Clipping paths are a necessary evil, as there is no such thing in PostScript as translucent fills. When you place a figure or some text, no matter how light a shade of gray, on top of another object, the lower one will be obscured. So for special effects, you build up your images in layers using clipping paths. The really difficult part is deciding, artistically, what should happen within all those layers. What part of the lower level should seem to bleed through, what should be obscured, and in what order must the layers go down on the page? To do this you need to know how the tools—clipping paths—work.

Think of a clipping path as a stencil sheet you put on a piece of paper. You then spray a liberal amount of paint on the sheet and all that comes through is the form on the stencil. Nice and neat. Anything not inside the region defined by the clipping path is not affected at all. This means that you can be as messy as you like, and not ruin what you've already got on the page.

Let's explore a simple example. You want to draw a maple leaf with the top and bottom of the leaf being white and the middle being red. So you draw your maple leaf with white paint. Then you make a stencil, cutting out the shape of the part of the leaf that you wish to make red. You place the stencil on the white leaf and let go with the red paint. The shape and size of the blotch of red makes no difference, since the stencil effectively masks the red everywhere except in the areas you cut out.

Getting a bit more practical, let's dissect the *Graphic Perspective* title bar. Visually it looks like a transparently grayed bar with the word, "Perspective" placed over the larger word, "Graphic." The parts of the letters behind the bar show through.

(Just to add some subtlety, the "Perspective" lettering has a black shadow behind it, but that is so easy to do we don't even need to describe it.)

The mechanics are as follows. Place down the "Graphic" word and plop a gray bar through the middle of it. Using the same bar as a clipping path (i.e., stencil, i.e., mask) place the word "Graphic" down again in a darker shade than the filled bar. Using the same path, stroke the outline of the box with black to define the box. Then put the word "P·E·R·S·P·E·C·T·I·V·E" into the bar, in black. Shift the position up and to the right a little and do the bulleted word again in white.

Look at the second program listing. It's definitely an improvement over the one created for the first issue. Comments, even. And yet none of that programming "sin exch cos pop div she bop she walla walla" stuff. The only part that might need explaining is the use of the DefineBar routine. Rather than retyping the coordinates for the bar over and over (programmers are a lazy lot), I type them in once and call the routine whenever I need it. This also cuts down on adjustments, since the coordinates are only in one place in the program.

Initially I use it to fill the bar, then to define the clipping path, and finally to draw the box around it. By not specifying what I want to do with the defined path within the definition, I can use it generically. After each use of the definition, you'll see either *fill*, *clip*, or *stroke*, the three most fun things to do with paths.

So much for typing text within clipping path boxes. Another more fun use is to define text as a clipping path, and draw something within the text. There are some drawbacks. For one, this operation takes a long time to do. My favorite example came up when I was first starting this PostScript programming stuff. I wanted to take the outline of the word, "Kilroy," and fill it with the words "was here" repeated over and over in very small type. I didn't know much at the time about the speed of things like this, so every time I sent the program to the LaserWriter I'd get impatient and cancel the job. Finally I couldn't take it any more. I had pored over the program as much as I was going to. So I let the thing run. It took two hours! Just for a simple effect.

The reason is that there are very complex curves within most text, and the math involved to decide whether to draw within the lines or not is just that—involved. So either start the job with a lot of patience, or limit the use of text as clipping paths.

By the way, to define text as a clipping path, you just do the following:

```
(The Text) true charpath clip
```

Using clipping paths is the only way to do some very special effects, and if you're going to do any PostScript programming at all, you'll have to get to know them.

Modules within Modules

The GP logo is only one element on what could quite possibly be a huge page. Though each program—such as the one to create the logo—might comprise several modules, the program is, in itself, one of a larger group of modules. Other PostScript modules might include a TIFF file, an EPS file, some subtitle effects scattered around the page, and, of course, the PostScript code for your text. Imagine preparing a page featuring all these elements, ending up with a 500k file, then sending it to the printer for proofing.

It's probably not going to work.

If there is just one syntax error anywhere in that 500k file (and it can even be as small as a missing space), the page won't print. Confidence and eagerness to see your page come out of the printer don't speed up the process. You can get hopelessly mired hunting for errors when you do your initial tests with large files. The modular approach is best. Write little programs for effects, proof them on the printer until they work the way you want them to, then tack them all together. PostScript pages are built that way. Code errors are found and squashed way before they hit the final page.

Start with something that you know works, then gradually build it up until you have what you wanted in the first place. It's a great way to learn, too. Modifying other people's code (and there are numerous examples in this book) allows you to see just what visual parameters are changed by which groups of numbers.

2 / PostScript as a Programming Language   *Bill Woodruff*

This chapter offers three answers to the question, "What is PostScript?"

It's an Imaging Model. The first answer is that it is a device-independent imaging model, a way to create images composed of dots. It is a modern imaging model using a delightfully general method of describing the structure of the space in which dots are made. This method involves a very simple data structure called the "current transformation matrix," and relatively simple mathematical operations upon it. Of particular interest to our study is understanding the nature of a path in PostScript, because here the imaging model is quite different from our physical experience, in which our hand moves a pen and leaves marks on a flat, unchanging page. And it is quite different from other modern computer graphic imaging models, like Apple's QuickDraw or the GKS (graphics kernel system), in which a drawing act is not conceptually separate from creating dots.

The imaging model has been well covered elsewhere, notably in the green book, so I won't go into depth on the subject here. Instead I'll concentrate on PostScript as a programming language.

It Controls Raster Marking Devices. The second answer is that PostScript is a device-control environment that has a mix of device-independent and -dependent machine control functions. In chapter 3, Michael Fryd does a good job of introducing you to these aspects of PostScript, and we won't repeat that here. But let's do add that one source of confusion about what PostScript is has been that people interpreted its structure and behavior in the context of the typical "device-driver scenario," where a dumb marking engine with a simple repertoire of dot-making behaviors is controlled by a low-level piece of software code optimized for speed to image static page descriptions.

It's a Language. The third answer is that PostScript is a general-purpose, very high level interpreted computer programming language in which you can do any of the mundane and sublime things done in other computer languages: write a spreadsheet, process some data, create mathematical simulations, draw a circle, etc. We shall find rich rewards here, because PostScript is a unique synthesis of structural elements and styles found in other traditional programming languages.

Have no doubts, PostScript is a historically deviant language that unites elements of LISP, FORTH, and C in remarkable ways. This type of analysis may help us to understand some of the early misconceptions and criticisms of PostScript that were based upon its larval stage employment—digesting relatively simple descriptions of pages and making dots inside a printer engine.

How PostScript Does What It Does

Just as describing a pair of pants, a coat, and a vest generates only trivial hypotheses about sex and work behavior, so our analysis must be more than descriptive and attend to how PostScript does what it does. We will compare the way you create variables, data structures, loops, and IF-THEN-ELSE tests in PostScript with the way you create them in other languages.

Two dynamic views of the language are offered here. The first is an easygoing overview designed to be a general literacy model to help you understand how PostScript typically constructs a file, makes objects, executes the objects, and makes marks on a page by turning bits on or off and, finally, telling a device to print the page.

(In case this last remark raised hopes for magic bullets and amulets, let us say that the problems of file compatibility and encapsulated PostScript EPS interchange that turn desktop publishing houses into bedlams are not addressable here. Those problems at least have the value of creating consulting work of the Roto-rooter variety for a number of people who master the infernal arcana of various prep files and headers.)

Next I get into a second level of focus with considerably more technical depth, designed to be of service to the professional programmer who needs to fully understand the nature of naming and binding in

PostScript in order to construct programs that are efficient and that make the best use of PostScript's computational resources. Understanding the dictionary structure of PostScript and how naming and binding are freed from the syntactical constraints of traditional languages is, in my opinion, the royal road to PostScript mastery.

The temporary artificial distinction between the language itself and the imaging model it embodies is an educational ploy. In reality, the imaging model framed the design of the language; the language shaped the robustness and generality of the imaging model. The need to use PostScript, as printer controller, to facilitate the mapping of an application's internal data structures to printed page also shapes PostScript's identity as an environment for building translators, and partially accounts for its LISP-like plasticity.

For example, the imaging model uses matrices to translate points in a user-defined coordinate space to an underlying fixed device space. PostScript has a complex matrix math package and a variety of operators to let users perform transformations of points from one type of space to another. These facilities, inherent in the imaging model, enable PostScript's elegantly general way of scaling, rotation, and translation of any object. They also provide a generic solution for mapping from a different cartesian coordinate system (like Apple's QuickDraw) to PostScript's internal system that does not require individual manipulation of data points (which would be costly).

PostScript at Work: The Sidewalk Superintendent's View

On a simple level, we can use the following as a metaphor for how the PostScript interpreter works—A person reading a book: eyes moving across a page; visual perception; construction of sub-units of meaning; combinations of meanings leading to larger meaning; the internal sense of having perceived, having "read"; another page.

The PostScript interpreter has an innate behavior pattern called the server loop (actually a program written in PostScript and running in the interpreter itself). The server typically cycles through a simple set of behaviors:

Is there a job to be done?

Yes: Execute a save so all definitions will be temporary. Read in the job and construct a file object. Set a read pointer to its start. Turn control over to the scanner/interpreter, within a stopped context, which intercepts errors in the execution of the file

Keep interpreting and executing the file until you reach end of file; then execute a restore to match the save, and terminate the job

Go back to the start of the loop

No:

Are all the default characters cached in the font cache?

Yes: Go back to start of loop

No: Cache the default characters, then go back to start of loop

The input to the PostScript interpreter is a group of ASCII characters traveling over a serial channel. These must be "framed" so that the interpreter can work on them. This is done by constructing a file object with a read pointer set to its beginning and an end-of-file character at its end.

THE LIFE OF AN OBJECT

This file object goes on the execution stack on top of the server loop, and the PostScript interpreter applies its scanner to the file, constructing one object at a time and advancing the read pointer as it moves.

The scanner applies the syntax and grammatical rules of the language to determine what type of object is constructed and whether it is executed or left on the operand stack. The start and end of an object are determined by a single unit of white space (any number of contiguous spaces, tabs, carriage returns, etc.).

The interpreter uses the operand stack to build procedure objects and arrays. When the interpreter encounters a name object with the executable attribute, it searches the dictionary stack until it finds the object as a key, and then returns the value associated with the name. If this value is itself an executable procedure body, then the interpreter puts it on the execution stack and executes it step by step.

Part of the clean elegance of the PostScript model is this structural similarity between the way the interpreter/scanner works on a file object on the execution stack, and the way a procedure is executed. As a PostScript programmer you have access to the *token* command, which will apply to a string object the same operation that the scanner applies to the file object. You will find a detailed explanation of this technique and an example of its use in an embedded control-code text formatter in Part IV, "Projects from the Pros."

THE LIFE OF A PATH

As the file object is executed and drawing commands are carried out, paths are created in PostScript's memory. A drawing act occurs in the context of the current definition of page space. The PostScript page is a rubber sheet that can be stretched, contracted, twisted away, rotated, etc. At the moment of the drawing act, the coordinate points that define the line or curve are internally translated by PostScript from the way the user has defined the page into the underlying way the PostScript device defines the page.

A path is not a drawing! A path is just a collection of points in the fixed coordinate system peculiar to each printing engine (known as device space). It is very important for you to realize that creating a path creates no dots. Dots are created only at the moment of rendering the path, when PostScript is told to fill the path or to stroke the path. At the moment of stroking or filling a path, PostScript looks up the current values of a number of fill-model or pen-model parameters, which tell it what gray value to use in a fill, what line width and line style to use for a stroke, etc. Stroking or filling consumes the current path and destroys the current point in space.

Here our "reading" model fails us. A better analogy is the creation of a set of blueprints drawn to scale, which are then used in the field as a guideline for cutting actual-size beams for a house.

Text objects represent a special case of the general PostScript model because they function as compound objects that have special properties like automatically updating the current point after each character is filled. They also have a special private spatial scaling mechanism, which means they can be scaled independent of the global page scaling, and their strokewidths are maintained independent of the font's internal scaling.

There are only three elements of paths: moves, lines, and curves (arcs are decomposed internally into curves). PostScript uses Bezier curves, named after a French engineer whose curve drawing templates (known today as French curves) embody a form of mathematical function called a cubic spline.

WHERE DOTS COME FROM

Stroking and filling (and the special case of imaging a bitmapped image) are the only ways to set the bits in the printer's raster memory that result in physical dots imaged on the page. Perhaps you can, even from this sidewalk superintendent's window, grasp the wonderful simplicity of the internal representation of paths in PostScript, and the flexibility that separating the rendering of the path from the construction of the path allows. You, the user, are free to create pages that are arbitrarily and very complexly scaled and rotated. Yet this twisted, turned page is an illusion propped up by a simple internal list of fixed addresses.

The end of our simple view is, of course, the triggering of the actual printing of the page. Here machine-specific hardware takes over and maps what is in raster memory to a charge on a drum or a laser beam striking photo-sensitive paper. Voilá: the page.

PostScript as a Programming Language

The texture of PostScript reminds me of a picture in a medieval bestiary showing a magical animal, a collage of parts of real animals. Take the power of abstraction of LISP and SmallTalk, the stack and reverse Polish notation of FORTH, some of the file-stream and input-output flavors of UNIX, and the terseness and pointer usage of C. Marry them all to a vector-based imaging model employing the most advanced graphic algorithms; digitally emulate the century-old method of producing gray levels from ordered clusters of dots (halftoning); add a model of type based on scalable outlines created by world-class typographers. Now let this mythical beast consume static descriptions of pages to produce—giant bitmaps!

RPN: JERZY KOZINSKY, PLEASE REPORT TO MATH CLASS

A person who has programmed in other languages looking at PostScript for the first time is likely to focus first on its use of post-fix (RPN, or reverse Polish) notation. BASIC, C, and Pascal use infix notation, where operators are put between the values they operate on. LISP uses prefix notation, where the operator comes before arguments. Here's code to determine a hypotenuse of a right triangle with sides 10, 20:

```
PASCAL      SQRT ( (10 * 10 ) + ( 20 * 20 ) )
LISP        ( SQRT ( + ( * 10 10 ) ( * 20 20 ) ) )
POSTSCRIPT  10 10 mul 20 20 mul add sqrt
```

LISP and Pascal use parentheses to force one clause to be executed before another. PostScript needs no parentheses because the stack accumulates intermediate results, and what is executed is always determined by when an executable object goes on the stack.

The complex imaging model of PostScript could be implemented in another language. Having post-fix notation means that the interpreter does not have to be recursive (it does not have to parse nested expressions delimited by special characters); it means that what is to be done next is always crystal clear.

John Warnock has commented that Adobe felt post-fix design was appropriate to a language that would frequently be used as a translator between the high-level data structures of an application program and control of a marking engine. It definitely simplifies the internal operation of the language. It is my experience as a teacher of PostScript that in three months or less of use, RPN notation becomes transparent and users begin to appreciate the simplifying nature of life without clouds of parentheses.

SMOKE FROM THE STACK

The explicit presence of a stack where objects "pile up" until used or destroyed is a novelty to many programmers, except those who are familiar with FORTH or who have implemented their own stacks in assembly language programming. Explicit access to a stack allows a programmer to accumulate intermediate results of computation without creation of complex data structures in memory, and enables a terse, efficient programming style. The PostScript stack is an object stack, unlike the FORTH stack which is primarily a data stack. Technically it is a LIFO stack (last in first out), and is analogous to piling up books by placing one on top of another.

Stacks (there are several) in PostScript are a key feature of the language. You can write your programs so that stacks are virtually ignored, using the operand stack to temporarily hold values that are immediately consumed by operators. We'll present a brief simulation of Pascal-style parameter-passing by *value* and *var* later, in the section on the dictionary mechanism.

Most languages, internally, use stacks; you just have no access to them. Explicit access to a stack lets you eliminate multiple references to data by duplicating it, or to construct "nameless procedures" (like LISP's lambda functions), which can be executed on the fly.

Many PostScript programmers use complex stack manipulations instead of creating named variables and procedures. Timing studies suggest that it is as fast or faster to keep the stack shallow and to make generous use of named variables and small procedures. Maintaining and debugging code that makes exotic use of stack manipulations is as wasteful as handling bad code in any other language, and destroys the potential conviviality of sharing your clean and readable code with others.

One hypothesis: the tendency to write stack-deep code is a reflection of the "device-driver" mentality of those who historically have dealt with the need to send lengthy, but simple, streams of tokens.

HOW THE FLOW GOES

A sequence refers to the ability of the computer to execute a series of instructions one after the other. In all modern computer languages a sequence is inherent in the way programs are written. They are executed from top to bottom, just as you read lines on a page.

One variation in handling sequences involves the way the interpreter or compiler executing or compiling the program treats white space (carriage returns, tabs, spaces, etc.). In many BASIC interpreters there is a maximum line length of 255 characters or so, and the carriage return marks the end of the line. The carriage return in PostScript terminates a comment line.

Modern languages like C, Pascal, and PostScript treat any arbitrary amount of white space as one unit of white space. This lets you use tabs and carriage returns to make your programs visually reflect their logical organization, and to make it easier to debug and maintain them.

As in most modern computer languages, there are no line numbers in PostScript, and there is no facility to use a *goto*-like statement (as in BASIC) or an internal label in a procedure body (as in LISP) to which you can redirect execution of a sequence. There is a generic way to exit from an inner loop or from an IF-THEN-ELSE-type clause by use of the command *exit*, as we'll see.

INVIDIOUS COMPARISONS

Let's compare the way objects are made and initialized in PostScript, LISP, and Pascal. The LISP and Pascal examples are not taken from one strictly defined dialect, but are freely adapted.

1. Create a constant value to be used globally throughout a program:

```
PostScript   /golden_mean .618034 def
LISP         (SETQ golden_mean .618034)
PASCAL       CONST golden_mean = .618034;
```

2. Create a four-element string variable:

```
PostScript   /somestring 4 string def ... or /somestring (abcd) def
LISP         (setq somestring "abcd")
PASCAL       VAR somestring : STRING[4]; somestring := 'abcd';
```

3. Create a four-element array object whose values can be accessed by
   index:

```
PostScript   /anarray 4 array def ... or /anarray [ null null null null ] def
LISP         (setq anarray (make-array 4) )
PASCAL       VAR anarray = ARRAY [1..4] OF INTEGER;
```

4. Assign an integer value (100) to the first element of this array:

```
PostScript   anarray 0 100 put
LISP         (setf (aref anarray 0) 100)
PASCAL       anarray[1] := 100;
```

5. Create a function that takes a Fahrenheit temperature as input and
   returns a Celsius temperature.

```
PostScript   /ftoc { 32 sub 5 mul 9 div } def
LISP         (defun ftoc ( f ) ( / ( * 5 ( - f 32 ) ) 9 ) )
PASCAL       FUNCTION ftoc ( f : REAL ) : REAL ;
             ftoc := ( f - 32 ) * 5 / 9;
```

Whether or not PostScript "returns" anything from a call to a
procedure object is strictly up to the programmer. If you wish to return
something, you can place it on the stack or assign it to a name object
in an active or inactive dictionary. There is no inherent distinction in
PostScript between a function and a procedure that is called for side
effect only, as in Pascal. Some dialects of LISP (and LOGO) return a
value whenever a procedure is called (or any object is evaluated);
PostScript's procedures can be designed to make PostScript also behave in this way.

HERE WE GO LOOP-DE-LOOP

POSTSCRIPT provides a simplified and clean set of operators that control iteration, or flow-of-control as it's sometimes called. Here, for economy of space, we will not give examples from Pascal or LISP. POSTSCRIPT loop forms remove the procedure body to be repeated and the controlling arguments from the stack prior to their execution. You can "jump out" of any of these loop forms at any time by using the *exit* operator.

The *repeat* loop is the simplest form of loop, used when you know (or can calculate) exactly how many times something is to be done, and you don't need to keep track of the current repetition number as you loop. Here's an example that would call our temperature conversion program four times. It assumes that four temperature values would be on the stack:

```
4 { ftoc 4 1 roll } repeat
```

This example converts one temperature and pushes it to the bottom of the stack. At the end of the program, the four converted values are on the stack in original order. Note that the number of repetitions must be an integer.

Most traditional languages implement a loop with a built-in counter called a FOR loop. POSTSCRIPT provides a classic FOR loop that leaves the current counter value on the stack before calling the procedure each time:

```
1 % counter start value
1 % counter increment or decrement
4 % counter final value to stop at
{ 50 mul ftoc 4 1 roll }
for
```

The direction of counting is determined by the sign of the middle parameter (positive = up, negative = down). Error checking is done by POSTSCRIPT prior to the first execution of the loop, and the loop will not be executed at all if, for example, the counter start value is greater than the final value (and the direction of counting is up).

POSTSCRIPT's *loop* operator is a flexible tool that you can use to emulate the classic REPEAT-UNTIL and DO-WHILE forms found in Pascal. The *loop* operator sets up a repeating form that will not stop until it encounters the *exit* operator. Examples:

```
% repeat...until        % while...do
{                       {
do some stuff           test { exit } if
test { exit } if        do some stuff
}                       }
loop                    loop
```

You'll find examples of the use of *loop* in the graphing program and the embedded-control-code word processor in Part IV.

POLYMORPHIC BUT NOT KINKY: *FORALL*

One of the strongest resemblances between PostScript and LISP is in the operators that, given some complex structure such as a dictionary, put each element of the structure on the stack and call a procedure that the programmer supplies. These are known as polymorphic (because they work, with slight variations, on a number of different forms), and they are called mapping operators, probably because, in LISP, you speak of "mapping" a function onto a list. An example:

```
% our re-usable array
/temp 8 array def

% fill it with 8 initial values
10 22 34 67 89 101 234 312 temp astore

% for every element of 'temp: convert to Celsius
temp { ftoc } forall

% put results back into 'temp
temp astore
```

With the exception of dictionaries, the data argument to *forall* is a structure that you could process by using a *for* loop:

```
% our re-usable array
/temp 8 array def

% fill it with 8 initial values
10 22 34 67 89 101 234 312 temp astore
```

```
% for every element of 'temp: convert to Celsius
0 1 temp length 1 sub
{
       temp exch get ftoc
}
for
% put results back into temp
temp astore
```

The *forall* operator provides the only way to get at every element of a dictionary (it puts each key/value pair on the stack before calling your procedure with the value on top of the stack).

There are a number of other operators in PostScript that have a "mapping" function at an operating system level (*filenameforall*) or in special cases of handling strings (*kshow* particularly). They are a wonderfully elegant tool that allows the programmer to abstract the flow of control and to focus on problem-solving rather than mechanical details of program structure. They are also quite appropriate to a language that frequently deals with input data (page descriptions) of varying length.

THE MISSING CASE

PostScript lacks a high-level form for evaluating multiple conditions, the equivalent, say, of the "cond" form in LISP or the "case" statement in Pascal. This is a peculiar gap to this writer, given the other very advanced features of the language. Researchers into programming science, like McCabe in England, have suggested that programs with more than seven or eight nested IF-THEN-ELSE structures are likely to be a source of error.

Of course, you can, in any language, create a complex set of modules rather than write nested IF-THEN-ELSE clauses (passing complexity on to the call tree rather than the code). If your problem lends itself to generating an integer code in PostScript, you can pull out a procedure from an array or another procedure using the code, and then execute it:

```
% procedure definitions
/p0 { ... } def /p1 { ... } def
% procedure of procedures
```

```
/pofp { p0 p1 ... pn } def
% calculate an integer result and get stuff to do
pofp exch get exec
```

You'll find other ideas about using dictionaries and redefining PostScript operators to handle situations that have complex testing and control structure in the naming and binding section of this chapter.

Dictionaries: A Beginning Overview

A key feature of PostScript is the implementation of a dictionary structure that is under explicit user control and that regulates the scope of a name. It is very similar to the way dictionaries are used in FORTH, and similar to what happens just underneath the surface in the implementation of LISP or C or any language that allows recursion or subtle manipulation of local and global naming.

PostScript has, at any given time, a dictionary stack: the top dictionary on this stack is the first place that a name object is looked up and its value retrieved (as in accessing the value of a variable) or executed (procedure). The PostScript interpreter retrieves or executes the value associated with the name in the first dictionary it finds, starting from the top of the dictionary stack and going down. If it does not find the name, it executes the "undefined" error.

You have the complete power and freedom to redefine any name in PostScript, even those of system-level primitives. PostScript has two dictionaries that are always present: systemdict and userdict. All user-created objects come to being in userdict unless you have created and activated your own dictionary context. A dictionary is not indexable and is a random-access structure where only the key—any PostScript object except the null object or a string—can retrieve or reference the value stored with the key.

NAMING AND BINDING IN POSTSCRIPT

Earlier in this chapter I said that an understanding of naming and binding in PostScript is "the royal road to PostScript mastery." It is the aspect of PostScript (along with the accompanying imaging model) that most sets it apart from other languages, and I think it deserves a more complete discussion in its own right. So, herewith, a more complete discussion.

Every computer language provides facilities to create names that are associated with data (variables), and to create names associated with sequences of executable instructions (procedures or functions). And all computer languages have mechanisms for regulating the scope of a name, the value or procedure associated with the name at any given point in the computer program.

We use the word "binding" here to refer to the act of associating a name with a particular piece of data or sequence of instructions. This usage is distinct from the PostScript *bind* command, though it does encompass that command. The act of creating a named variable or procedure in any language is a "binding" act. Our focus will be on how names that occur within user-defined procedures are evaluated. Keep in mind that some of these names will be defined by the language itself (primitives or operator names); others will be user-defined (variables and procedure names).

In many modern languages, names are evaluated and values (or pointers to complex structures) are substituted as the procedure is internally massaged into executable form. Hence we can refer to these languages as "early binding."

PostScript is a "late binding" language, where the value associated with a name is looked up in a stack of dictionaries which is searched from top to bottom when that name is encountered by the PostScript interpreter. PostScript is extensible: you can redefine the operators or primitives that compose the language itself. This is not permitted in languages like C and Pascal.

A goal of this chapter is to demonstrate how extensibility and late binding create much of PostScript's power and distinguish it from other modern computer languages. This is not only of academic interest: the key to writing fast and memory-efficient programs is understanding how to manipulate the binding of names.

WEAK, SENSITIVE TYPING

The most widely used structured computer languages, C and Pascal, are strongly typed languages. Each name used as a variable name must be declared by type and can hold only that type of data. Names for procedures and functions must be specified as you write the sequence of executable instructions they contain. A function, in these languages, is a type of procedure that returns an unnamed result that can be used by some other procedure or function. From a POSTSCRIPT point of view, you might say they have a stack that has a maximum depth of one!

These languages vary in the extent to which they allow you to change one type of data into another. In general, you can't break a procedure or function down into its component elements. Binding in these traditional languages is regulated by the syntax and grammar of procedure/function definitions, and by the inner structure of the language itself. In Pascal, for example, a function or procedure can create "local" names through internal declaration or by specifying the names in a required way in the parameter list that follows the name of the procedure/function.

POSTSCRIPT, like LISP and LOGO, is a weakly typed language: any name can be bound to any type of object without pre-declaration. There is no specialized "function" form of procedure, since any procedure can return any number of results (on the stack). The act of naming is independent of the act of creating a sequence of instructions, and not tied to the syntax and grammar of procedure construction. You can name at any time.

By design, POSTSCRIPT, like LISP, offers powerful mechanisms by which procedures can be decomposed into their objects, and procedures can be composed from groups of objects—while your program is executing. POSTSCRIPT procedures are arrays with an executable attribute; they can be disassembled, appended to, and modified as easily as lists in LISP. Both of these modern languages offer a rich set of operators to convert one type of object to another. As you would expect of a language that does not require pre-definition of the type of a name, POSTSCRIPT has operators that allow you to determine the type of any object dynamically.

Default control of naming and binding in POSTSCRIPT is done by the dictionary mechanism. The way this is done makes POSTSCRIPT a more radically "first-class" language than LISP! In POSTSCRIPT, any object (except a string) can be a key in a dictionary. The objects we use for keys will usually be literal name objects (which do not contain white space), and the naming process will be like that in other languages.

Figure 2.1 shows an example of how the POSTSCRIPT interpreter searches the dictionary stack for a matching key when an executable name is encountered. When the name is found, the value associated with the key is executed. In this example, the key "show" is located in systemdict, and a pointer is found to the executable code that

(destiny waits for no string) show

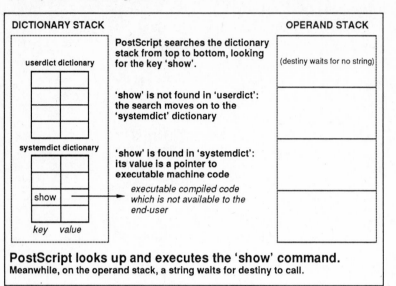

DICTIONARY STACK   **OPERAND STACK**

userdict dictionary

PostScript searches the dictionary
stack from top to bottom, looking
for the key 'show'.

(destiny waits for no string)

'show' is not found in 'userdict':
the search moves on to the
'systemdict' dictionary

systemdict dictionary

'show' is found in 'systemdict':
its value is a pointer to
executable machine code

show ———→   *executable compiled code
                          which is not available to the
                          end-user*

key   value

PostScript looks up and executes the 'show' command.
Meanwhile, on the operand stack, a string waits for destiny to call.

Figure 2.1. The POSTSCRIPT interpreter encounters ASCII characters and builds a string on the operand stack. It then recognizes an executable name and begins a search through the dictionary stack.

actually takes a string off the stack and images it in the current font from the current point.

IN A BIND

POSTSCRIPT provides several other explicit mechanisms for binding control. On the most global level, the *bind* command can be applied to a procedure object. It goes through a procedure, finds all executable operator names, and substitutes pointers to the executable code, which enacts the operator inside the procedure body. This substitution occurs only for POSTSCRIPT operators that have not been redefined in a higher-level dictionary. If the operator has been redefined, *bind* leaves it at it is.

This is done recursively so that even deeply nested operator names are replaced by pointers. The obvious purpose of using *bind* is to eliminate dictionary searches and name lookups, making your procedures execute faster. For *bind* to work on an inner procedure, it must be both executable and have write access (in other words it must not have been made literal or read-only). Figure 2.2 shows the result of binding the show operator in a procedure.

{ (destiny waits for no string) show } bind

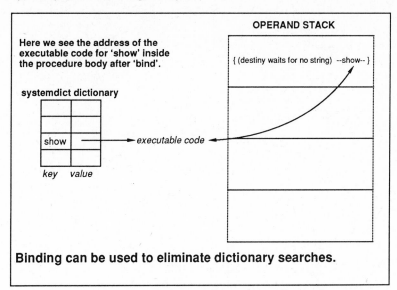

Here we see the address of the
executable code for 'show' inside
the procedure body after 'bind'.

systemdict dictionary

show ──────► *executable code* ◄──

key   value

OPERAND STACK

{ (destiny waits for no string) --show-- }

Binding can be used to eliminate dictionary searches.

Figure 2.2. The PostScript
interpreter builds a
procedure object and the
bind command substitutes
the address of the
executable code for show,
which eliminates the
dictionary stack search and
name lookup.

Another way to force replacement of any name with its current value
appeared beginning with version 38 of PostScript, the // macro. //
tells the interpreter to immediately substitute the current value associated with the name as it constructs the procedure body. I think of
this command as a macro because it modifies the interpreter's behavior
and is not a defined name in userdict or systemdict.

Using the *load* command is another way to pull out the value of a
name. All the techniques we've mentioned for binding have implicitly
behaved as if they used *load* (with the exception of *bind* ignoring
redefined operators). *load* will search the dictionary stack and return
the value associated with the first key match it comes to.

Another way to consciously manipulate the context in which names
are evaluated is to put the dictionary you want on top of the dictionary
stack so it will be searched first for names. In a context where you
have redefined some operators but wish to make sure you use the
original PostScript definitions, you might use a form like:

```
% revise show
/show { newstufftodo show } bind def      % or { newstufftodo //show } def
...
```

```
% make sure we use the old show here
systemdict begin show end
```

Think for a moment what would have happened if we had not used the *bind* command when we redefined *show*. The execution of our revised *show* operator would have contained an instruction to execute itself, generating an endless loop!

In some situations, such as the construction of a piece of code that will be executed in a loop a great number of times, it is essential that the code be as efficient as possible. How can we best use the variety of naming and binding techniques available to produce the fastest code?

One way to build a tightly bound procedure object to serve as the body of a loop is to assemble it piece by piece into an array and then convert it to a procedure by using *cvx*. The problem with this is that we would have to use the form "/operator cvx " to make an executable name that would execute not immediately but when the procedure was run. If the procedure is simple, this is not a problem:

```
/hyp { dup mul exch dup mul add sqrt } bind def
/distance 0 def
/tightloop0
[ /hyp cvx /distance
      /dup cvx /load cvx 3 -1 /roll cvx /add cvx /def cvx
] cvx bind def
```

Note that this style rapidly gets tedious and obscure and we still have an unwanted name lookup in the call to hyp. We could use the // operator on the name hyp, but this would not work on an earlier version of PostScript, and it would have to be followed by a call to *exec* to actually execute the procedure object returned by //.

Glen Reid of Adobe Systems has suggested the technique of loading procedures then following them with a call to "/exec cvx:"

```
/tightloop0 [ /hyp load /exec cvx ... ] cvx bind def
```

This method shares some of the awkwardness of the previous method: procedure bodies are left inside the procedure, and extra work is done by the call to *exec*.

Nothing stops us from constructing our own "superbinding" function that lets us write our loop body code in the style we are accustomed to, and that will automatically substitute operator code pointers for operator names and load and unpack calls to procedures we have defined. The trade-off in using this technique is that a new array, which takes up virtual memory, is created; the original procedure call is wasted.

```
/superbind {
        % put a mark below the procedure object
        [ exch
        % go through procedure and for each object
        {
        % is it a name ?
        dup type /nametype eq
            {
                    % load its value on the stack
                    load
                    % is the value a procedure ?
                    dup type /arraytype eq 1 index xcheck and
                        % unload its contents on the stack
                        { aload pop }
                    if
            }
            if
        } forall
        % put everything down to mark into an array
        ]
        % convert to procedure and bind
        cvx bind
} bind def
```

In summary, we find that PostScript has several mechanisms for substituting a value for a key name and controlling the context in which a name is evaluated. And by its dictionary structure, it allows us to redefine any operator in complex ways.

Procedure, Modify Thyself

The structural flexibility of naming and binding in PostScript allows us to write procedures that modify themselves and to create event handling structures quite different from the complexly nested IF-THEN-ELSE forms used in other languages. By defining dictionaries that contain redefined operators, and activating those dictionaries based on some test of events, we can avoid complicated massage of data under special conditions in our programs. In the real world, modifying the way an application writes out data can often require expensive software engineering.

You'll find real world examples of these techniques if you look at the structure of EPS files imported by Macintosh applications. The host application redefines *showpage* as a null procedure inside a *save ... restore* context to prevent a spurious printing and disruption of page structure by the imported EPS file.

Classic instruction in traditional procedural languages often treats the idea of writing a self-modifying procedure as "original sin." It is true that one should exert cautious control over such code and debug in depth, but there is absolutely nothing wrong with the following form in PostScript:

```
/procedure {
      % initialize some structures once on
      % first call to this procedure only
      /counter0 0 def
      /workstring 100 string def

      % to be done this time and every time
      {
            stuff to do every time
      }
      % do it the first time
      dup exec
      % redefine this procedure so it doesn't initialize variables every time
      /procedure exch def
} bind def
```

EXPRESSION YOURSELF

In traditional procedural languages—BASIC, Pascal, C—the creation of named variables or data structures requires a statically defined symbol. This symbol is translated into an internal address by the interpreter or compiler and cannot be modified. The programmer must type the symbol name literally into the program. These languages cannot evaluate an expression, produce a symbol, and then use it. Pascal and C variable names and data structure names must be declared by type; an integer variable cannot hold a floating point number, for example. The limited evaluation involved in indexing a variable name by evaluation of subscripts, or in de-referencing a handle, or the chained assignment possible in C (of the form a = b = c = 1;), are still limited compared to what LISP and PostScript allow you to do. You do need to take into account the inherent differences between compiled and interpreted languages here.

In Pascal and C, local variables are created by the way they are named in the parameter lists of functions; global variables are created by declaring them outside the definition of functions at the top or enclosing level of the program. A few BASIC implementations now support local variables in a Pascal-like manner.

In LISP, a complex expression can be evaluated and the resulting symbol used to name any type of data or data structure. We can say that in LISP a name object, wherever it came from, can be bound to any object. Local variables are created by naming them in certain ways in the parameter lists of functions and by some internal forms (like let). LISP also has support for "anonymous" variable names (created by a call to gensym) and procedures (created by the lambda mechanism). These nameless forms allow the programmer to hide detail, prevent name conflicts in expanding macros, and conserve the use of names and memory.

Here are some PostScript examples of naming and binding:

```
/myarray 100 array def
/string0 (Post) def
/string1 (Script) def
/myproc { 1 2 add } def
/myinteger 100 cvi def
/myfloat 100.00 def
```

In these first examples we make PostScript behave like other procedural languages. The literal form of a name becomes a key in a dictionary, and the value associated with the key is of varying type. Here we've used names that remind us of what type of object we have placed in them. Let's look at a more complex example:

```
% create a new string big enough to hold both
% string0 and string1, preserving string0's length
```

```
/newstring string0 length dup /s0len exch def string1 length add string def

% insert string0 into new string at its start
    newstring 0 string0 putinterval

% insert string1 at end of string0 in new string
    newstring s0len string1 putinterval

% make new string a variable and assign to it
    newstring (is an object oriented language!) def
```

We created a new string object (PostScript) from two string objects, and made it a key in a dictionary with a value consisting of another string. String objects are automatically converted to name objects when they become keys in dictionaries. Normal name objects do not have white space, but you can, if you wish, construct a name object from a string that includes newline, space, and/or tab characters.

Exotic technical note: even though a string object cannot be a key, the PostScript interpreter knows what you really want:

```
(under the sea) (in an octopus' garden with you) def
userdict (under the sea) get
```

This works properly even though the key in userdict is not a string object.

With the exception of string objects and the null object, every PostScript object can become a key in a dictionary without conversion into a nametype object. Conceptually, this means that PostScript is more "first class" than any other commonly used computer language. Study this carefully:

```
/x { 1 2 add } def
/x load { 3 4 mul } def
/x load load exec
```

The first statement is a simple binding of a procedure to a literal name. The second statement loads the procedure object bound to x and puts it on the stack. The second procedure object then goes on the stack, and the *def* command makes the first procedure object a key in a dictionary whose value is the second procedure object. The third statement loads the first procedure object and then loads its value—

which is the second procedure object—which is then executed. The result would be the value 12 left on the stack

What if we want every PostScript dictionary we create to "remember" its own name? Let's create a dictionary building command that creates a dictionary one slot larger than requested. The key for this extra slot will be the dictionary object itself and its value will be its own literal name:

```
/smartdict { 1 add dict dup dup 3 index put } bind def
/dictname { dup get } bind def
Let's show how we would use this to "ask" a dictionary its own name:
/anydict 10 smartdict def
anydict begin
      /a 100 def
end
anydict dictname
```

The *smartdict* command creates an eleven-slot dictionary. When we call *dictname*, we duplicate the dictionary object on the stack. The *get* command treats the bottom one as the source dictionary and the top one as a key name, and returns the value associated with the key name. Freud would love it.

We talked of how both functional and procedural languages create local variables through placing names in parameter lists. In PostScript, the dictionary structure, a stack, provides a very simple yet elegant control for the scope of names, which is independent of the form of procedures or functions. Yes, we can make PostScript behave like a Pascal function with local variables:

```
/pascalform {
      /scratchdict 4 dict def
      scratchdict begin
            /param1 exch def
            /param2 exch def
            /internal_param 0 def
            % procedure body goes here
      end      % end local dictionary
} def
```

In this example we create a dictionary inside the procedure, and parameters on the stack, as well as one internal parameter, are defined

within it. When this procedure is completed the names used within it
are not available (though they are still defined). There is a potential
problem here. If such a procedure were used in a loop, a new dictionary
would be created each time through the loop; this could be very wasteful of virtual memory. Here are better forms to use:

```
/scratchdict 4 dict def
/form0 {
      scratchdict begin
            /param1 exch def
            /param2 exch def
            /internal_param 0 def
      % procedure body goes here
      end
} bind def


/form1 {
      xxx begin
            /param1 exch def
            /param2 exch def
            /internal_param 0 def
      % procedure body goes here
      end
} def
/form1 load bind 0 4 dict put


/form2 {
      save /form2_save exch def
            /param1 exch def
            /param2 exch def
            /internal_param 0 def
      % procedure body goes here
      form2_save restore
} bind def
```

This second example is more interesting because a nameless dictionary is created outside the procedure body and inserted with a *put*
command, replacing a symbol xxx which serves only as a place marker.
In this way we prevent duplication of the dictionary structure each
time the procedure is called. We could have any number of nameless

dictionaries active at one time without any possibility of a conflict of scope. Local dictionaries used in this way are desirable in PostScript for the same reason that creating local names is desirable in any structured language: to create tightly controlled modular code and to eliminate naming conflicts. Note that we use the command *bind* to eliminate name lookups of system-level primitives just before inserting the nameless dictionary into form2.

Example two uses the *save ... restore* technique. Every object in PostScript is tagged (has a pointer to a special field) with the integer number of its save level. When a *restore* is encountered, the virtual memory of objects with the current save level tag is freed up, and the global save level counter is decremented. This is PostScript's only method to reclaim memory, and it is quite unlike the dynamic garbage collection done in other interpreted high-level languages. You, as a programmer, should feel free to use the *save ... restore* mechanism, since you already pay, as it were, for its use with every object.

SAVE ... A VISIT WITH THE BEARDED LADY

We'll talk a bit more about *save ... restore*, but first a side trip. PostScript gives you all the rope you need to lower yourself into chaos. In that spirit, here is example three for creating a dictionary:

```
/form3 {
     4 dict begin
          /param1 exch def
          /param2 exch def
          /internal_param 0 def
     % procedure body goes here
     % put copy of current dictionary on stack
     currentdict
     end
     % redefine this procedure
     /form3 {
          xxx begin
               /param1 exch def
               /param2 exch def
               /internal_param 0 def
          % procedure body goes here
          end
```

```
        }
        % insert the dictionary into the procedure and re-define
        dup 0 5 -1 roll put bind
        def
} def
```

This monstrosity works. It does the right thing the first time and then redefines itself so that the dictionary created by the first call is in the right place in the revised version of itself. It also has the benefit that the call to allocate the dictionary only happens if the procedure is called once. The tradeoff is the wasteful duplication of commands inside the procedure and the extravagant squandering of unused procedure bodies.

. . . RESTORE

A specific benefit of using *save . . . restore* occurs in the common situation of using global scratch variables which you want reset to some default value after every use. Creating the scratch variable and initializing it once outside your procedure calls, and changing it only within *save . . . restore* contexts, means you can assume it is correctly initialized in every procedure:

```
/counter0 0 def
/counter1 255 def

/process
{
save /process_save exch def
        % do some stuff in here with counter variables
process_save restore
} bind def
```

In this example, two counter variables are defined outside a *save . . . restore* and used within it. Note that we name the save object after creating it. Leaving a save object hanging around on the stack is an invitation to disaster (unfortunately, this is often done). Because we named the save object after it was created, when the *restore* is encountered, the save name is reclaimed—a sensible economy.

There is a limit of twenty or so dictionaries active on the dictionary stack in PostScript (there are always at least two active, systemdict and userdict). Practically, this means that you cannot implement LISP-like recursive processes that depend on continual activation of dictionary after dictionary within a loop.

You can, however, freely insert dictionaries within dictionaries to create complex random-access data structures like a binary tree:

```
/put4 { 4 dict put } bind def
/buildnewnode {
     /node exch def
     node /left put4
     node /right put4
     node /parent 3 -1 roll put
     node /value 3 -1 roll put
} bind def


/binarytree 4 dict def
1 /root binarytree buildnewnode
2 binarytree dup /left get buildnewnode
3 binarytree /left get dup /left get buildnewnode
```

The dictionaries in this sample tree are never activated with *begin*, so there is no danger of producing a dictionary stack overflow error. Still, dictionaries are expensive: you pay at least twenty bytes per key/value pair, plus a few bytes of overhead. This VM use is always based on the declared size of the dictionary; you can't save bytes by leaving a key value pair slot empty. Arrays (cost: eight bytes per slot plus overhead) are much less expensive and can consist of arbitrarily nested stuff, but, of course, must be manipulated through indices rather than being randomly accessible through keys.

Stack It Up

The operand stack in PostScript is used for purposes that in other languages are met by using named variables (or lists or lambda functions in LISP). The point is well taken that recursion is implemented by means of address stacks and value stacks in other languages. Use of the stack as a data structure is a fine way to use PostScript and to avoid paying for arrays or dictionaries. The dangers of using the stack are that it is more difficult to maintain and modularize your code; that exotic stack manipulations are more costly than frequent references to named variables; that you can lose the distinction between data and other objects that are not data; and, finally, that you can overflow the operand stack (limit: five hundred objects, or so). One technique to preserve a place on the stack as a boundary between your data and other objects is to use the mark:

```
/usestack {
      % get the procedure to call off the stack
      /dothis exch def
      % place mark on stack
      mark
      % push mark to bottom of stack
      count 1 roll
      % do something until you hit the most recent mark
      {
            counttomark 0 eq { cleartomark exit } { dothis } ifelse
      }
      loop
} def


data0 data1 data2 .... datan
{ procedure to call to act on data on stack } bind
usestack
```

Here a bunch of data goes on the stack, followed by a procedure definition. The usestack procedure defines the procedure from the stack and then enters a loop where, if the *counttomark* operator returns 0, the stack is cleared to the mark and the mark is cleared (by cleartomark). As long as there's something on the stack above the mark, the stub procedure dothis will be called. The dangers here are: stack overflow; the stack may never get down to the mark; a new mark could somehow get on the stack, etc. Extensive use of the operand stack as a data structure requires increased vigilance by the programmer and may demand more debugging and maintenance.

First-Class PostScript

In other languages, as we've seen, there is far less flexibility and control over naming, and no access to the internal operation of the interpreter or compiler (not strictly true of LISP, which has facilities like macros and *eval*).

The freedom to use objects that are not names as keys in a dictionary is an important, radical step in the evolution of computer languages. On a practical level, there is little need to use this technique in the execution of page descriptions, which are usually static collections of data. This technique is used in the PostWord text formatter in the projects section (Part IV) of this book, both for educational reasons and because it solves a problem elegantly.

I think the "radical first-classness" of PostScript will be understood and widely used only when Display PostScript has fully evolved and users are able to write a complete application with internally defined data structures. Data structures with non-name keys will be appropriate in the highest-level, most indeterminate computational problems, like expert systems and asynchronous, event-driven windowing interfaces. There is no reason that a SmallTalk or Prolog could not be written in PostScript!

In this light, the criticism by some in the desktop publishing trade that PostScript is slow because it spends time looking up names in dictionaries rather than getting busy making marks in raster memory is valid. Programmers writing translators that take page descriptions as their input can, through judicious use of binding and the stack, eliminate many name lookups. Here are a few heuristics for making your code faster and smaller:

1. Carefully evaluate and eliminate, if possible, all occurrences of ( ) { } [ ] or string array and *dict* operators inside a loop.

2. Use *bind* on every procedure definition you can.

3. Carefully evaluate the trade-offs between using the stack to hold data and intermediate results of computation, and using named variables. Too many rolls, dups, or indexes may indicate a situation where a few temporary definitions will produce smaller, more efficient code that is much easier to maintain and debug.

   Each name you use will cost you forty or so bytes when you create it, but reusing a name costs nothing. This is a bargain if one or two names will eliminate exotic stack manipulations at key places in your code.

4. Locate the most repeated sections of your code and minimize the use of subroutine calls in those sections.

5. Create named variables holding pointers to frequently used fonts.

6. Set the most frequently used graphic state parameters and fonts as defaults and change them only inside *gsave . . . grestore* contexts.

7. Use the *save . . . restore* mechanism to manage virtual memory and to avoid unnecessary reinitialization of scratch variables

8. Consider using some of the advanced binding techniques presented here when creating a frequently executed critical loop.

9. Consider the use of local "nameless" dictionaries to manage local variables.

3 / Writing Device-Independent PostScript   *Michael Fryd*

Although PostScript is advertised as a device-independent way of describing pages, it is possible to write PostScript programs that will successfully print on some PostScript printers and fail to print on others. The most useful PostScript programs are those that print properly under all circumstances. Ideally it should be possible to:

- Print a PostScript file on *any* PostScript printer (not just a 300 dpi LaserWriter)

- Merge a PostScript file into a composite document. The original file may need to be rescaled, repositioned, or rotated

- Use a utility program to extract and/or reorder individual pages in a PostScript file

  This flexibility is available only in programs written in the subset of PostScript that I call "generic PostScript".

Generic PostScript

Many people don't see an advantage to generic PostScript. These same people create PostScript programs that will work only on the printer they have, cannot be included in another document, and don't work with utility programs. These people experience major problems whenever one of the following occurs:

- Their printer breaks and they need to use the one down the hall

- Their company buys a new printer and expects the existing files to work

- Their company decides to print the final copy on a high-resolution Linotronic 300

- The boss wants the great-looking logo they designed to appear in the annual report—only he wants it smaller than they intended

- Their offset printing house offers them a discount if they can print the pages in signature order.

It's really quite easy to write in generic PostScript; there are four simple concepts to keep in mind:

- *Context Independence*—Do trust that your initial environment is correct

- *Device Independence*—Don't make any assumptions about the device your file will be printed on

- *Page Independence*—Wrap each page with *save* and *restore* to make sure pages are independent of one another

- *Spooler Friendly*—Follow Adobe's Document Structuring Conventions.

These concepts sound very simple, and for the most part they are. It is just a matter of knowing which PostScript operators are to be avoided, and which must be used with care. Most PostScript operators are safe to use, some operators are always unsafe, and the remaining fall into a gray area and may only be used with care and under certain circumstances.

Page Description Languages vs. Printer Control Languages

PostScript is not only a Page Description Language (PDL), but also a Printer Control Language (PCL). The PDL features of the language are used for describing, in an ideal fashion, how the page should look, while the PCL features are used for describing how to realize that image on the current printer. Most PostScript operators can be easily categorized as either PDL or PCL commands, but a few iffy operators can be used as either PDL or PCL.

The normal PostScript drawing and painting operators (*setgray, lineto, moveto, stroke, fill,* etc.) all fall into the PDL category and may be used freely. PostScript operators that control how the printer is set up (*setsccbatch, setdefaulttimeouts, setidlefonts, manualfeed*, etc.) fall into the PCL category and should not be used.

The remaining operators (*settransfer, setscreen*, etc.) were intended by Adobe to be PCL commands; however these commands may be carefully used to achieve certain special effects (posterizations, reverse video, pattern fills, etc.). When carefully used to control the look of an image, these commands are, effectively, PDL commands.

Generic PostScript files should contain only PDL commands (or the PDL uses of the iffy commands). If your particular setup requires the use of PCL commands, do not imbed them in every PostScript file you produce; rather keep the PCL commands in separate files and use those separate files as needed.

For example, when you buy a LaserWriter you may need to set up the LaserWriter's communication parameters to match your computer's communication parameters. The method to change the Laser-Writer's communication parameters is to create a PostScript file containing the *setsccbatch* command.

```
% This command sets the LaserWriter to 9600 bd odd parity.
% This only works outside of the server loop.
25 9600 1 setsccbatch
```

If you were to embed the *setsccbatch* operator in all of your PostScript files, then you would have no trouble as long as you were printing from your computer. Your file would not, however, work on a printer that was connected via AppleTalk or Ethernet.

The correct method is to have separate files for the PCL functions from the PDL functions. If your printer setup requires that they be sent together, have a small command file on your computer to merge them temporarily just before printing.

Remember, a generic PostScript file describes what to print (the image), not how to print it (the communication parameters).

Context Independence

One of the big advantages of the PostScript language is that it allows the user to describe images in an ideal abstract environment; PostScript automatically handles the translation from the abstract description to the printed page. Although the abstractions are the same regardless of what printer is being used, the translations differ from PostScript printer to PostScript printer.

Composite documents add another layer of abstraction to the situation. You may intend for your file to produce an image that fills the entire page, but your image might be reduced to become a small part of a composite document. This reduction is accomplished by changing the initial context (i.e., translations) that your file sees.

You may think of a PostScript program as painting onto an 8½-by-11-inch page, but actually it is painting into a 612-unit by 792-unit rectangle. The default context maps the 612-by-792 rectangle to the 8½-by-11-inch page. Components of composite documents are positioned by providing the component with a nonstandard initial context that has the 612-by-792 rectangle carefully positioned and sized on the page.

If your file was to be reduced to fifty percent and placed in the top left corner of a composite page, the following code might be used to set up an initial context with the 612-by-792 rectangle reduced and positioned at the top left corner of the page:

```
396 translate        % move origin halfway up page
.5 .5 scale          % use 50% scale so image fits
% insert included file here
```

A context-independent PostScript program will work regardless of what its initial environment is, and will conform to that initial environment.

The general rule is to avoid assumptions about the initial state of the PostScript environment (context). When you make such assumptions, you limit your program to functioning correctly only when those assumptions are true.

NEVER USE INIT OPERATORS

The various PostScript init operators are PCL operators used internally by the printer to reset the printer to the standard state before each job. These PCL commands should never appear in a Generic PostScript file, although there are two circumstances where people are tempted to use them: at the start of the file, and to undo a series of changes.

The most common assumption that destroys context independence is "*initgraphics* can be used to undo graphics state changes."

Many people have a habit of always starting their PostScript files with *initgraphics* (or *initclip*, or *initmatrix*) to make sure the PostScript environment is in its default state. The problem is that this practice assumes the default environment is the appropriate environment with which to start. If your file is being printed by itself, your *initgraphics* is superfluous because the PostScript environment will already be in its default state. If your file is being included as part of a composite document, then the appropriate initial state will have been specially prepared to properly position your file on the page, and your use of an init command will undo that preparation.

The second common use of *initgraphics* (or *initclip*, or *initmatrix*) is in the middle of a file to undo a long series of changes and return to the original environment. The problem is that the init command doesn't return to your file's original environment; it returns to the printer's default environment. If your file is part of a composite document, your file's initial environment may not be the same as the printer's default environment.

The proper way of restoring the PostScript environment to its original state is to start your file with a *gsave* to save your initial context, and then use *grestore* to return to the saved context.

RIGHT	WRONG
Resets graphics context to file's initial context	Resets graphics context to printer's default context

```% save the graphics state```	```% restore default graphics```
```% we started with```	```% state```
```gsave```	```initgraphics```
```...```	```...```
```% restore starting g-state```	```% restore default g-state```
```grestore gsave```	```initgraphics```
```...```	```...```
```grestore gsave```	```initgraphics```
```...```	```...```
```grestore```	```initgraphics```
```...```	```...```

The same reasons for not using *initgraphics* also apply to *initmatrix* and *initclip*. *Initmatrix* is sometimes used to restore the CTM (current translation matrix) to its original value without affecting the rest of the graphics state.

The correct solution is to avoid *initmatrix* and to treat the CTM the same as any other component of the graphic state. To save only a few components of the graphic state, just look them up with one of the *currentxxx* operators, and then use the corresponding *setxxx* operator to restore the previous value.

RIGHT
Resets CTM to
file's initial CTM

WRONG
Resets CTM to
printer's default CTM

```
% look up and save the
% CTM we started with
/StartCTM matrix                    % insure default CTM
  currentmatrix def                 initmatrix
...                                 ...
%return us to original CTM          % restore default TM
StartCTM setmatrix                  initmatrix
...                                 ...
%return us to original CTM          % restore default TM
StartCTM setmatrix                  initmatrix
...                                 ...
```

The fundamental rule in PostScript programming is "always augment the current environment; never replace it." This means that you should work from your initial environment, and not try to ignore it.

DON'T LOOK UP VALUES IN SYSTEMDICT

The PostScript environment includes more than just the graphics state; it also includes the definitions of the various PostScript operators.

PostScript keeps definitions in dictionaries, and always searches the dictionary stack to find the current definition of each name it encounters. The last dictionary in the dictionary stack (and hence the last dictionary searched) is called systemdict. This is where the standard definitions for built-in operators are stored. In order to retain context independence, you must always trust the current definitions of the various PostScript commands. Never explicitly look up definitions directly in systemdict.

Normally this rule is easy to follow. The typical scenario is to refer to all PostScript commands by name. PostScript takes care of finding the current definition. The one situation about which you must be wary is when you redefine one of the built-in operators.

For example, suppose you had a multi-page PostScript file and you wanted to print a copy with the word "DRAFT" ghosted in the background. In order for "DRAFT" to be in the background, it must be the first thing placed onto the page. An easy way to do this is to modify the *showpage* command so that it starts each new page by placing the word "DRAFT" in the background.

To do this, we first write a procedure called Print-Draft-Notice to ghost the word "DRAFT" onto the background:

```
/Print-Draft-Notice
      {save
      200 72 moveto
      60 rotate
      /Helvetica-Bold findfont 200 scalefont setfont
      .95 setgray
      (DRAFT) show
      restore
} bind def
```

Then we define a new version of *showpage*, which simply calls the original *showpage* followed by Print-Draft-Notice:

RIGHT	WRONG
Builds on current definition	Builds on standard definition

```
%Place notice on 1st page          %Place notice on 1st page
Print-Draft-Notice                 Print-Draft-Notice

% Look up current showpage
/Old-Showpage /showpage load def

% define new showpage               % define new showpage
/showpage{                         /showpage{
% invoke original showpage          %invoke standard showpage
Old-Showpage                       systemdict /showpage get exec
% Put "draft" on new page           % Put "draft" on new page
Print-Draft-Notice                 Print-Draft-Notice
} bind def                         } bind def
```

This is not the only useful customization that can be made to *showpage*. Some sites modify *showpage* to put a corporate logo and copyright notice on each page, while other sites modify *showpage* to report timing statistics back to the host. Some Linotype owners change *showpage* to count pages and to stop every fifteen pages so they can change paper rolls.

If you use the built-in definition of *showpage* from systemdict, then you will bypass any other *showpage* customizations. If you use the definition you started with, you can combine the customizations however you like.

THOSE IFFY PCL FUNCTIONS

Adobe was very good in designing the PDL operators to work by modifying the current environment rather than replacing it. The command 2 2 scale stretches the coordinates system by a factor of 2, rather than setting it to 2.

However, most PCL commands ignore the current environment and simply replace the existing value with a new one. This makes sense, as you are less likely to need to double the baud rate of the communications channel than to set it to a particular rate.

The "iffy" commands are PCL commands that can be used to alter the way the page looks. When using a PCL command for PDL functions, you must be very careful to take the current environment into account. Usually this means that you must look up the current environmental values manually, and then modify those values to get the new value. You can then safely use this computed value with the PCL command.

Failure to take the current value into account when using a PCL function will destroy your file's context independence and device independence.

DON'T BLINDLY REPLACE THE TRANSFER FUNCTION

The PostScript transfer function defines the relationship between the gray level requested by the user and the percentage of printer rasters set to white. Typically this is a one to one mapping; i.e., .25 setgray will usually result in twenty-five percent of the printer rasters in each halftone cell being white. The transfer function was intended to be used by Adobe to compensate for nonlinear makes of marking engines (thus making it a PCL-only command.)

Regardless of what Adobe intended, the transfer function is very useful for achieving special effects, such as posterizations, high contrast, and reverse images (black for white and vice versa.) This is a PDL use and places the transfer function in that area of iffy commands that may only be used with care in generic PostScript files.

The *settransfer* operator is used for changing the transfer function, but because it was intended to be a PCL command it ignores the current transfer function when setting the new one.

For example, reverse image (black for white and white for black) requires only a simple change to the transfer function. The typical mistake the user makes is to simply replace the current transfer function, reasoning that "The default transfer function doesn't do anything anyway." Of course, the fallacy is that you don't really know what your initial context is. Your program might be part of a composite document, or might be sent to a printer with an atypical default transfer function.

The correct procedure is to have your new transfer function modify the current transfer function. The easiest way to accomplish this is to assign a name to the current transfer function, and then have your new transfer function refer to the old function by this name.

Remember that the transfer function takes one argument, a number between 0 and 1; this is the current gray. The transfer function should return a single number between 0 and 1 that represents the percentage of pixels to be white. For a transfer function that produces reverse video, we do the following:

RIGHT
Modifies existing transfer function

WRONG
Ignores existing
transfer function

```
% remember original transfer function
/initial-xfer currenttransfer def
{1 exch sub % reverse number
initial-xfer % call old xfer
} bind settransfer
```

```
{1 exch sub % reverse number

} bind settransfer
```

Remembering to use the original transfer function is particularly important when printing high-quality work on a laser typesetter like the Linotronic. The photographic process used is not always linear;

different batches of paper and processing chemicals can alter the densities of the halftones. The easiest way for the operator to compensate is to adjust the transfer function, and it is important that your file doesn't erase these adjustments. Remembering the original transfer function is also important when your file has been included in another document, in which case that document might already be applying a special effect of its own.

DON'T OVERSPECIFY

Don't set the values in the graphics state unless you need them to be a particular value. If your PostScript program always paints in the same color, don't start by setting the current color to black. In the typical case, the default color will already be black, and if you don't change it your program will be able to paint images in the default color, regardless of what it is.

On the other hand, if your program makes use of color (or different gray levels), and contains elements of colors other than the default black (white counts as another color), you can certainly make sure that the initial color is whatever you need it to be.

SPEAK IN WHISPERS, LEAVE NO FOOTPRINTS

Always assume that your file will be included in a composite document. Follow your mother's advice and clean up after yourself.

You can get away without cleaning up after yourself when your file is printed stand-alone. No matter what shape the PostScript environment (graphics state and various stacks) is left in, it will be cleaned up by the server loop before the next job is executed. When your file is part of a composite document, however, the server loop does not clean up for you, and you must clean up after yourself. The only changes your PostScript file should make are to the page; everything else should be left the same.

Leave the operand stack the same as you found it. Don't leave the stacks cluttered with items. If you have put anything on a stack, make sure you take it off. If you don't want to keep track, start your file with a *mark* command and end with a *cleartomark*.

Leave Dictionary, Graphic, and Exec stacks the same as you found them. If you have used *begin*s to add to the dictionary stack, make sure you have a matching *end* for every *begin* to remove the dictionary from the stack.

Leave VM the same as you found it. You should not leave any definitions modified, and you should not use up lots of VM. This is easy to implement. Just start your file with a *save* and end it with a *restore*. The *save* operator allows you to change virtual memory (VM) as much as you like, with the *restore* undoing the changes.

You can think of *save* as taking a snapshot of all of your existing definitions, and the *restore* as resetting the definitions to match the snapshot. This may sound like an expensive (slow) process, but it isn't. POSTSCRIPT doesn't really take a snapshot; instead it uses a tagging scheme whose implementation is built into all POSTSCRIPT commands. You incur the overhead of the *save . . . restore* mechanism whether or not you use it, so you may as well use it to your advantage.

Leave the Graphics State the same as you found it. It is quite normal to change the graphics state while creating your image. Most POSTSCRIPT files change the coordinate system, create paths, change the gray level, etc. When your file is included in a composite document, you want to be careful to undo all of these changes so that subsequent parts of the composite document will not be affected. In practice, you don't need to worry about this; the *save* and *restore* commands that you should use to protect VM also save and restore the graphics state.

Don't stretch the printer to its limits. The red book (occasionally referred to as *The POSTSCRIPT Language Reference Manual*) lists the guaranteed minimum limits for various POSTSCRIPT resources. These are minimums for the amount of VM on which you can depend, how deep all the stacks are, how complex paths may become, etc.

These are limits for the machine as a whole. If your file is included as part of a composite page, many resources may already be used, and there may be much less of these resources available for you. Always stay well within the published limits, and never use more resources than you need to.

Don't use all of stack space. Place items on the operand stack only as you need them:

RIGHT	WRONG
Uses only as much stack as needed	Uses as much stack as possible

```
20 moveto 37 86 lineto        4 37 86 10 20
4 setgray                     moveto lineto setgray
```

The correct example above never has more than two arguments on the stack at a time. The wrong example places all five arguments on the stack and then uses them. This is a simple example. Although placing five arguments on the stack won't get you into trouble, you shouldn't place more on the stack than you need to. POSTSCRIPT guarantees that the stack can hold up to five hundred items, but that's no excuse for you to try to use all five hundred items. If your document is part of a composite document, part of the stack may be in use by the master document.

Don't forget that when you define a POSTSCRIPT procedure (commands inside of { } brackets), POSTSCRIPT uses the stack as temporary storage of the procedure. This means that you can't easily have a procedure with more than five hundred commands in it (less if the stack is being used for other things too). Of course, you can always break up a procedure into two smaller procedures, which are in turn called by a master procedure:

RIGHT	WRONG
Uses small amounts of stack space	Uses large amounts of stack space

```
/MyProc {                     /MyProc {
 MyProc-Part-1                    [...very big procedure...]
 MyProc-Part-2                } bind def
} bind def
/MyProc-Part-1 {
 [ ... first small portion
  of very big procedure...]
} bind def
/MyProc-Part-2 {
 [ ... next small portion
  of very big procedure...]
} bind def
```

In addition to limits on the operand stack, there are limits to how many *saves* or *gsaves* may be active at one time, and, in composite files, some of the available *saves* will be used by the master document.

One situation where you may be tempted to have many active *saves* is when you need to *save* (or *gsave*) the environment and return to it many times. The problem is that each *save* should have a matching *restore*, so the temptation is to put many *gsaves* up front, and then spread the *grestores* throughout the rest of the file. The correct technique is to do a single *gsave*, and then follow each *grestore*, except the last, with another *gsave*. This technique allows you unlimited returns to the same context, yet never has more than one active *gsave* at a time:

RIGHT	WRONG
Uses 1 slot on gsave stack	Uses 3 slots on gsave stack

```
RIGHT                                  WRONG
Uses 1 slot on gsave stack             Uses 3 slots on gsave stack

gsave                                  gsave
                                       gsave
                                       gsave

.5 setgray                             .5 setgray
fill                                   fill
grestore                               grestore
gsave
0 setgray 3 setlinewidth stroke        0 setgray 3 setlinewidth stroke
grestore                               grestore
gsave
.5 setgray 2 setlinewidth stroke       .5 setgray 2 setlinewidth stroke
grestore                               grestore
1 setgray 1 setlinewidth stroke        1 setgray 1 setlinewidth stroke
```

Keep paths short. There is also a limit to how complex a path may be. Unfortunately, path complexity is tied to size and resolution. If a file is magnified, or printed on a higher resolution printer, path complexity is increased. A file that prints on a LaserWriter may not print (limit-check errors) on a Linotronic 300. The solution is to assume that you will be printing on a high-resolution device and always to break up complex paths into many simpler paths.

If you have a single path that is an outline for an octopus, you would be better off making each arm (and the body) an independent path, and operating on each independent path separately. By concentrating on one small path at a time, you reduce the complexity of the current path. It is important to deal completely with one path before moving on to the next, because the path complexity limit applies to the combination of the current path, the clipping path, and all paths saved by *gsave* and *grestore*.

Character outlines are very complex paths. The *charpath* operator allows you to turn character outlines into paths. If you use *charpath* on a string of many letters you run the risk of exceeding path complexity. The solution is to use *charpath* on one letter at a time.

RIGHT

```
/Times-Bold findfont 200 scalefont
setfont 100 100 moveto
(H) false charpath
currentpoint        % save cp
stroke              % clears cp
moveto              % restores cp
(e) false charpath
currentpoint        % save cp
stroke              % clears cp
moveto              % restores cp
(l) false charpath
currentpoint        % save cp
stroke              % clears cp
moveto              % restores cp
(l) false charpath
currentpoint        % save cp
stroke              % clears cp
moveto              % restores cp
(o) false charpath
stroke
```

WRONG

```
/Times-Bold findfont 200 scalefont
setfont 100 100 moveto
(Hello) false charpath

stroke
```

The correct method is more work, but will actually work on a high-resolution PostScript printer. To save programmer effort, we can, of course, define a procedure to perform the *charpath* and *stroke* on each character of a string.

Device Independence

Never assume that your document will always be printed on a partic-ular type of printer. This means:

- Never assume that you know the resolution of the device
- Never assume that you can tell what features are present from the product name.
- Never assume anything that isn't specified in *PostScript Language Reference Manual* (red book)
- Don't use anything from statusdict.

Never assume you know what the resolution of the PostScript printer is. You never really need to know. There are times when the resolution of the printer needs to be considered (printing thin lines or device resolution bitmaps), but even this can be handled in a device-indepen-dent fashion.

Zero Width Lines. Many people make assumptions about the resolu-tion of the device without even realizing it. The most common method is to use 0 setlinewidth to get hairlines. When you ask PostScript for a line width of zero, PostScript gives you the thinnest line that the printer is capable of printing. This is, by definition, resolution-depen-dent. On a 300 dpi printer, you get a nice, visible hairline; on a 2500 dpi printer you need a magnifying glass to see the line. The correct approach is to specify the size of the hairline you want.

If you like the LaserWriter's 1/300-inch hairline, just ask for it with .24 setlinewidth (1/300th-inch is .24 points).

Printing Thin Lines. PostScript is very good at hiding the fact that you are really using a raster printing engine, but there are some minor problems when printing objects (such as thin lines) that are very close to the device's resolution.

For instance, on a 300 dpi printer, a vertical line .36 points wide should be exactly 1.5 pixels wide. Unfortunately, 1.5 pixels is not a possibility. The line will be either exactly 1 or exactly 2 pixels wide. The choice of 1 or 2 depends on where the line happens to be with respect to the nearest pixel. One three-hundredth of an inch doesn't sound like much, but the human eye can easily see the difference between a 1-pixel- and a 2-pixel-wide line. The situation is compounded if you are creating a form with many lines of equal width.

The wrong solution is to make sure that all positions you use are multiples of a 1/300-inch. This works only on a 300 dpi printer, and only if you are not scaled as part of a composite page.

The correct solution is to specify the position that you really want, and then, at the last moment, to adjust the position to the nearest pixel. As long as all of your addresses have the same alignment with the physical pixels, POSTSCRIPT will always round the same way, and all lines of a given requested width will be the same number of pixels wide. You do lose a smidgen of accuracy, as the position of the center of the line may be off by up to half a pixel. This is a good compromise, as the eye will notice the difference in line thicknesses, but it won't notice the difference in spaces between lines.

The trick is to do this adjustment in such a way that it will work for all POSTSCRIPT printers, not making any assumptions about what the resolution is.

The following routine expects an X and a Y position on the stack. It adjusts both positions so that they line up with the physical pixels.

```
/SnapToPixel {
        transform           % convert from user coordinates to device coordinates
        round .25 add       % adjust Y coordinate to just past nearest pixel
        exch                % move X to top of stack
        round .25 add       % adjust X coordinate to just past nearest pixel
        exch                % put Y back on top
        itransform          % convert back to user coordinates
} bind def
```

This routine works by using the *transform* operator to run the specified coordinates through the CTM to give us the coordinates expressed in pixels. We use the round operator to throw away any fractional component, which gets us the exact address of the nearest pixel. We then add a fudge factor of .25. POSTSCRIPT sometimes uses lines that are an even number, and sometimes an odd number of pixels wide. If we didn't add the .25, POSTSCRIPT would always produce lines that were an odd number of pixels in width. If we added .5, POSTSCRIPT would always make lines an even number of pixels in width. By choosing .25, POSTSCRIPT gets us much closer to the desired line width.

This routine should be called whenever positioning a thin line. It could also be used for thick lines, but there isn't any need. Half-pixel variations are not noticeable with thick lines. You do not need to use this routine when positioning text, because PostScript's font machinery has this optimization built-in, at least for Adobe typefaces.

```
%sample use of SnapToPixel
100 200 SnapToPixel moveto
100 300 SnapToPixel lineto stroke
450 256 SnapToPixel moveto
0 210 rlineto stroke
```

You should note that the SnapToPixel is needed only for absolute positions such as those passed to *moveto* and *lineto*. It is not needed by relative positions such as those passed to *rlineto* or *rmoveto*.

Printing Bitmaps at Device Resolution. The next most common reason for wanting to know the device's resolution is to be able to quickly print bitmaps. When PostScript notices a bitmap being imaged at exactly the physical resolution of the device, it uses some shortcuts that allow it to process the page faster.

If you download a 300 dpi bitmap to a 300 dpi printer, PostScript will handle it very quickly. But what about 400 dpi printers? There are two choices: shrink the image to seventy-five percent of its original size so that it will print quickly, or print it at its original size.

If you shrink the image to fit, you will save time in printing, but your file prints differently on different printers. On a 2,500 dpi printer, you would have to shrink the file to about twelve percent of its original size. Your best bet is not to shrink the picture and to let PostScript print it at the size you really want. PostScript can even handle bitmaps that are a higher resolution than the intended output device, using its halftoning mechanism to produce a reasonable representation.

Never assume that you can tell what features are present from the product name. Most PostScript programs never need to know about the printer they are using, but some utility programs do need to know about various features the printer has. For instance, a PostScript program that listed all fonts available on a particular printer needs to know if the printer has a hard disk so it can check the hard disk for fonts.

The correct way to determine if a feature (such as a hard disk) is available is to find out whether the PostScript operators that control it exist. The wrong way is to check the product name to find out whether it is the printer you are looking for:

RIGHT	WRONG
Checks to see if the feature is available	Checks to see what model printer is in use

```
% Check to see if there              % if we are on a Linotype
% is a file system                   % then there is a file system


systemdict/filenameforall known      product (Linotype) eq
```

Both fragments of code put a true on the stack if they think there is a file system, and a false if they think there isn't. Both pieces of code worked when Linotype made the only printer that had a hard disk. Only the fragment on the left works on the Varityper VT600 (600 dpi with hard disk).

Never assume anything that isn't specified in PostScript Language Reference Manual (the red book). The red book contains the public definition of PostScript. Anything in the red book (except for Appendix D, which covers the Apple LaserWriter specifically) will continue to be supported by future PostScript printers. If it isn't in the manual, don't use it. Undocumented PostScript operators or features which "just happen to work" or "work on both printers we have in the office" may not work on future PostScript printers.

A few companies are marketing PostScript look-alikes (clones). These printers contain an implementation of PostScript that was created without Adobe's help. The clone makers have only the red book to work from. If you use a feature that is not in the red book, the clone manufacturers may not have known about it and it won't be in their printers.

A useful but undocumented feature is the =string. Some PostScript printers have a string called =string in systemdict that is 128 bytes long. This string is used as a scratch string by some of the built-in routines (like "=="). Don't try to use this string yourself. Adobe has never guaranteed that =string will exist, so it may not exist in future printers (or future ROM revisions of current printers).

Don't use anything from statusdict. Printer setup and other printer-specific operators are stored in the dictionary called statusdict. The available operators (and their effects) differ from one model printer to another. Don't use anything from statusdict or you will be tied to machines that have that particular statusdict entry.

Don't assume you know how the printer is connected. It is always wrong to assume that you know how the printer is connected to the host computer. In fact, you shouldn't assume that the printer is connected to a local computer. This means that you have to worry not only about how the host will talk to the printer, but also about how the file will get from your machine to the machine with the printer.

CHARACTER LIMITATIONS

In order for a PostScript file to be printed, it must be communicated to the PostScript printer. This task consists primarily of sending the contents of the file to the printer, but there are some administrative functions which must be added in as well.

- The host must tell the printer where jobs begin and end
- The printer must tell the host when it is and isn't ready for more of the file (flow control)
- The host may tell the printer to abort a job
- The host may ask a printer for its status (busy, idle, etc.)
- The printer may inform the host of unusual conditions such as paper out, or a paper jam

The actual mechanism for this administrative overhead depends on how the printer is connected. The four most common methods for connecting a PostScript printer to a host are Serial, AppleTalk, Centronics Parallel, and Ethernet connection. AppleTalk and Ethernet printers split your file into packets. Administrative functions are handled by special packets which don't interfere with your file. Serial and Parallel communications use "in-band" signaling for administrative functions. Certain ASCII control characters are mixed in with your file to signal the various conditions. For example the character Control-D (Octal 004) is used to signal the end of a job. This means that if your PostScript file contains a Control-D, and it is printed via a serial printer, the printer will interpret the Control-D as the end of the print job.

Putting a Control-D at the beginning and end of every file to insure that the printer will reset before and after your job is a bad idea because it will ensure that your file will only print on a serial printer. Marking where files begin and end is the job of the spooler program, not the creator of the PostScript file.

The characters Control-C, Control-T, and sometimes Control-S and Control-Q are also reserved. If your file contains any of these characters, it will not correctly print over a serial connection (unless it was relying on a Control-D to signal End-of-Job, then it will *only* print on a serial printer).

Some serial printers can only pass characters in the range 1 to 127 (decimal), while nonserial can typically pass all 256 possible characters (0 to 255).

What this all means is simple: stick to the ninety-five printing ASCII characters, plus space, tab, and new-line. To be specific:

- Do not include characters whose code is above 128 (high bit on)

- Do not include control characters in your file

- Do not place a Control-D in your file to indicate end-of-job (this works only with serial printers)

There are two cases where it is tempting to place unusual characters in your file: for getting at unusual characters and for printing bitmap data.

If you need to access an unusual character, don't place the character directly in your file; use PostScript's string escape mechanism instead. To get at the cent sign (¢) in character position octal 242, use:

RIGHT	WRONG
Uses 7-bit ASCII	Uses 8-bit ASCII

```
(only 24\242 if you order now) show          (only 24¢ if you order now) show
```

The correct method uses four normal characters (\242) to represent one unusual character (¢), but will work on all printers. The wrong method places the 8-bit character directly in the file, and may not work on a serial printer.

Always encode bitmap data as printing characters. PostScript has built-in functions to handle hexadecimal data, and you can write your own for other schemes (including compression.) Just make sure you stick to the set of printing characters.

Don't set communication options. Never start your file by setting up the printer's communication parameters. After all, the communication parameters must have been right in the first place, or the printer wouldn't be executing your file.

Host Limits. In addition to the limits imposed by the various communication methods, some host computers have limitations of their own. You should stay within these limitations so your files are more transportable.

- Keep line length below 132 characters (PostScript allows you to freely insert new-lines in hex data). Many hosts may truncate long lines, or insert new-lines in inconvenient places

- Keep line lengths longer than a few characters (60 to 70 is ideal). Some hosts have overhead associated with each line, and very short lines can slow down printing.

Change device parameters in a device-independent fashion. Sometimes you will need to change a device parameter. If you are doing color separations, you will need to change screen angles. The important point is not to change anything you don't really need to. If you need to change the screen angle, leave the spot function alone:

RIGHT
Leaves spot function alone

```
currentscreen % get current
3 1 roll pop  % throw away angle
75     % replace with 75
3 -1 roll  % put in proper order

setscreen   % set new angle
```

WRONG
Changes spot function and frequency

```
60 % frequency

75 % angle
{dup mul exch dup
mul add 1 exch sub}
setscreen
```

Spooler Friendly

In a multi-user environment, a *spooler* is a program that will accept printing requests from many users and process the requests as the resources become available. A good spooler allows users to make a print request even when the printer is in use; the spooler will hold the file until the printer is available, allowing the user to continue with his or her work.

A good spooler will do more than just hold print requests; it will download fonts on an as-needed basis, print pages in reverse order, and automatically select the first available printer from a group.

The spooler must be able to determine your file's organization and needs if it is to successfully perform all of its tasks. Most spoolers don't try to understand the PostScript in your file, they just look for certain standardized comments.

These comments are described in Appendix C, "Document Structuring Conventions," of the red book. All PostScript files should follow these conventions.

Page Independence

A PostScript file is actually a computer program. It can allocate memory and/or affect its environment in many ways. Although a PostScript file consists of an ordered group of pages, it is frequently desirable to print the pages out of order, or to print only a subset of the pages.

Usually this is accomplished with a utility program that looks at your PostScript file and extracts only the desired portions in the desired order. In order for a PostScript file to work with one of these utility programs, it must be organized according to Adobe's guidelines.

- The file should start with a prologue
- The prologue should be followed by a series of independent pages
- The file should end with a trailer
- Adobe Document Structuring Comments must be used to identify the various portions

The prologue contains any definitions or setup needed by the rest of the file. No matter how the pages are shuffled, the prologue will remain at the beginning, so you can use procedures defined in the prologue on any page.

The trailer should undo any environment changes made by the prologue. No matter how the pages are shuffled, the trailer will remain at the end, so it won't take effect until all of the desired pages have printed.

Pages must be independent of one another. Setting the line width on one page and relying on it still to be set on the next page will lead to trouble if the pages are printed out of order. A good technique is to start every page with a *save* and to place the matching *restore* just before the *showpage*. The *restore* will undo any environment changes made on that page, so you are guaranteed that the page cannot possibly affect subsequent pages. When your pages are guaranteed independent, it is safe to reorder them however you like.

RIGHT	WRONG
Independent page	Dependent pages

```
%%Page 1 1
save
3 setlinewidth                    3 setlinewidth
newpath                           newpath
400 400 45 0 360 arc stroke       400 400 45 0 360 arc stroke
restore
showpage                          showpage
%%Page 2 2
save
3 setlinewidth                    % assume line width is still 3
newpath                           newpath
400 400 25 0 360 arc stroke       400 400 25 0 360 arc stroke
restore
showpage                          showpage
```

The *showpage* should always come after the *restore*. The reason is that in some environments it is useful for *showpage* to keep track of how many pages have been printed. On a Linotype, *showpage* might be redefined to stop every fifteen pages and to wait for a new roll of typesetter paper to be loaded. If *showpage* is outside of the *save-restore*, it can keep the page count in a variable. If the *showpage* were inside the *save-restore*, then the *restore* would undo any changes *showpage* tried to make to the counter.

Rules of Thumb

- Follow Adobe's Document Structuring Conventions (Appendix C of the red book)

- Start every page with a *save*, and put the matching *restore* just before the *showpage*

- Keep PCL functions in their own separate files

- Don't use device setup commands: *exitserver, erasepage, grestoreall, start, banddevice, clear, closefile, erasepage, initclip, initmatrix, defaultmatrix, initgraphics, renderbands*, and *quit*

- If you think you want to use *erasepage*, use the following instead:

```
gsave       % save current context
newpath     % clear any current path
clippath    % get current clipping path (typically page boundary)
1 setgray   % set color to white
fill        % fill with white
grestore    % restore context
```

- If you think you want to use *initclip*, use instead an initial *gsave* to remember your initial clipping region and then use *grestore* to restore it.

- Be very careful when using *transform, itransform, dtransform*, and *ditransform*. These printer control commands should be used only when computing the appropriate arguments for other PCL commands that take arguments in inches or rasters (like *setscreen*), or for fine positioning of thin lines

- Don't explicitly set the CTM (*setmatrix* operator). Setting the CTM assumes you know the resolution of the device, the laser scan direction, paper feed direction, and whether or not your program is part of a composite document. The only time it is alright to use *setmatrix* is when you pass *setmatrix* a value that you previously (i.e., in this print job) looked up with *currentmatrix*

- Your file should consist entirely of the ninety-five printing ASCII characters, plus space, tab, and new-line.

- Don't assume that FontDirectory contains all available fonts. This especially isn't true on printers with a hard disk

- Avoid *setscreen*. If you must use it, use *currentscreen* to determine current parameters and change only what you need to. Remember, the screen frequency does not follow the current scale. If you want it to scale, you must use look up the current scale (compare *currentmatrix* to *defaultmatrix*) and manually determine the scaled frequency

- Avoid *settransfer*. If you must use it, make sure you modify, not replace, the existing transfer function

- Avoid *setflat*. If you must play with flat, use *currentflat* to determine old value and change that.

- Avoid paper size selection

Part II

Working with Type

Kerning is the art of adjusting the space between letters in a word so that the letters appear to be uniformly well-spaced. Shortly after placing our first text on a page, most of us learned about kerning. In awe of our new ability to place text anywhere on a page, we showed it to a professional graphic artist or typographer. The pro looked at it and asked why there was so much space between the letters. Score: technology, 0; tradition, 1.

Typographers have known for centuries that optimal letterspacing depends on the letters being kerned. One of the most visible examples is seen in the word "To." Note the difference between the two words in Figure 4.1.

The pros are right; kerning matters. The larger we set type, the more it matters. Fortunately, although kerning is not an automatic feature of PostScript, PostScript has the capability to help us solve this problem. This chapter will discuss what PostScript has to offer. Application developers will benefit most from the material presented here, although anyone writing custom PostScript who is concerned about optimal type spacing will find it of interest.

AVATAR

AVATAR

AVATAR

Figure 4.1. The same word is shown three ways: unkerned, kerned based on the Adobe font metrics accompanying the face, and with additional manual kerning to taste.

If we generalize the definition of kerning a little to say it is anything that changes the letterspacing set by the type designer, we can define four types of kerning: pairwise kerning, track kerning, letterspacing, and manual kerning.

Pairwise Kerning

Pairwise kerning is what most people think of when they discuss kerning. It operates on pairs of letters, and adjusts the spacing between a pair such as T and o. Operating from kerning tables defined by the type designer, this technique automatically corrects the spacing to account for the context in which a letter finds itself in a word. The driving program simply looks up each character pair in a kerning pair table and adjusts the character positions on a letter-by-letter basis.

Pairwise kerning works well over a range of type sizes, but breaks down for very large type, and is unnoticeable for very small type. The problem with large type is caused by the nonlinearity of human perception. Really large type needs much tighter overall spacing to appear balanced. Enter track kerning.

Track Kerning

Track kerning is not concerned with pairwise spacing, but rather with the relationship between overall spacing and point size. Again, the motivation is to define tables that can automate good letterspacing. Track kerning tables specify ranges of sizes and percentage adjustment factors for those ranges. The spacing rules then modify the natural spacing by the percentage appropriate to the point size. Often these tables come in three or more varieties, to provide tight, normal, and loose spacings, in addition to compensating for the type size. Adobe has defined a format for track kerning tables, but most, if not all, of their fonts are released without track kerning tables. We can define our own tables, but it is not normally worth the effort.

Letterspacing

Most applications, rather than defining or accessing track kerning tables, implement letterspacing. Like track kerning, letterspacing alters the space between all characters in a font. But unlike track kerning, this is done on a one-shot basis, under user control. This allows the user to set the space between characters as tightly or as loosely as desired for each specific block of text.

Programs that support letterspacing allow us to insert positive or negative space between all the characters, usually expressed in fractions of the point size (or em-square) so that it can be scaled along with the type.

Manual Kerning

For the most discerning designers, no automatic technique works well enough. They want to position each letter independently according to their artistic judgment, using full manual kerning. Each letter is positioned where it looks the best. The adjustment is sometimes specified in absolute units (points), while other applications allow for adjustment using fractions of an em, which is a relative measurement that changes when the type size changes

With the current display resolutions of 72 dots per inch or less, manual kerning is difficult to do properly on screen and typically requires printing test pages to get the right spacing.

Space Adjustment in POSTSCRIPT

Enough background. Let's see how we can use POSTSCRIPT to do kerning. The POSTSCRIPT font definition contains no kerning information, since it is optimized for storage efficiency in the printer. All kerning information is found in the auxiliary Adobe Font Metrics (AFM) files delivered with POSTSCRIPT fonts. AFM files are text files that contain pairwise kerning tables and track kerning tables, as well as character width and bounding box information for each character. On the Macintosh, kerning pair tables, but not track kerning tables, are stored in the FOND resource associated with the bitmap screen font.

The format of the pair kerning table is quite simple:

```
KPX first letter second letter distance
```

The KPX entry defines a horizontal kerning pair, which is followed by the character names and a distance. Another form is defined, which supports both horizontal and vertical kerning, but is not normally used. As with the other numbers in the AFM, this distance is relative to the font's em-square. Convert these numbers to points by dividing by 1,000 and multiplying by the desired point size. Mapping the character names to actual character numbers is dependent on the font encoding vector; see chapter 8 on font encoding for details.

Let us now split out discussion of automatic pair kerning from track kerning. Track kerning and letterspacing are done via the *ashow*, *widthshow*, or *awidthshow* operators and will be discussed later. Pairwise and manual kerning are normally handled quite differently.

PostScript defines the *kshow* operator to handle kerned pair letterspacing, but it is rarely, if ever, used for that. The reason is simple. Kerning tables are quite large, and looking up kerning pairs at print time is very slow in PostScript. It is much better to do the calculations in the host computer and generate PostScript to do the proper spacing. This method also allows for manual kerning adjustments.

The trick is to generate a show for a group of nonkerned letters, do an *rmoveto* by the appropriate amount, then do another show for the next group of nonkerned letters. An example should make this clear. Let us print the word "Torn" in the 24-point Bookman-Demi typeface. We will first print the unkerned string for comparison:

```
/Bookman-Demi findfont 24 scalefont setfont
36 700 moveto
(Torn) show
showpage
```

Now we look up the kerning tables in the AFM file. The relevant kerning tables are as follows:

```
    . . .
    KPX T o -28
    . . .
    KPX r n 20
    . . .
```

Thus the kerning values for the "To" pair tell us to move them together by 28/1000 of an em so the o is tucked under the overhang of the T. The kerning pair "rn" is moved apart by 20/1000 of an em, so the r and the n don't appear to join and become an m.

Now we must break the text and apply the kerning values scaled by the point size. Using the formula

kern distance = table_value * point_size / 1000,

we find the kerning distance should be −0.672 points and 0.480 points. This results in the following PostScript:

```
/Bookman-Demi findfont 24 scalefont setfont
36 700 moveto
(T) show
-0.672 0 rmoveto
(or) show
0.480 0 rmoveto
(n) show
showpage
```

If we were doing manual kerning, we would break the text in an identical fashion and apply the desired adjustment factor.

Pairwise kerning is easy in PostScript; the only hard part is looking up the kerning pairs to get the adjustment factor. Oh yes—building the tables may take a little programming as well, but the C programming we use for the purpose is beyond the scope of this chapter.

Using FOND Tables

On the Macintosh, most programs extract this kerning information from the FOND. Very few programs read the AFM file directly. Other systems must read the AFM file and convert it into internal tables which drive the kerning process. The Macintosh FOND is much easier to read and is always accessible, and so is the table of choice. *Inside Macintosh Volume IV* (Addison-Wesley, 1986) describes the format of the FOND kerning pair table, so it won't be repeated here.

There are two potentially serious problems, which require care when using the FOND. The first is that not all kerning pair tables are sorted, making binary search worthless. Efficient programs should sort the kerning tables before using them, so looking up kerning entries can be done quickly.

The second problem is far more serious. The numbers in the FOND are not always what they should be. Early fonts released by Adobe used an unusual representation (sign-magnitude) for their negative numbers. Altsys' Fontographer font editor followed this numbering convention as well, so early third-party fonts have the same number format. In early 1987, programs started to read the FOND information as normal (two's complement) numbers, and had wildly overkerned characters due to the confusion over number representation.

Negative sign-magnitude numbers, when interpreted as standard two's complement numbers, appear to be terribly wrong. Minus 1 looks like -32767 and -32767 looks like -1, while -100 looks like -32667.

Apple decided all numbers should be uniform, and changed the version of the FOND from version zero to version two. All numbers in a version two FOND are two's complement, so this problem is resolved. Unfortunately, there are still thousands of the old FOND versions in use. Programs that read the FOND must be prepared to handle either kind of number. The numbers used for kerning values can be identified as sign-magnitude or two's complement by their absolute values; sign-magnitude numbers are much larger. The sequence we use, in the C programming language, is:

```
if ((number<0) && ((unsigned) number < 0xC000)
    number = -(number & 0x7FFF);
```

This adjustment should be performed on all kerning values when the table is built. Since reasonable kerning values should never be more than one em (the height of the font), the one's complement and two's complement number ranges never overlap and this test will always work.

TRACK KERNING AND LETTERSPACING

Track kerning and letterspacing require a different approach. Since every letter's space must be changed, the driving program would have to split strings into one character per line, interspersed with *rmoveto* commands—not a pretty sight. POSTSCRIPT has three operators that do just what we need: *ashow*, *awidthshow*, and *widthshow*. All three print a string with a specified positive or negative space added between each character, but the last two allow for additional effects.

The *ashow* operator is the simplest of the three. It is typically used for inserting extra space between every letter of a string to stretch a word or line. The POSTSCRIPT reference manual shows a simple example using a fixed letterspace of four points. More interesting cases come about by calculating the letterspace on the fly. For example, let us assume we want to fit a line of text to a fixed-width column by uniformly adjusting the space between each character. We will use the string, "A very stretched line," and justify it to be five inches long:

```
% Define conversion function
/inch {72 mul} def


% Define function to show a string in a column of
% fixed length by uniformly adjusting letter space.
% calling stack setup: column_width string --
% first is column width in points
% second is string to be printed
% (set up the desired font before calling this)
/lsshow {    % letter space show
     /str exch def     % save string

     % calculate the natural string width, toss Y value
     str stringwidth pop    % column_width string_width --
     sub                    % adjustment --

     str length  % count all characters in string
     1 sub       % except for last character
                    % stack is: adjustment character_count --

     dup 0 eq        % check for string with no characters
          {pop 0}    % 0 adjust if no characters
          {div} % divide adjustment by character_count
     ifelse
               % stack is: adjustment_per_character --

     0     % vertical adjustment is zero
     str   % get string
          % stack is: adjustment_per_character 0 string --
     ashow
} def

% Set up the font
/Helvetica findfont 24 scalefont setfont

% Position to starting point
36 700 moveto
```

```
% print string in 5 inch column
5 inch (A very stretched line) lsshow
```

```
showpage
```

The *widthshow* operator allows spaces (or any other selected character) to be handled differently from all other characters in the string. This is typically used to add more spaces between the words in a line. Contrast this with the previous example, which added space between each letter. By adding word space, the original letterspacing set by the font designer is maintained, but lines of text still can be justified. We will use the same sample scenario as before, printing the string "A very stretched line" in a five-inch column:

```
% Define conversion function
/inch {72 mul} def
```

```
% Define the blank character
/blank 32 def
```

```
% Define function to count occurrences of a character.
% calling stack: count character_number string -- count
% first is a count, usually initialized to zero
% second is a character number (not a character!)
% third is the string to be searched
% Function returns an updated count on the stack
/countchar {
        {1 index eq        % count char_num char char_num --
        {exch 1 add exch} % increment count if char match
        if
        } forall    % examine all characters in string
        pop    % toss char_num
} def
```

```
% Define function to show a string in a column of
% fixed length by adjusting word space.
% calling stack setup: column_width string --
% first is column width in points
% second is string to be printed
% (set up the desired font before calling this)
```

```
/wsshow {    % word space show
    /str exch def    % save string

    % calculate the natural string width, toss Y value
    str stringwidth pop    % column_width string_width
    sub                    % adjustment

    % count the number of blanks (char code 32)
    0 blank str countchar
    % stack is: adjustment blank_count

    % check for string with no blanks
    dup 0 eq
        {pop 0}    % 0 adjust if no blanks
        {div}      % divide adjustment by blank_count
    ifelse
    % stack is: adjustment_per_blank

    0     % vertical adjustment is zero
    blank % extra goes into 'blank' character
    str   % get string
    % stack is: adjustment_per_blank 0 blank string
    widthshow
} def

% Set up the font
/Helvetica findfont 24 scalefont setfont

% Position to starting point
36 600 moveto

% print string in 5 inch column
5 inch (A very stretched line) wsshow

showpage
```

The *awidthshow* operator adds a uniform amount between all characters of the string, and adds an additional space after occurrences of one special character, usually the blank. This allows us to improve on the previous example. We can put most of the adjustment factor into the word spacing, but still allow some adjustment between letters, as in the first *ashow* example. This often results in an improved appearance for the line, even though the original letterspacing is changed. The *widthshow* operator left wide spaces between words, but *awidthshow* allows us to distribute the spaces as letter space or word space. We continue with the same sample text:

```
% Define conversion function
/inch {72 mul} def


% Define the blank character
/blank 32 def


% Define function to count occurrences of a character.
% calling stack: count character_number string -- count
% first is a count, usually initialized to zero
% second is a character number (not a character!)
% third is the string to be searched
% Function returns an updated count on the stack
/countchar {
        {1 index eq       % count char_num char char_num
            {exch 1 add exch}
        if    % increment count if char match
        } forall    % examine all characters in string
        pop          % toss char_num
} def


% Define function to show a string in a column of
% fixed length by full justification.
% calling stack setup: column_width string --
% first is column width in points
% second is string to be printed
% set up the desired font before calling this
/fjshow {   % full justification show
        /str exch def     % save string

        % calculate the natural string width, toss Y value
        str stringwidth pop     % column_width string_width --
        sub dup     % adjustment adjustment --
```

```
% now we want to put 80% of the adjustment into
% the blanks, and 20% between letters of the words.
0.8 mul      % adjustment blank_adjust

% count the number of blanks (char code 32)
0 blank str countchar
% stack is: adjustment blank_adjust blank_count

% check for string with no blanks
dup 0 eq
        {pop 0}     % 0 adjust if no blanks
        {div}       % divide adjustment by blank_count
ifelse
% stack is: adjustment adjust_blank

0            % vertical adjustment is zero
blank        % extra goes into 'blank' character
% stack is: adjustment adjust_blank 0 32

% now calculate extra space for other characters
4 -1 roll    % adjust_blank 0 32 adjustment --
str length   % count all characters in string
1 sub % except for last character

% check for string with no characters
dup 0 eq
        {pop 0}     % 0 adjust if no characters
        {div}       % divide adjustment by character_count
ifelse
0.2 mul           % put 20% of delta between characters
% stack is: adjust_blank 0 32 adjust_all --

0       % vertical adjustment is zero
str     % get string
% stack: adjust_blank 0 32 adjust_all 0 string --
awidthshow
} def

% Set up the font
/Helvetica findfont 24 scalefont setfont
```

```
% Position to starting point
36 500 moveto

% print string in 5 inch column
5 inch (A very stretched line) fjshow


showpage
```

Try combining these three examples, removing all duplicate definitions and all but the final *showpage*. Printing all three lines on one
page clearly shows the difference (see Figure 4.2). Try different strings
and different lengths to demonstrate the effect of varying letter and
word space. In particular, try a very long string and a short line to see
the effect of negative letter spacing. Try adjusting the split between
letter and word space in the last example.

A very stretched line

A   very   stretched   line

A   very   stretched   line

Figure 4.2. The same line is justified using three different methods. The first uses the ashow operator to add space between every character (including spaces). The second uses widthshow to add space only between words. The last uses awidthshow, resulting in 80 percent of the adjustment between words and 20 percent between characters.

5 / Precise Character Bounding Boxes   *Bill Woodruff*

Suppose you want to force-justify some very large type on a page, so that both the left and right edges are perfectly flush—right down to the pixel. It's a simple enough matter to measure the width of the string, measure how much total space is left to fill, and apportion that space between the characters.

What you'll find, though, is that the results aren't perfect. Each character has a "sidebearing"—part of the character that extends to the right or (more often) left of the origin. There is also sidebearing to the right of the character, which I'll call letterspacing for clarity (see Figure 5.1). The sidebearing and letterspacing mean that type you set may not be aligned right down to the edges of the characters (see Figure 5.2).

Fine typography and aesthetic page layout involve careful selection and placement of type. Styles of justification are both aesthetic and cultural choices. If you are setting type left-justified ("rag right," a typographer would say), and you have each line clearly defined and are content that the left margin is not a perfectly straight vertical line, then you do not need to measure type down to the pixel. You can use a simple program like this:

```
/leading 20 def
/crlf { 0 currentpoint exch pop leading sub moveto } def
line1 show crlf
line2 show crlf
```

This prints a line at a time and calls a "carriage return line feed" routine between lines.

Getting the Length with *stringwidth*

To go a step further, you can use the *stringwidth* operator. *stringwidth* returns the length of a string of characters in current user space units.

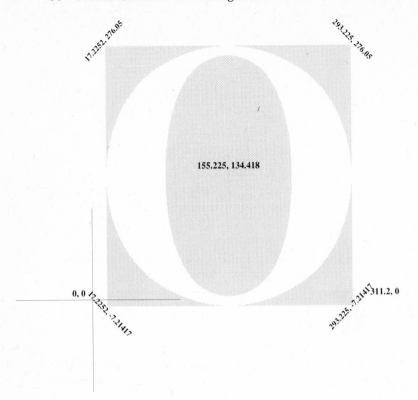

155.225, 134.418

0, 0   311.2, 0

Figure 5.1. The parts and coordinates of PostScript characters. (The letter O is set in Times Bold and, on the following page, the letter S in Palatino Italic.)

The same units are returned independently of the scaling or rotation of user space. The length vector returned extends from the origin of the first character in the string (which is not necessarily at the lower left corner of the character—in fact, it probably isn't) to the origin of the next character, if another character is to be shown.

I've done a lot of testing to make sure that even in an extremely complex rotated and scaled user space, the value returned by *string-width* is identical to the value returned by executing the character's path and observing the displacement of the current point in that space.

It may be helpful if you think of the *show* command as a macro that says, for each character in a string:

1. Starting at currentpoint, follow the character outline path

2. Note the maximum horizontal displacement along the x axis. Add to that value the letterspacing information built into the charwidths

Figure 5.1. Continued.

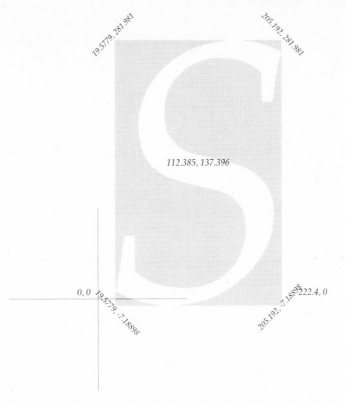

Figure 5.2. The problem with stringwidth for precise justification is that it fails to take into account the sidebearing of the first character in a string and the letterspacing of the last.

dictionary entry for this character. Add the total to the old current-point, and reset currentpoint

3. *fill* the character's path in current gray level using current halftoning

4. *moveto* revised currentpoint ready to start another character

If you wish to perform simple right and center justification in PostScript—with no font changes in a line—you can just use *string-width*. It operates on one or many characters, returning the length of that string. Here's a simple example:

```
/leading 20 def
/crlf { 0 currentpoint exch pop leading sub moveto } def

/sw { dup stringwidth pop }def       % get the stringwidth
/showcenter { sw 2 div 0 rmoveto show } def      % move 1/2 the width
/showright { sw neg 0 rmoveto show } def  % move the full width
line1 showcenter crlf
line2 showright crlf
```

Here two simple routines take the *stringwidth* of the current line, discard the unused axis displacement value it returns, then operate on the width to create values for right or center justification.

For simple type placement, you don't need to measure characters down to the pixel. The eye might see a line justified by pixels, rather than by character origins, as odd—perhaps too precise. However, when you take on projects like creating a vertical column of text with each character centered horizontally, or you want to drop a gray screen perfectly around the outlines of a character, or simply get perfect justification, then deeper techniques are required. The sidebearing and letterspacing of characters, which can amount to several points with large type, will throw off the alignment. As I'll explain below, the problem is even worse in rotated or scaled space. To get things perfect, you need a method to precisely measure character widths, the bounding boxes that surround individual characters, exclusive of sidebearing and letterspacing.

The following sections show how to precisely measure a character, to isolate its sidebearing and letterspace, to know exactly where the highest and lowest pixels fall. Even if you never use these techniques, understanding them will serve you well in having a clearer sense of how POSTSCRIPT operates.

What's Wrong with *stringwidth*

The first problem with *stringwidth* is that it doesn't take into account the sidebearing and letterspacing, so we cannot determine with accuracy where the character pixels start and stop. Also, we have no way to get vertical information about the highest or lowest pixel in the character. *stringwidth* doesn't really tell us where the character itself starts and stops.

On a pragmatic graphic level, using *stringwidth* may be adequate where we deal in large lines where the cumulative length it returns is only off by the possible values of the sidebearing of the first character and the letterspacing of the last character. For projects using large type and special modes of justification, however, we need to measure the bounding box of the character path. The bonus of measuring the path this way is that we get the vertical information "for free."

PostScript provides the *pathbbox* operator for returning the user space locations of the lower-left (llx,lly) and upper-right (urx,ury) co-ordinates of a path. At first glance it seems this would give us the measurements we need. There are two complicating factors, though, that must be eliminated for these measurements to be accurate (see Figure 5.3).

First, if a path contains a Bezier element, then the control points for that element may be included in the points returned by *pathbbox*. And those control points may lie well outside the boundaries of the char-acter. The solution for this is to call the *flattenpath* operator before calling *pathbbox*. *flattenpath* converts the character's curved path into a series of straight lines, eliminating the outlying Bezier control points.

The second problem deals with using *pathbbox* in a rotated and/or scaled coordinate space. PostScript maintains its current path as a series of points in device space. The bounding rectangle constructed by the call to *pathbbox* has its axes parallel to the fixed x and y axes of device space. So the values returned may be inaccurate.

One can imagine a general solution to the problem of actual path size measurement based on reading through the points in the path and recording maximum or minimum displacements from the starting point in current user space. But for characters in Adobe typefaces, we cannot use *pathforall* to visit all the elements of the path—they are encrypted. The best we can do is to restore a "normalized" coordinate space temporarily and measure the character in its current font scaling. Then we can use these measurements in the current user space (see "Tech-nical Notes" section).

Figure 5.3. You can use pathbox to find the bounding box of a character, but you can run into problems in rotated space. Outlying control points can also throw off the resulting coordinates.

Let's develop a routine for reading out precisely all measurement information about a single character. Of course we'll perform this ritual in a context that will preserve and restore user space. And as long as we are going to the trouble to measure all parts of the character, we might as well compute offsets for horizontal or vertical centering of the character from the origin:

```
% measure a character precisely
% assume that a single character is in a variable 'ch
% and that the user has selected and scaled a font
% and made it the current font by using 'setfont

/cmeasure {
        % preserve current user space
        gsave
                % measure bounding box in default user space
                % set currentpoint at 0,0 in new space
                % so we can then use vectors with
                % 'rmoveto, 'rlineto
                currentpoint initmatrix translate 0 0 moveto

                % obtain character path
                % use 'true if Courier, else use 'false
                currentfont /FontName get /Courier eq
                % get the path of the current character
                ch exch charpath

                % just after obtaining character the current point
                % is displaced to the start of the next character
                % we preserve this so we can later isolate
                % 'letterspacing
                /next_ch currentpoint pop def

                % flatten the path and get pathbbox
                flattenpath pathbbox

                % get four values off stack
                /ury exch def /urx exch def
                /lly exch def /llx exch def
```

```
      % true height of character is ascent - descent
      /ht_ch ury lly sub def

      % true width of character is
      % rightmost pixel - sidebearing
      /wd_ch urx llx sub def

      % letterspacing of character is total width
      % less the distance to the rightmost pixel
      /ltrspc next_ch urx sub def

      % x center offset is
      % -(half true width) - sidebearing
      /xch wd_ch -2 div llx sub def

      % y center offset is
      % -(half true width) - sidebearing
      /ych ht_ch -2 div lly sub def
   % restore previous user space
   grestore
} def
```

Let's quickly construct a routine to create a vertical column of characters where the descent of the top character is a fixed number of pixels below the ascent of the next one:

```
% on stack: (string object) gap between
% characters in user space pixels

/column_text {
   % preserve current user space
   gsave
      % get gap
      /gap exch def
      % define string
      /str exch def

      % for each character in string from start to end
      0 1 str length 1 sub
      {
```

```
                    % get the character (See Tech Notes)
                    str exch 1 getinterval /ch exch def

                    % measure it
                    cmeasure

                    % horizontally center and
                    % and move down so its ascent
                    % just touches current baseline
                    % preserve currentpoint, show character
                    gsave
                            %optional call to "cbackbox" here
                            xch ury neg rmoveto ch show
                    grestore

                    % start next character down from current
                    % position by full character height + gap
                    0 ht_ch neg gap sub rmoveto
            } for
        % restore previous user space
        grestore
} def
```

Here's a sample call for using column_text. You can see the output in Figure 5.4.

```
306 390 translate 0 0 moveto
/Helvetica-Bold findfont 48 scalefont setfont
(REALWORLD!) 10 column_text
showpage
```

A logical use of our bounty of character measurements is to drop a box behind the character that fits it to the pixel. Here's a sample procedure that assumes you are at the point where you will show the character (the origin), and that you have, of course, previously called *cmeasure* for the character.

```
/cbackbox {
gsave
        llx lly rmoveto
        0 ht_ch rlineto
```

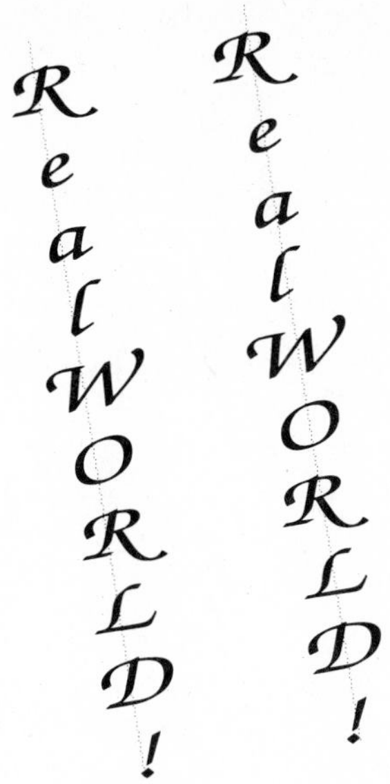

Figure 5.4. The same string
is centered two different
ways: using stringwidth and
by measuring the precise
character bounding boxes.
Notice that the text remains
centered even in rotated and
scaled space.

```
            wd_ch 0 rlineto
            0 ht_ch neg rlineto
            closepath
            .5 setgray fill
grestore
} def
```

You can insert a call to this procedure just before the character is shown in the procedure column_text.

A final idea: If you are working with a multi-character string, there is no need to determine exact bounding boxes for each character. You can figure the true length (pixel to pixel) by calling *stringwidth* for the entire string, subtracting the sidebearing of the first character, and then subtracting the letterspacing of the last character only.

Try working this one out as an exercise. Remember that a negative sidebearing means the character extends to the left of the origin. Subtract that sidebearing value from (or add the absolute value to) the stringwidth. The letterspacing will be positive; again, subtract that value from stringwidth to get the precise pixel-to-pixel string length.

Remember also that if you want the left edge of the leftmost character to align perfectly, before you place that character you will need to shift the currentpoint to the left by the absolute value of the first character's sidebearing.

A Better String Handler

You might have noticed the use of *getinterval* in the column_text program. For some reason, perhaps influenced by the first examples of POSTSCRIPT to be published, most POSTSCRIPT programmers use the more complex form of getting a character at a time, typically:

```
% convert character code to string by stuffing it
% into a scratch string at the 0th position
/scratch 1 string def
/code_to_ch { scratch dup 0 4 -1 roll put } def


(some string) { code_to_ch character_procedure } forall
```

It is true the use of the *forall* loop is elegant, but why not use the simpler *getinterval* form:

```
% sequentially access all string characters one by one
% put string in named variable
/str (some string) def
0 1 str length 1 sub
{
        str exch 1 getinterval
        character_procedure
} for
```

I ran a timing test comparing sequential access to each of 10,000 characters in a test string filled with random values from 0 to 255. The *forall*-based technique was slightly slower (by .4 milliseconds per iteration), and it used 24 more bytes of virtual memory. It's your choice.

Technical Notes

• To create a normalized space context in which to measure characters, we use the *initmatrix* operator. The *initmatrix* command restores the device's default matrix. It's a little shorter to type in than "matrix defaultmatrix setmatrix" and saves the VM that creating a new six-element array would consume.

While several PostScript documents warn against the use of *init-matrix*, particularly in code embedded in other code (like in an EPS file embedded in another file), Adobe also has said that it is valid to use *initmatrix* to read out character information in a graphically saved context, without creating marks on the page.

- The user space distance vectors returned by using *pathbbox* on the flattened character path can be exported directly to a transformed space. Keep in mind that the FontMatrix entry in the font dictionary is not affected by global coordinate system scaling, rotation, etc.

- Also remember that the *flattenpath* operator decomposes Bezier curves in the current path into a series of line segments. The number of segments per unit curve is governed by the *setflat* operator.

- We should always be careful not to use the *charpath* command on more than one character at a time : it can produce the deadly limit-check error caused by too many path elements at one time, and send our PostScript interpreters howling into the outer void. A complex character like a ZapfChancery "W" may contain many Bezier curves, and when *flattenpath* is used you may exceed the path element limit (1500 elements on an Apple LaserWriter).

- Maintaining character or path measurements as signed (positive or negative) user space vectors has the benefit that they are highly readable; a negative sidebearing for a character tells us unambiguously that the character's pixels extend to the left of the origin.

6 / Building Fonts

Michael Mace

The first and most important thing to understand about making a POSTSCRIPT font is that you're not just creating a font data file; you're making a POSTSCRIPT program that will image font characters. At the precise moment that one of your font's characters prints, the font program is in total control of the POSTSCRIPT interpreter. It can use any POSTSCRIPT command in the book, and can also produce any POSTSCRIPT error.

This gives you a tremendous amount of power in terms of what you can do in a font; your imagination is literally the limit. But it also gives you a lot of responsibility. If your font is inefficient or poorly written, it can severely reduce the speed of the POSTSCRIPT interpreter. Try whenever possible to make your font programs operate efficiently. Because they will be invoked hundreds of times to fill a single page of text, even a small inefficiency can add up to create a very long print job.

The Structure of a Font

Adobe's font construction rules are surprisingly flexible. Although there is a suggested data format for fonts, you don't have to follow it strictly, and in fact you can cook up a number of improvisations of your own, as long as you follow a few specific rules.

A font must meet the following conditions:

1. It must be a single POSTSCRIPT file, so that it can be downloaded automatically by the Macintosh print driver or other drivers. It should consist of a single dictionary (possibly containing other dictionaries) with certain required entries.

2. If it is to be permanently downloaded, it must begin with the *exit-server* command, which will load the file into a memory location

99

that won't be cleared after each job. This is usually the case for fonts that are downloaded manually . The syntax for this command is:

```
serverdict begin 0 exitserver
```

If you are creating a font that will be dynamically managed (loaded automatically by the driver), omit this line. The Macintosh LaserWriter print driver, among others, downloads fonts automatically.

3. The font dictionary must include a procedure called BuildChar, which will image each font character when invoked. The font dictionary and character to be printed are placed on the stack when the font is invoked; it is the responsibility of your BuildChar to image the character from the information given. This process is followed for each character printed.

4. There must also be an encoding array that matches character procedure names to the numerical character codes fed to the font by POSTSCRIPT (see chapter 8, "Font Encoding Vector Compatibility").

That's all you have to do. The internal workings of BuildChar, and the way you store your font data, are more or less up to you. However, Adobe does supply a suggested font structure, and that's what we will demonstrate here.

Adobe's suggested font includes the following:

1. Several convenience operators in the font dictionary, some of which are mandatory for Macintosh fonts.

2. A CharacterDefs dictionary, which is an array of POSTSCRIPT path procedures, one for each character. The procedure names in this dictionary are the ones referenced by the Encoding array.

3. The BuildChar procedure, which works by taking the character number and font dictionary given to it by the interpreter, using the character number to find a character name in the Encoding array, and then using that name to find the character drawing procedure in the CharacterDefs dictionary. This procedure is executed in order to draw the character.

Here's a sample font file using this format. POSTSCRIPT comments are used to explain sections of the file.

```
%An example font.  Copyright 1988, Michael Mace.
```

Most commercial fonts have a copyright notice here. Most also include the EPS file header, but it's not mandatory.

```
0 serverdict begin exitserver
```

Remember, the line above is omitted in automatically-downloaded fonts.

```
/BuildCharDict 17 dict def
/ExampleFont 11 dict def
```

This allocates the dictionaries used by BuildChar and the font itself.

```
ExampleFont begin
/FontType 3 def    % a mandatory entry
```

This tells POSTSCRIPT how the font is set up. 3 must be your font type; other values are used by Adobe's encrypted fonts.

```
/FontMatrix [.001 0 0 .001 0 0] def        % mandatory
```

This matrix maps your font characters to a one-unit coordinate space, which enables POSTSCRIPT to scale font characters properly. Adobe suggests that fonts use a 1,000-unit grid, but what you use is up to you, so long as you adjust the FontMatrix accordingly.

```
/FontBBox [0 -200 1238 800] def       % mandatory
```

This is used by POSTSCRIPT's font caching mechanism. The bounding box must be large enough to enclose every character in the font. If you want, the box can be set to all zeros, and the POSTSCRIPT interpreter in the printer will calculate the bounding box for you, but this may make the font management process a little less efficient.

```
/PaintType 0 def  % optional Adobe, mandatory on Macintosh
```

This determines whether a font is outlined. When the Macintosh driver wants a font to print outlined, it changes the PaintType to 3. Your BuildChar procedure should always check the PaintType value, then print accordingly.

```
/FontName (NewFont) def %optional
```

You can omit this entry to save space. There are several other optional entries we won't bother with.

```
/Metrics 256 dict def   % optional
```

This is a dictionary that can be used to alter the font's preset character widths by increasing or decreasing characters' letterspacing. Each character must be altered individually. We will not use it in our example.

```
/UniqueID 123456 def    % 1 to 9 digits - optional
```

Assigning your font a unique ID number between 0 and 16777215 will allow the character cache to be managed more efficiently. Unfortunately, if two fonts share the same "unique" ID numbers, you may get one font's character images appearing in another font's text.

Adobe, to its discredit, has provided no mechanism for registering third-party font IDs, so you assign an ID number to your font at your own risk. (Figuring about a thousand fonts on the market by the end of 1988—not an unreasonable number—this translates into a one in 16,000 chance of two fonts even sharing the same ID number, let alone ending up in the same printer at the same time. Still the risk is there.)

```
/FontInfo 2 dict def    % optional dictionary
/FontInfo begin
/UnderlinePosition -100 def
/UnderlineThickness 10 def
end
```

This dictionary can contain a lot of housekeeping information, which you don't need to worry about, and also these two important underline entries, which are used to position the underline and set its thickness. If you don't include these entries, underline position and thickness will be set arbitrarily for you, but you may not like the results. Light fonts in particular should always reset the thickness; it's fairly bold by default.

```
/Encoding 256 array def % mandatory for Macintosh
0 1 255 {Encoding exch /.notdef put} for
Encoding 32 /space put
```

```
Encoding 33 /exclam put
Encoding 34 /quotedbl put
 .

 .

 .
Encoding 250 /dotaccent put
Encoding 251 /ring put
```

This is the encoding array mentioned above and discussed further in chapter 8, "Font Encoding Vector Compatibility." Note that any undefined (blank) characters are named .notdef, the name of an empty procedure in the CharacterDefs dictionary.

```
/CharacterDefs 166 dict def    % mandatory
CharacterDefs /.notdef {} put
CharacterDefs /space {286 0 0 -200 1000 800 setcachedevice} put

CharacterDefs /exclam
{286 0 0 -200 1000 800 setcachedevice
newpath
5 0 moveto
53 90 lineto
143 90 lineto
95 0 lineto
5 0 lineto
5 190 moveto
143 333 lineto
143 661 lineto
190 709 lineto
53 571 lineto
53 243 lineto
5 190 lineto
} put

CharacterDefs /quotedbl
{238 0 0 -200 1000 800 setcachedevice
newpath
53 619 moveto
95 661 lineto
95 571 lineto
```

```
53 524 lineto
53 619 lineto
196 619 moveto
238 661 lineto
238 571 lineto
196 524 lineto
196 619 lineto
} put
        .

        .

        .

CharacterDefs /dotaccent
{238 0 setcharwidth
.5 setgray
243 614 92.5936 360 0 arcn
0.9473 1 scale
257 614 50.2656 0 360 arc
} put
```

   The CharacterDefs dictionary includes a POSTSCRIPT drawing procedure for each character. Even the space character has one (it has a
width, even though it doesn't print anything). The *setcachedevice*
operator is always preceded by a numeric arguments. The first number
tells POSTSCRIPT the width, or horizontal displacement, of the font
character that follows; the second number, usually 0 for western languages, determines the vertical displacement of the character; the last
four numbers are the character's bounding box.

   This operator stores the bitmapped image of the character in the
printer's font cache, for reuse later in the print job (it's a lot faster to
cache a bitmapped character than to rebuild it each time it's printed).
However, *setcachedevice* won't work if you use any gray fills. In such
cases, you should instead use *setcharwidth*. The two numeric arguments that precede *setcharwidth* are the same as the first two for
setcachedevice. Characters that use setcharwidth are not stored into
the font cache, and as a result print very slowly.

```
/BuildChar
        {BuildCharDict begin
        /char exch def
        /fontdict exch def
```

```
/charname fontdict /Encoding get char get def
/charproc fontdict /CharacterDefs get charname get def

fontdict /PaintType get 0 eq
        {charproc fill}
        {charproc 10 setlinewidth stroke}
    ifelse

end
} def
```

This BuildChar procedure (a very simple one compared to those of most third-party fonts) accepts the character number and font dictionary passed to it by PostScript, looks up the procedure name in the encoding array, looks up that name in the CharacterDefs dictionary, and then executes the associated procedure. Note that BuildChar checks the PaintType variable in order to see if the font should be filled or outlined.

```
end    % end of dictionary for this font

/NewFont ExampleFont definefont pop
```

This final line enters the font's name in the font dictionary, and then associates your new dictionary with that name. The *pop* operator is required to clean up because *definefont* returns a copy of the font dictionary on the stack.

Font Compression

Adobe's modular font structure makes it easy to change character definitions. Unfortunately, fonts also hog memory, an important consideration in an environment full of hundred-kilobyte scanned images and end users who love to fill their pages with fonts. It is horribly easy to overrun the memory limits of a PostScript printer using downloaded fonts; in the original LaserWriter, three large fonts could do it easily. More recent printers are better behaved, but the memory problem is by no means behind us.

Almost all commercial fonts on the market today use compression schemes in order to reduce their demands on the printer's memory.

Since the CharacterDefs dictionary is the largest one in the font, it is the logical one to attack.

One very simple compression scheme is to truncate the operator names used within the character definitions. Replace *lineto* with l, *moveto* with m, and so on. Then at the start of your BuildChar dictionary, define /l as *lineto*, and /m as *moveto*, etc.

The next step in compression is to encode the numbers and operators into hex strings, which are then stored in the CharacterDefs entries in lieu of drawing procedures. A procedure invoked within the BuildChar procedure is responsible for unencoding these compressed strings, and executing the commands. The technique is a little complicated to go into here, but it is used by Fontographer, and if you read through the POSTSCRIPT code of a Fontographer-generated font, you should be able to figure it out.

Beyond the hex compression technique, it is possible to make a supercompressed font using assembly language and a lot of effort. That's what Adobe does. Unfortunately their technique is proprietary and beyond the purview of this book.

Although compressed fonts are good for professional font sellers, they involve trade-offs in speed; generally, the more compressed the font, the longer it takes to decode, and therefore the longer it takes to print. If you are practicing or hacking around, you probably shouldn't bother with the effort involved in compressing your font.

Playing with Character Definitions

Although the vast majority of font definitions include simple outlines in their font procedures, you need not stick to that. Remember, your BuildChar procedure is in complete control of the POSTSCRIPT interpreter; you can use any POSTSCRIPT operator.

One simple thing you can do from within a font is call another font. You can easily call another font, image a character from it, and then add to or change it. This is the procedure Apple uses to map some of the Symbol characters into other fonts.

Here's how you call a font from within a font:

```
CharacterDefs /cent
{286 0 0 -200 1000 800 setcachedevice
/Times-Roman findfont 1000 scalefont setfont
(c) show
```

```
0 0 moveto
300 500 lineto
10 setlinewidth
stroke
} put
```

This is a rough attempt to construct a ¢ sign. Note that it's difficult to outline this character properly, although you could probably construct something by stroking it all in black, then filling in white.

A more useful thing you can try is special effects with built-in fonts. You can make complicated outline effects, various gray levels, and fonts that are twisted or even reversed by manipulating the transformation matrix.

Other people have made "bolder" versions of fonts by outlining and filling them. To make a bolder version of a letter in Times, for instance, you might use the following procedure:

```
CharacterDefs /a
{286 0 0 -200 1000 800 setcachedevice
/Times-Roman findfont 1000 scalefont setfont
(a) charpath 50 setlinewidth
save stroke restore fill
} put
```

Of course, this is not a true bold version. It tends to wipe out the fine details in a letter and, if carried to extremes, can make your work look trashy. But you can achieve some interesting results. (If the line-width of 50 seems large to you, remember that in describing characters you typically are working in a coordinate system that has 1,000 units to the point.)

Let your imagination work for a while, and you will probably be able to think of other interesting things a character procedure can do. Imagine, for instance, a font that simulates handwriting by randomly changing some curves and lines. Or one that consists of scanned images instead of outlines.

WORKING WITH *DEFINEFONT*

In addition to making new fonts, the *definefont* operator can be used to alter existing ones. By changing the parameters within an existing font, you can cause it to outline itself, or change its spacing, or do a number of other things. One nice application would be to change the ugly underline positioning in Times-Bold.

Here's an example that alters the FontMatrix to make a stretched font (in this case, fifty percent fatter than the original). This is the sort of thing that makes a professional typographer turn livid; the line widths of fonts are carefully balanced, and stretching or shrinking them arbitrarily destroys that balance. But with desktop publishing technology you have the freedom to ignore the old fogies and do what you like.

```
%Fat Times Copyright 1988, Century Software.
/Times-Roman findfont dup length dict /newdict exch def
{1 index /FID ne
      {newdict 3 1 roll put }
      {pop pop }
ifelse
} forall
newdict /FontMatrix [.0015 0 0 .001 0 0] put
/FatTimes newdict definefont pop
```

The FID entry is an internal font ID number assigned by POSTSCRIPT; a new one is created by the *definefont* operator, so you are safe omitting the old one when you copy the original font.

7 / Building Smart Fonts *Michael Mace*

To people who don't understand it, programming a computer often looks like a black art. The trouble with programming in PostScript is that, even after you understand it, it still looks like magic.

A very prominent case in point is the construction of PostScript fonts. If you have a magnifying glass, dig it out and examine some text printed by the built-in fonts in a PostScript printer—say, in 10-point Times. Look at the smooth bowls on the curved letters like b and d. Note the uniform width of the legs on the m and n. Note the stable size and positioning of the serifs everywhere.

Now try the same trick with a downloadable font, made by some company other than Adobe. Or better yet, use Illustrator or Free-Hand to draw some letters yourself, then shrink them down very small and print them. Look through that magnifying glass, and what do you see?

Disaster! Those smooth bowls are jagged, with pixels jutting out at odd angles. Those beautiful serifs have turned into awkward hooks. And the once uniform vertical strokes are actually different widths.

The average user often doesn't notice these imperfections, simply because most people aren't very sophisticated about type. But be warned: once you learn to spot good type, you'll never be completely satisfied with lower-quality output again.

What's Going On?

What makes otherwise beautiful letters fall apart when they are printed small? And why don't Adobe's fonts do the same thing?

The problem is actually related to the mathematical foundation of PostScript. Because it is a numerical problem, it is completely predictable. Adobe takes advantage of that predictability to make fonts that work around the mathematical problems. Adobe's font-smoothing routines are proprietary, but with a little thinking, you can cook up your own. This chapter shows you how.

The fundamental problem with printing text on most POSTSCRIPT printers is the printers' limited resolution. If you have a Linotronic (1,270 or more dots per inch) or even a higher-resolution laser printer (like the Varityper VT600), you probably won't be able to tell the difference between an Adobe font and a good third-party font. But a standard 300 dpi printer just doesn't have the resolution necessary to faithfully display a font outline.

As you can see in Figure 7.1, the problem is a mismatch between the infinitely accurate mathematical outline of the font, and the relatively coarse 300 dpi grid. In our example, the left-hand leg of the letter H starts at the point 0,0 and is 1.4 pixels wide. Since the printer can't print fractional pixels, it will round this to a 1-pixel-thick line. But on the right side, the left-hand edge of the leg starts at the point 4.4, and goes to 5.9. Although it is mathematically the same width as the left-

1a.

1b.

1c.

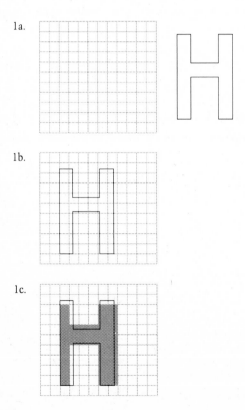

Figure 7.1. (1a.) A 300 dpi pixel grid and a letter outline drawn to full precision. (1b.) As you can see, the mathematical outline does not match the pixel grid. (1c.) The gray area shows what happens when POSTSCRIPT rounds every point on the outline to the nearest pixel: the imaged letter looks uneven. The pixel grid is too coarse to represent the letter properly.

2a.

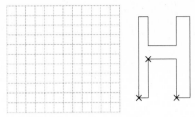

Figure 7.2. (2a.) The X's show the restraining points, one at the lower left corner of each stroke. (2b.) The restraint points are rounded to pixel boundaries. The remainder of the character outline, which is drawn relative to the restraint points, follows their rounding. (2c.) The letter, when imaged, now looks uniform. Because each stroke starts at a pixel boundary, rounding affects them all the same way.

2b.

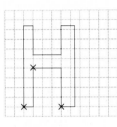

2c.

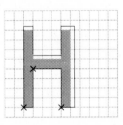

hand leg, it will print as two pixels thick, because PostScript has to round the coordinates to whole pixels.

You can set PostScript to round in different directions—up, down, or to the nearest integer—but they all produce the same effect. You could, of course, set up the line widths to match exactly a certain pixel grid, but a font outline that works properly at one size will fail at other sizes. Since a standard PostScript font uses a single set of outlines to print every size, there will always be some sizes that fail. This is why third-party fonts often look good at some sizes, but not at others.

Font Magic

So how does Adobe do it? Does the company have "that special Adobe font magic" (as one employee put it)? Actually there's no magic involved, but there is a fair amount of obfuscation. Adobe's fonts are not outlines; they're algorithms.

The details of Adobe's system are secret, but apparently their fonts use an outline that mathematically modifies itself, depending on the font size and printer resolution, to fit the pixel grid perfectly. Adobe's fonts are smart; they contain information telling themselves how to look their best.

You can make your own intelligent fonts, but for now you have to write them directly in PostScript, because no font-drawing program on the market today generates true algorithmic fonts. Here's an example of one font-smoothing algorithm, using what are sometimes called "restraint points."

In this scheme, every vertical and horizontal stroke is stored relative to a fixed reference point. Each letter stem has its own reference. These reference points are individually rounded to the nearest pixels first, and all measurements are made relative to them.

This system, in effect, shifts the position of each stroke so that (in our example here) the left bottom corner of each stroke fits the grid exactly. Because each stroke starts at the same point, each will be rounded in the same way.

This probably sounds confusing, but it's actually fairly simple when you have an example to look at. Let's use the H from Figure 7.1. The reference points are placed at the Xs shown in Figure 7.2. Each point serves a single stem. For instance, all the points on the left leg of the H are drawn relative to point number one.

The code for the character is as follows:

The Original

```
0 0 moveto
0 100 lineto
10 100 lineto
10 55 lineto
50 55 lineto
50 100 lineto
60 100 lineto
60 0 lineto
50 0 lineto
50 45 lineto
10 45 lineto
10 0 lineto
closepath
```

With Restraint Points

```
% Round two points on stack to nearest pixel in device space
% and transform back to user space
/roundproc {transform round exch round exch itransform} def


0 0 roundproc /point1y exch def /point1x exch def      % Establish
10 45 roundproc /point2y exch def /point2x exch def    % three points
50 0 roundproc /point3y exch def /point3x exch def     % for X and Y


% Now build a character off those six points
newpath
point1x point2x moveto
point1x 0 add point1y 100 add lineto
point1x 10 add point1y 100 add lineto
point1x 10 add point2y 10 add lineto
point3x 0 add point2y 10 add lineto
point3x 0 add point3y 100 add lineto
point3x 10 add point3y 100 add lineto
point3x 10 add point3y 0 add lineto
point3x 0 add point3y 0 add lineto
point3x 0 add point2y 0 add lineto
point1x 10 add point2y 0 add lineto
point1x 10 add point1y 0 add lineto
closepath
```

This is an inelegant, brute-force approach to the problem, but it does work, and that counts for a lot. Unfortunately, there are two important features of this "solution" that make it less than practical:

1. You have to tune every character by hand (imagine doing this with a script font)

2. The resulting font outline is bulky to store and slow to execute

How slow? An algorithm much like this one doubles the print time of a font I tested it on. Adobe's fonts are speedy in part because they are written in assembly language, not POSTSCRIPT. They can thus access the processor very efficiently, allowing them to do more calculation than any third-party font could. What the world is waiting for is a computer whiz to cook up an algorithm that executes quickly and can be applied automatically by a program like Fontographer. Then we'd be talking about POSTSCRIPT's font magic, not just Adobe's.

The standard ASCII character encoding used for computer characters has one minor drawback; it defines only the first 128 of the possible 256 characters. The meaning of the last 128 characters was left undefined by the ASCII standards committee. Presumably the rigors of agreeing on 128 characters exhausted the committee, and they decided that manufacturers should be free to use the last 128 however the manufacturers saw fit.

This has led to a proliferation of non-standards. IBM uses these character positions for line graphics, Apple uses them for foreign characters, and Adobe leaves most of them unused. Other computer and printer vendors have their own proprietary encodings, no two of which are alike. Of course, we should be grateful for the standardization even of the first 128 characters . . . .

Using Nonstandard Characters

If we wish to use any of these non-ASCII characters, such as ™, ®, ©, ß, Å, and so on, we have to manipulate POSTSCRIPT's "encoding vector." The characters in a POSTSCRIPT font are defined by name (e.g., A), but referenced by number (e.g., 65). The link between character number and name is handled by the font's *BuildChar* procedure. It looks up the number in the font's encoding vector and gets the character name from there. The character name is then used to look up the actual definition of the character. This definition contains the information needed to draw the character. Separating the character number from its definition allows different character mappings to be specified.

Unfortunately, this awkward and inefficient encoding procedure complicates the process of accessing characters and forces us to write relatively complex procedures for changing font encodings. Furthermore, many of the characters Macintosh users take for granted, such as the ®, are defined only in the Symbol font (see Table 8.1). QuickDraw automates the substitution for you. However, if you are writing your own PostScript, an explicit font change is necessary to print one of these characters.

Table 8.1. Macintosh encoding vectors

This table shows Apple's standard font encoding for PostScript fonts, as of System 4.3. The first three columns list the decimal character number, hexadecimal character number, and printed character. The Name column contains the remapped PostScript character name of the character encoded at that character number. When followed by numbers in parentheses, this represents a remapping of a character from the Symbol font, and the number is the hexadecimal Symbol font character number (the Macintosh borrows several characters from the Symbol character set). The Default name column shows the Post-Script name of the character in that position in the default Adobe encoding. The Keyboard column shows how to type that character on the Macintosh keyboard.

Dec	Hex	Print	Name	Default Name	Keyboard
0	00		NUL		Ctl-@
1	01		SOH		Ctl-a
2	02		STX		Ctl-b
3	03		ETX		Ctl-c
4	04		EOT		Ctl-d
5	05		ENQ		Ctl-e
6	06		ACK		Ctl-f
7	07		BEL		Ctl-g
8	08		BS		Ctl-h
9	09		HT		Ctl-i
10	0A		LF		Ctl-j
11	0B		VT		Ctl-k
12	0C		FF		Ctl-l
13	0D		CR		Ctl-m
14	0E		SO		Ctl-n
15	0F		SI		Ctl-o
16	10		DLE		Ctl-p
17	11		DC1		Ctl-q
18	12		DC2		Ctl-r
19	13		DC3		Ctl-s
20	14		DC4		Ctl-t
21	15		NAK		Ctl-u
22	16		SYN		Ctl-v
23	17		ETB		Ctl-w
24	18		CAN		Ctl-x
25	19		EM		Ctl-y
26	1A		SUB		Ctl-z
27	1B		ESC		Ctl-[
28	1C		FS		Ctl-/
29	1D		GS		Ctl-]
30	1E		RS		Ctl-^
31	1F		US		Ctl-_
32	20		space		

Dec	Hex	Print	Name	Default Name	Keyboard
33	21	!	exclam		!
34	22	"	quotedbl		"
35	23	#	numbersign		#
36	24	$	dollar		$
37	25	%	percent		%
38	26	&	ampersand		&
39	27	'	quotesingle	quoteright	'
40	28	(	parenleft		(
41	29	)	parenright		)
42	2A	*	asterisk		*
43	2B	+	plus		+
44	2C	,	comma		,
45	2D	-	hyphen		-
46	2E	.	period		.
47	2F	/	slash		/
48	30	0	zero		0
49	31	1	one		1
50	32	2	two		2
51	33	3	three		3
52	34	4	four		4
53	35	5	five		5
54	36	6	six		6
55	37	7	seven		7
56	38	8	eight		8
57	39	9	nine		9
58	3A	:	colon		:
59	3B	;	semicolon		;
60	3C	<	less		<
61	3D	=	equal		=
62	3E	>	greater		>
63	3F	?	question		?
64	40	@	at		@
65	41	A	A		A
66	42	B	B		B
67	43	C	C		C
68	44	D	D		D
69	45	E	E		E
70	46	F	F		F
71	47	G	G		G
72	48	H	H		H
73	49	I	I		I
74	4A	J	J		J
75	4B	K	K		K
76	4C	L	L		L
77	4D	M	M		M
78	4E	N	N		N
79	4F	O	O		O
80	50	P	P		P
81	51	Q	Q		Q
82	52	R	R		R

Dec	Hex	Print	Name	Default Name	Keyboard
83	53	S	S		S
84	54	T	T		T
85	55	U	U		U
86	56	V	V		V
87	57	W	W		W
88	58	X	X		X
89	59	Y	Y		Y
90	5A	Z	Z		Z
91	5B	[	bracketleft		[
92	5C	\	backslash		\
93	5D	]	bracketright		]
94	5E	^	asciicircum		^
95	5F	_	underscore		
96	60	`	grave	quoteleft	`
97	61	a	a		a
98	62	b	b		b
99	63	c	c		c
100	64	d	d		d
101	65	e	e		e
102	66	f	f		f
103	67	g	g		g
104	68	h	h		h
105	69	i	i		i
106	6A	j	j		j
107	6B	k	k		k
108	6C	l	l		l
109	6D	m	m		m
110	6E	n	n		n
111	6F	o	o		o
112	70	p	p		p
113	71	q	q		q
114	72	r	r		r
115	73	s	s		s
116	74	t	t		t
117	75	u	u		u
118	76	v	v		v
119	77	w	w		w
120	78	x	x		x
121	79	y	y		y
122	7A	z	z		z
123	7B	{	braceleft		{
124	7C	|	bar		|
125	7D	}	braceright		}
126	7E	~	asciitilde	(none)	~
127	7F		(none)	(none)	(none)
128	80	Ä	Adieresis	(none)	Option-u A
129	81	Å	Aring	(none)	Shift-Option-a
130	82	Ç	Ccedilla	(none)	Shift-Option-c
131	83	É	Eacute	(none)	Option-e E
132	84	Ñ	Ntilde	(none)	Option-n N

Dec	Hex	Print	Name	Default Name	Keyboard
133	85	Ö	Odieresis	(none)	Option-u O
134	86	Ü	Udieresis	(none)	Option-u U
135	87	á	aacute	(none)	Option-e a
136	88	à	agrave	(none)	Option-` a
137	89	â	acircumflex	(none)	Option-i a
138	8A	ä	adieresis	(none)	Option-u a
139	8B	ã	atilde	(none)	Option-n a
140	8C	å	aring	(none)	Option-a
141	8D	ç	ccedilla	(none)	Option-c
142	8E	é	eacute	(none)	Option-e e
143	8F	è	egrave	(none)	Option-` e
144	90	ê	ecircumflex	(none)	Option-i e
145	91	ë	edieresis	(none)	Option-u e
146	92	í	iacute	(none)	Option-e i
147	93	ì	igrave	(none)	Option-` i
148	94	î	icircumflex	(none)	Option-i i
149	95	ï	idieresis	(none)	Option-u i
150	96	ñ	ntilde	(none)	Option-n n
151	97	ó	oacute	(none)	Option-e o
152	98	ò	ograve	(none)	Option-` o
153	99	ô	ocircumflex	(none)	Option-i o
154	9A	ö	odieresis	(none)	Option-u o
155	9B	õ	otilde	(none)	Option-n o
156	9C	ú	uacute	(none)	Option-e u
157	9D	ù	ugrave	(none)	Option-` u
158	9E	û	ucircumflex	(none)	Option-i u
159	9F	ü	udieresis	(none)	Option-u u
160	A0	†	dagger	(none)	Option-t
161	A1	°	degree(B0)	exclamdown	Shift-Option-8
162	A2	¢	cent	cent	Option-4
163	A3	£	sterling	sterling	Option-3
164	A4	§	section	fraction	Option-6
165	A5	•	bullet	yen	Option-8
166	A6	¶	paragraph	florin	Option-7
167	A7	ß	germandbls	section	Option-s
168	A8	®	registered(D2)	currency	Option-r
169	A9	©	copyright(D3)	quotesingle	Option-g
170	AA	™	trademark(D4)	quotedblleft	Option-2
171	AB	´	acute	guillemotleft	Option-e
172	AC	¨	dieresis	guilsinglleft	Option-u
173	AD	≠	notequal(B9)	guilsinglright	Option-=
174	AE	Æ	AE	fi	Shift-Option-'
175	AF	Ø	Oslash	fl	Shift-Option-o
176	B0	∞	infinity(A5)	(none)	Option-5
177	B1	±	plusminus(B1)	endash	Shift-Option-=
178	B2	≤	lessequal(A3)	dagger	Option-,
179	B3	≥	greaterequal(B3)	daggerdbl	Option-.
180	B4	¥	yen	periodcentered	Option-y
181	B5	µ	mu(6D)	(none)	Option-m
182	B6	∂	partialdiff(B6)	paragraph	Option-d

Dec	Hex	Print	Name	Default Name	Keyboard
183	B7	Σ	summation(B5)	bullet	Option-w
184	B8	Π	product(D5)	quotesinglbase	Shift-Option-p
185	B9	π	pi(70)	quotedblbase	Option-p
186	BA	∫	integral(F2)	quotedblright	Option-b
187	BB	ª	ordfeminine	guillemotright	Option-9
188	BC	º	ordmasculine	ellipsis	Option-0
189	BD	Ω	omega(57)	perthousand	Option-z
190	BE	æ	ae	(none)	Option-'
191	BF	ø	oslash	questiondown	Option-o
192	C0	¿	questiondown	(none)	Shift-Option-/
193	C1	¡	exclamdown	grave	Option-1(digit)
194	C2	¬	logicalnot(D8)	acute	Option-l(letter)
195	C3	√	radical(D6)	circumflex	Option-v
196	C4	ƒ	florin	tilde	Option-f
197	C5	≈	approxequal(BB)	macron	Option-x
198	C6	Δ	Delta(44)	breve	Option-j
199	C7	«	guillemotleft	dotaccent	Option-\
200	C8	»	guillemotright	dieresis	Shift-Option-\
201	C9	...	ellipsis	(none)	Option-;
202	CA		blank	ring	Option-(space)
203	CB	À	Agrave	cedilla	Option-A
204	CC	Ã	Atilde	(none)	Option-n A
205	CD	Õ	Otilde	hungarumlaut	Option-n O
206	CE	Œ	OE	ogonek	Shift-Option-q
207	CF	œ	oe	caron	Option-q
208	D0	–	endash	emdash	Option--
209	D1	—	emdash	(none)	Shift-Option--
210	D2	"	quotedblleft	(none)	Option-[
211	D3	"	quotedblright	(none)	Shift-Option-[
212	D4	'	quoteleft	(none)	Option-]
213	D5	'	quoteright	(none)	Option-]
214	D6	÷	divide(B8)	(none)	Option-/
215	D7	◊	lozenge(E0)	(none)	Shift-Option-v
216	D8	ÿ	ydieresis	(none)	Option-u y
217	D9	Ÿ	Ydieresis	(none)	Shift-Option-`
218	DA	⁄	fraction(A4)	(none)	Shift-Option-1
219	DB	¤	currency	(none)	Shift-Option-2
220	DC	‹	guilsinglleft	(none)	Shift-Option-3
221	DD	›	guilsinglright	(none)	Shift-Option-4
222	DE	fi	fi	(none)	Shift-Option-5
223	DF	fl	fl	(none)	Shift-Option-6
224	E0	‡	daggerdbl	(none)	Shift-Option-7
225	E1	·	periodcentered	AE	Shift-Option-9
226	E2	‚	quotesinglbase	(none)	Shift-Option-0
227	E3	„	quotedblbase	ordfeminine	Shift-Option-w
228	E4	‰	perthousand	(none)	Shift-Option-e
229	E5	Â	Acircumflex	(none)	Shift-Option-r
230	E6	Ê	Ecircumflex	(none)	Shift-Option-t
231	E7	Á	Aacute	(none)	Shift-Option-y
232	E8	Ë	Edieresis	Lslash	Shift-Option-u

Dec	Hex	Print	Name	Default Name	Keyboard
233	E9	È	Egrave	Oslash	Shift-Option-i
234	EA	Í	Iacute	OE	Shift-Option-s
235	EB	Î	Icircumflex	ordmasculine	Shift-Option-d
236	EC	Ï	Idieresis	(none)	Shift-Option-f
237	ED	Ì	Igrave	(none)	Shift-Option-g
238	EE	Ó	Oacute	(none)	Shift-Option-h
239	EF	Ô	Ocircumflex	(none)	Shift-Option-j
240	F0		apple†	(none)	Shift-Option-k
241	F1	Ò	Ograve	ae	Shift-Option-l
242	F2	Ú	Uacute	(none)	Shift-Option-;
243	F3	Û	Ucircumflex	(none)	Shift-Option-z
244	F4	Ù	Ugrave	(none)	Shift-Option-x
245	F5	ı	dotlessi	dotlessi	Shift-Option-b
246	F6	ˆ	circumflex	(none)	Shift-Option-n
247	F7	˜	tilde	(none)	Shift-Option-m
248	F8	¯	macron	lslash	Shift-Option-,
249	F9	˘	breve	oslash	Shift-Option-.
250	FA	˙	dotaccent	oe	Option-h
251	FB	°	ring	germandbls	Option-k
252	FC		cedilla	(none)	(none)
253	FD		hungarumlaut	(none)	(none)
254	FE		ogonek	(none)	(none)
255	FF		caron	(none)	(none)

† The Apple character is not defined in non-Apple printers. In particular, the Linotype RIPs do not have an Apple character.

The most frequent application for changing the encoding vector occurs when printing text with special characters or foreign characters. Macintosh users frequently need to do this and can type most of these characters directly from the keyboard. IBM users who need special characters such as ß must type the octal character equivalent into their POSTSCRIPT programs. In either case, the POSTSCRIPT font must have these characters defined in its encoding vector.

The process of changing the encoding vector for a font begins by defining the new encoding vector and some helper functions. This is non-trivial POSTSCRIPT since the recoding process is much harder than it could have been. Had the encoding process been defined simply as a table mapping new character numbers to font character numbers, this would be a simple array of numbers. However, unless we want to create our own fonts using our own conventions, we are compelled to do it the way POSTSCRIPT wants it done. We have chosen to use the standard Macintosh encoding vector for this example. It defines several characters that must actually be fetched from the Symbol character set. We name them here simply for completeness.

```
/NewCodes 256 array def    % define the character name array
NewCodes 0                 % stack: NewCodes 0 --
StandardEncoding           % use standard encoding as a base
0 128 getinterval          % get first 128 names from standard
putinterval                % put first 128 names into NewCodes
% PostScript defines typographical single quotes (`´), but
% Apple and ASCII want straight quotes ('`) and accent graves
% We can remap these while we are at it:
NewCodes 16#27 /quotesingle put
NewCodes 16#60 /grave put % redefine single quote & accent grave
% now we stack up the last 128 character names
/Adieresis /Aring /Ccedilla /Eacute
/Ntilde /Odieresis /Udieresis /aacute
/agrave /acircumflex /adieresis /atilde
/aring /ccedilla /eacute /egrave
/ecircumflex /edieresis /iacute /igrave
/icircumflex /idieresis /ntilde /oacute
/ograve /ocircumflex /odieresis /otilde
/uacute /ugrave /ucircumflex /udieresis
/dagger /degree /cent /sterling
/section /bullet /paragraph /germandbls
/register /copyright /trademark /acute
/dieresis /notequal /AE /Oslash
/infinity /plusminus /lessequal /greaterequal
/yen /mu /partialdiff /summation
/product /pi /integral /ordfeminine
/ordmasculine /Omega /ae /oslash
/questiondown /exclamdown /logicalnot /radical
/florin /approxequal /Delta /guillemotleft
/guillemotright /ellipsis /nbspace /Agrave
/Atilde /Otilde /OE /oe
/endash /emdash /quotedblleft /quotedblright
/quoteleft /quoteright /divide /lozenge
/ydieresis /Ydieresis /fraction /currency
/guilsinglleft /guilsinglright /fi /fl
/daggerdbl /periodcentered /quotesinglbase /quotedblbase
/perthousand /Acircumflex /Ecircumflex /Aacute
/Edieresis /Egrave /Iacute /Icircumflex
/Idieresis /Igrave /Oacute /Ocircumflex
/apple /Ograve /Uacute /Ucircumflex
```

```
/Ugrave /dotlessi /circumflex /tilde
/macron /breve /dotaccent /ring
/cedilla /hungarumlaut /ogonek /caron
% now we have top 128 names on stack - store them
NewCodes 128 128 getinterval astore pop
% now 'NewCodes' is our new encoding vector
```

Now we continue by defining a helper function to copy the font. Since a finished font is write-protected, we have to make a copy in order to do anything to it. This copy must consist of all the entries in the original font dictionary except for the font ID ("FID"), which is unique to each font. Our code to copy a font expects the source font dictionary on the stack at entry, and leaves the new font dictionary on the stack at exit.

```
% CopyDictionary - copies font dictionary
% source_font_dict -- new_font_dict
/CopyDictionary {
      dup maxlength dict        % create new dictionary as long as source
      /NF exch def              % save new dictionary in NF
      {1 index /FID ne          % copy everything except 'FID' entry
            {NF 3 1 roll put} % store entry into new dictionary
            {pop pop}             % don't copy FID entry
      ifelse
      } forall     % copy source font, gobbles dict off stack
      NF     % leave new dictionary on stack
} def
```

Next we define a function to recode the new font. We must also change its name at this time so we don't have duplicate font names. Apple uses the convention of preceding the font name with a vertical bar followed by six underscores (|_____). This identifies the font as one recoded with Apple's character encoding. It is best not to write PostScript code that relies on that convention, since Apple often indulges its urge to change conventions.

Our code names the font with a preceding vertical bar and a single underscore (|_). This function takes one argument, the new font name, and returns nothing. As a side effect, it creates a new font object with the desired name and new encoding. The original source font is assumed to have the same name, less the vertical bar and underscore.

```
% Recode a font with our own encoding vector
% calling stack: new_name --
/Recode{
     dup cvn /NewName exch def        % save new name
     (|_) anchorsearch          % split name into |_ and actual name
          {pop                            % toss |_ part
          findfont CopyDictionary       % copy base font to new dictionary
          dup /Encoding NewCodes put  % place encoding into new font
          NewName exch definefont
     } if      % this 'if' clause only executed if name had |_ prefix...
     pop    % toss font or improper name
} def
```

Now at last we are ready to define the actual recode function that ties all the above work together. This first looks up the font to see if it is already defined. If so, it does nothing. Otherwise it calls the Recode function to complete the recoding process. This function expects the new name on the stack and returns nothing.

```
% RecodeFont - create a newly recoded font if none exists with
% the same name already.
% calling stack: new_name --
/RecodeFont{
     dup FontDirectory exch known
          {pop}
          {Recode}
     ifelse
} def
```

Now we are finally ready to recode a font. As a test, we will recode Helvetica and print the first eight characters from the top 128 ASCII character codes. This should result in a line that looks like Figure 8.1.

```
% test recoding code...
(|_Helvetica) RecodeFont    % now its recoded
/|_Helvetica findfont       % find our new font
24 scalefont setfont        % set up to use it
36 700 moveto               % go to left top
(\200\201\202\203\204\205\206\207) show    % print recoded chars
36 600 moveto               % drop down a few lines
(ÄÅÇÉÑÖÜá) show              % this is an alternative on the Mac
```

ÄÅÇÉÑÖÜá

Figure 8.1. Output to test
font encoding vectors.

ÄÅÇÉÑÖÜá

A test to show other characters are OK

```
36 500 moveto              % drop down a few more lines
(A test to show other characters are OK) show
showpage
```

Our font recoding example is complete. Any PostScript program can now print most of the characters defined on the Macintosh by simply including them in a show statement. Try this in plain Helvetica and you will simply get blanks for the first two lines, since the default encoding for Helvetica does not define these characters.

Unfortunately, this still does not solve the problem of the characters from the Symbol font, such as $\leq$ or Σ. It is possible to build a composite font that calls characters from other fonts. The basic mechanism involves building a font full of characters that contain references to other fonts instead of drawing commands. For example, the letter A might be from Times-Roman. The code for this letter would indicate Times-Roman, character name "A." The letter S might be the symbol Σ from the Symbol typeface. The code for this letter would indicate Symbol, character name "summation." By applying our earlier recoding code to the base Times-Roman font, we can arrange to refer to letters by their character code rather than by name. The Symbol font is best referred to by character code without recoding, since its character names are all different and the recoding technique would not work.

9 / Geom: Building a PostScript Typeface   *Bill Woodruff*

In this chapter we're going to go through the process of building a PostScript typeface—though not your run-of-the-mill typeface. This face actually calls a procedure that draws a spirograph based on our supplied parameters. It demonstrates that a PostScript typeface truly is a program in its own right. You can see some sample characters in Figure 9.1.

The goal of building this sample face is to apply what we've learned about font construction from Michael Mace's chapters (6 and 7) on building fonts—to demonstrate how a PostScript font can take advantage of every aspect of the language, including control by user-defined variables external to the font.

Our sample font has a FontType of 3 since it is user-defined, and a PaintType of 3, which means that the character descriptions themselves are responsible for calling *stroke* or *fill*. We will exploit that by having flags defined outside the characters that will trigger either filling, stroking, or both. In this example, we will show how to put gray level into a character, so we will use *setcharwidth*, rather than *setcachedevice* because gray information cannot go in the cache.

It is a great benefit to be able to use the cache, since printing may be up to a thousand times faster. You could modify this code easily to use the cache as long as you did not change the *fill* command so that it called *setgray*.

Our font, Geom, will do some neat things:

1. Every character in it will call a procedure spi that will use variables side, angle, and inc if they are user-defined. If they are not user-defined, it will use built-in defaults for side and inc and calculate a default for angle based on the character code.

2. It will dynamically limit drawing to the unit square, even if the arguments passed would cause it to draw outside the unit square.

Figure 9.1. Several characters printed from the Geom typeface, with various parameters modified.

It will do this by testing position, not by clipping, which is too expensive.

3. It will demonstrate a solution to the problem of letting a user-space-defined current linewidth be accurately preserved in the strokes of a character.

4. It will demonstrate a work-around to allow both user-defined values and default values. A character definition in a font cannot normally use *def* or *put* because a font is a read-only structure.

Eye Spi

First let's define a spirograph routine based on the program (usually called spi) that almost all students of the LOGO language study and play with. A spirograph is produced by a very simple programming structure, and is an example of a class of graphics known as "turtle-graphics." Here's a pseudo code version:

1. Go forward

2. Turn a constant angle

3. Go forward same as step #1, but a little farther, based on a constant increase factor

4. Go back to step 1

In PostScript, our spi drawing procedure will look like this:

```
/dospi {
% start loop
    side
    { quitspi?
        { pop exit }
        { dup 0 rlineto angle rotate inc add }
    ifelse
    } loop
    % end loop
} bind readonly def
```

The drawing loop is very simple: an initial value of side is put on the stack and it draws a line and increments this value on the stack until quitspi? returns true. Then it pops off the final copy of counter variable and exits.

Remember that when spi is called we will be in the 1,000-by-1,000-unit character space. We will draw each character centered around its origin, allowing it to grow 500 units in any direction so that it fills, as much as possible, the unit square. We will quit drawing if we exceed 500 units of movement. Here's our test to see if we should quit drawing:

```
% are we more than 500 out in any direction?
/gt500abs {
    abs 500 gt exch
} bind readonly def


% this function returns a boolean value: true means quit
/quitspi? {
    currentpoint 2 { gt500abs } repeat or
} bind readonly def
```

We need a way to maintain a set of default variables for side, angle, etc., but also we have to be able to update the definitions. We have to

create a dictionary structure as we define the font within the scope of
userdict so it can be modified during the character procedures:

```
% spi default parameters
userdict begin
        /spidict dup 6 dict def load begin
                % defaults for side, inc, etc.
                /side 10 def
                /inc 10 def
                /angle 90 def
                /defaultangle 90 def
                /stroke? true def
                /fill? false def
        end
end
```

Here's how we use this structure in the main call to spi:

```
/spi {
        spidict begin
        setangle
                userdict begin
                        % begin at origin
                        0 0 moveto
                        % do spi
                        dospi
                        fill? {
                                stroke? dup { gsave } if
                                fill { grestore } if
                        } if
                        stroke? {
                                maplw stroke
                        } if
                end
        /angle defaultangle def
        end
}
readonly def
```

We begin spidict and then call setangle to set the value of angle based
on the value in userdict or, if not defined in userdict, to synthesize it

via a call to *getangle*. We then begin userdict. If a name is not found in userdict, the next dictionary searched is spidict.

After drawing the spirograph, we end the scope of userdict, which leaves spidict on top of the dictionary stack, and we reset the value of angle to the defaultangle, a constant. Note that we do not bind this procedure; that way, if there are any special modifications of *stroke* or *fill*, they will be used on the character path.

Note that if we *fill*, and also plan to *stroke*, we surround the *fill* in a *gsave . . . grestore* context so the path is not consumed.

Since angle is the key parameter governing the shape of the spirograph, we would not want it to default to one value for all characters—they'd all look alike!

If we define the character code in the BuildChar procedure, we can use it to create an angle. Since printable character codes begin at about ASCII 33, let's use a default angle for those under 33 and the character code for all others:

```
% uses cc defined in BuildChar
/getangle {
        cc dup 33 lt {
                pop defaultangle
        } if
} bind readonly def


/setangle {
        userdict /angle known not {
                /angle getangle def
        } if
} bind readonly def
```

Here you can see how *setangle* looks to see if the angle is defined in userdict, and calls *getangle* if it is not defined there.

If we set the value for angle before we show the characters, that value will be used and the character code will be ignored. This means we can use a floating point angle, like 42.5, if we wish. If we want to use the character codes, to have a row with each spirograph being different, we can only have integers, since character codes must be integers. A simple function can generate the right character from a supplied code:

```
% make character given character code
/anglechar { cvi 1 string dup 0 4 -1 roll put } bind readonly def

% show a bunch of specified angles
% on stack: a variable length array of integers
% assumes that Geom is the current font
/spishow {
        { anglechar show } forall
} bind readonly def
```

   Note that this change in linewidth is local to the execution of the character.

   We used a typical Macintosh encoding vector in the font definition; then we created a dictionary, cd, to hold the character definition paths. We want the default behavior of all characters to be a call to spi, so we go through the encoding array and define every character that is not a .notdef to call spi; then we once define the /.notdef to also call spi. From then on, we can write as many of our own character definitions as we wish; for each one we write, the default call to spi is overwritten in the cd dictionary.

Moving Backward

To control movement after the character is shown in a user-defined font requires us to construct some kind of array of character width information. Copies of built-in PostScript fonts can have complex movement instructions written to a dictionary called Metrics inside the copy of the built-in font. The advantage is that these entries are automatically used after each character is shown.

   Unfortunately, a user-defined font cannot invoke this automatic behavior. We will create a dictionary and call it Metrics for consistency with the PostScript ethos, however. We will access the C entry for a given character code in our C procedure, passing its value to C to control horizontal movement after the character is shown:

```
/BuildChar {
    /cc x
    begin
          cd Encoding cc get dup Metrics
          exch get 0 setcharwidth
```

```
         get exec
     end
} bind readonly def
```

In the code, you'll see that the B character is defined as a full back-space, allowing us to overprint. Try defining some additional character offsets in Metrics and observe their effects on printing.

Some other interesting ideas that you could pursue using this font as a start:

1. Define characters to show bitmaps with or without gray levels

2. Define characters to generate random bitmaps

3. Redefine *fill* as *eofill* before calling the character to create interesting stripe effects

4. Produce interesting "Speedball nib" type strokes in the characters if you scale after imaging the path but before you stroke

5. Make entries in the metrics dictionary two-element arrays, and extract them in the BuildChar procedure, passing both values to *set-charwidth*, and make characters move vertically as well as horizontally.

One other interesting technical problem involves trapping out the error of possibly having too many path elements. A better quitspi might be developed that keeps track of the number of lines drawn and does an automatic "stroke and keep going" of the usual form:

```
... currentpoint stroke moveto
```

Take a look at the code for the graphing routine in chapter 15, "Graphing and Typesetting with PostScript," to see how this "path prophylaxis" is implemented there.

Full Code for "Geom"

```
%!PS-Adobe

% Creator: Bill Woodruff
% {Technical Document Design}
% 2437 Durant Ave. #208, Berkeley, Ca. 94704
```

```
% PostScript™ is a registered trademark of Adobe Systems, Inc.

% miscellaneous binding funs and abbrevs
/l /load load def
/d /def l def
/b /bind l d
/r /readonly l d
/brd { b r d } b r d
/x { exch d } brd
/ld { l d } brd
/+ /add ld
/- /sub ld
/* /mul ld
/÷ /div ld


/inch { 72 * } brd

% GEOMETRY FONT DEFINITION

/fgeom dup 19 dict def load begin

    % map to the whole unit square
    /FontMatrix [ .001  0  0  .001  0  0 ] d

    % a user-defined font
    /FontType 3 d

    % 1000 units centered on origin
    /FontBBox [ 0 0 1000 1000 ] d

    % use the typical macintosh encoding vector
    /Encoding
    [ /.notdef /.notdef /.notdef /.notdef /.notdef /.notdef /.notdef /.notdef
     /.notdef /.notdef /.notdef /.notdef /.notdef /.notdef /.notdef /.notdef
     /.notdef /.notdef /.notdef /.notdef /.notdef /.notdef /.notdef /.notdef
    /.notdef /.notdef /.notdef /.notdef /.notdef /.notdef /.notdef /.notdef
    /space /exclam /quotedbl /numbersign /dollar /percent /ampersand
    /quoteright /parenleft /parenright /asterisk /plus /comma /hyphen /period
     /slash /zero /one /two /three /four /five /six /seven /eight /nine
    /colon /semicolon /less /equal /greater /question /at /A /B /C /D /E /F
```

```
/G /H /I /J /K /L /M /N /O /P /Q /R /S /T /U /V /W /X /Y /Z /bracketleft
/backslash /bracketright /asciicircum /underscore /quoteleft /a /b /c /d
 /e /f /g /h /i /j /k /l /m /n /o /p /q /r /s /t /u /v /w /x /y /z
/braceleft /bar /braceright /asciitilde /.notdef /.notdef /.notdef
/.notdef /.notdef /.notdef /.notdef /.notdef /.notdef /.notdef /.notdef
/.notdef /.notdef /.notdef /.notdef /.notdef /.notdef /.notdef /.notdef
/.notdef /.notdef /.notdef /.notdef /.notdef /.notdef /.notdef /.notdef
/.notdef /.notdef /.notdef /.notdef /.notdef /.notdef /.notdef
/exclamdown /cent /sterling /fraction /yen /florin /section /currency
/quotesingle /quotedblleft /guillemotleft /guilsinglleft /guilsinglright
/fi /fl /.notdef /endash /dagger /daggerdbl /periodcentered /.notdef
/paragraph /bullet /quotesinglbase /quotedblbase /quotedblright
/guillemotright /ellipsis /perthousand /.notdef /questiondown /.notdef
/grave /acute /circumflex /tilde /macron /breve /dotaccent /dieresis
/.notdef /ring /cedilla /.notdef /hungarumlaut /ogonek /caron /emdash
/.notdef /.notdef /.notdef /.notdef /.notdef /.notdef /.notdef /.notdef
/.notdef /.notdef /.notdef /.notdef /.notdef /.notdef /.notdef /.notdef
/AE /.notdef /ordfeminine /.notdef /.notdef /.notdef /.notdef /Lslash
/Oslash /OE /ordmasculine /.notdef /.notdef /.notdef /.notdef /.notdef
/ae /.notdef /.notdef /.notdef /dotlessi /.notdef /.notdef /lslash
/oslash /oe /germandbls /.notdef /.notdef /.notdef /.notdef
] d


% we are proud parents of
/FontName /Geom d

% we will do our own stroking or filling, thank you
/PaintType 3 d

% no FontInfo entry

% our unique id is
/UniqueID 10101010 d

% dictionary for character path definitions
/cd dup 256 dict def load
begin

% define every name in encoding that is
% not 'notdef as a pointer to 'spi procedure
```

```
        Encoding { dup /.notdef ne { /spi cvx def } { pop } ifelse } forall

        % define /.notdef once
        /.notdef /spi cvx def

        % define 'B as null
        /B {} def

        % define space
        /space {} def
end

% dictionary for metric definitions

/Metrics dup 256 dict def load
begin
        Encoding { dup /.notdef ne { 1000 def } { pop } ifelse } forall
                % define 'B as backspace 500 units
                /B -500 def
                /.notdef 0 def
end

% we'll put a special dictionary into userdict to hold
% spi parameters
userdict begin
        /spidict dup 6 dict def load begin
                % defaults for side, inc, etc.
                /side 10 def
                /inc 10 def
                /angle 90 def
                /defaultangle 90 def
                /stroke? true def
                /fill? false def
        end
end

% at last, the BuildChar procedure
/BuildChar {
        /cc x
        begin
```

```
            cd Encoding
            cc get
            dup Metrics exch get 0 setcharwidth
            get exec
        end
} bind readonly def


/gt500abs { abs 500 gt exch } bind readonly def


/quitspi? { currentpoint 2 { gt500abs } repeat or } bind readonly def


/dospi {
% start loop
    side {
    quitspi?
            { pop exit }
            { dup 0 rlineto angle rotate inc add }
    ifelse
    } loop        % end loop
} bind readonly def


/spi {
    spidict begin
        setangle
                userdict begin
                0 0 moveto  %begin at origin
                % do spi
                dospi
                fill? { stroke? { gsave fill grestore } { fill } ifelse } if
                stroke? { maplw stroke } if
                end
        /angle defaultangle def
    end
} readonly def


% uses cc defined in BuildChar
/getangle { cc dup 33 lt { pop defaultangle } if } bind readonly def


% make character given character code
/anglechar { cvi 1 string dup 0 4 -1 roll put } bind readonly def
```

```
/setangle { userdict /angle known not  { /angle getangle def } if } bind readonly def

/maplw { currentlinewidth FontMatrix 0 get div setlinewidth } bind readonly def

% end of the geometry font definitions
end

% formally define the font
/Geom fgeom definefont pop

/tan { dup sin exch cos div } brd

106 590 translate 0 0 moveto

% scale it up to some desired point size
/Geom findfont 100 scalefont setfont

% set spirograph parameters

% comment out angle to have auto-angling by character code
% /angle 90 d

/side 10 d   /inc 10 def

/stroke? true def /fill? true def

% example of redefined fill
/fill { .5 setgray eofill } def

% example of redefined stroke
/stroke { 1 2 scale stroke } bind def

.24 setlinewidth

(tuvw) show

showpage
```

Part III

Gray Scales and Color

Steve Roth

One of the powers embodied in PostScript that you will be hard-pressed to find elsewhere is its handling of grays. It lets you employ "screens," much like traditional photographic screens (more on that below), that give the impression of gray. When this screening technique is applied to photographs and other "continuous tone" images (images that include gray, along with black and white), it is called halftoning. PostScript offers a great deal of control over the resolution of gray screens, and the orientation and shape of the patterns that make up those screens.

While PostScript can, theoretically, create almost any type of halftone screen, there are definite, real-world limitations when it comes to producing those screens on PostScript output devices. It is those limitations and ways around them that this chapter addresses.

Printing Grays

To backtrack for a moment, let's talk about how grays are handled in the printing process. The red and blue books don't really explain halftoning and digital halftoning (and the green book's pretty skimpy), so here it is. If you already understand screens and halftones, you can skip this. If you already understand digital halftoning, you can skip the next section as well.

This discussion applies to laser printing, photocopying, offset, almost any kind of printing, because they all have one thing in common: they can't print grays. They make an area either black or white, but not gray. There is either ink (or toner) in a given area, or there isn't.

So from that black-and-white printing process, we are faced with creating the *impression* of gray. The problem was solved long ago by the offset printing people, using a photographic technique called screening. To create a gray area, light is passed through a fine screen and onto photographic paper. What results is a pattern of black and

141

white areas that looks gray. The same technique applies to photographs; the image is photographed through a screen, converting that image to a pattern of black dots. These dots, together with the white area surrounding them, give the impression of gray. The size of the black dots in a given area determines how dark the gray in that area appears.

The word "screen" is a little tricky here. It describes the actual physical screen that is placed between the image and the camera, but it also refers to the result—a halftoned image has a "screen" applied to it.

The pattern of dots that results from screening (the screen) may actually be made up of dots, or dashes, or little Santa Clauses for that matter. The most common shape is round or elliptical dots. No matter what their shape, these dots are called halftone cells, and the cells in a halftone image are all equally spaced. There may be 75 cells per inch (common in newspaper work, since newsprint cannot reproduce a much finer screen), or 20 (it looks special-effecty), or 200 (though it's rare for offset printing to reproduce this fine a screen).

Take a look at the photographic halftones in Figure 10.1. Notice that the cell spacing, or frequency, remains the same; only the size of the cells changes.

Figure 10.1. The same image is shown halftoned photographically at 100 and 150 lines per inch with a zero-degree screen angle. The star is enlarged to 500 percent to show the halftone pattern.

That bears repeating: the cell spacing of a gray screen remains the same throughout. Only the size of the cells changes, not the number of cells per inch. In dark areas, the cells are large, to the point of overlapping; in light areas, they are small. Again, this applies to both photographic halftones and gray screens that you use to fill an area.

There are three variables that can be applied to gray screens:

- Frequency: the number of cells (dots, lines, or Santa Clauses) per inch
- Angle: the orientation of the cell pattern in degrees
- Cell shape: the shape of the halftone cells, be they circles, ellipses, lines, or Santas

By adjusting these three variables, you can create a variety of screen effects, from a close approximation of a photograph or a fine gray fill, to all sorts of special effects. Using traditional photographic methods, all three are easy to change, though you are limited by the (expensive) screens that are available for your camera. You use different screens in front of the photographic paper to change the frequency and cell shape. To change the angle of the halftone pattern, you can rotate the screen (if your stat camera allows for that), or use a screen with a different rotation.

The problem with photographic halftones is that you can't change them. If you have a 5-by-7-inch, 75-line halftone of an image, that's what you've got. You can't even reduce or enlarge that image photographically, because the screen frequency changes and the halftone pattern breaks down. If you enlarge it, the dot pattern becomes apparent; reduce it, and the dark areas fill in and go black. Your only option is to rescreen the image at the size and frequency you want.

POSTSCRIPT GRAYS

Enter PostScript. PostScript creates halftone cells using three parameters: frequency, angle, and a function, called the spot function, which lets you control the shape of the cell. These are equivalent to the three variables discussed above. Since the PostScript halftoning machinery works independent of the *scale* and *rotate* commands, you can scale and rotate gray-filled objects and halftoned images without affecting the screen angle, frequency, or cell shape.

When you start a PostScript device, a default screen is in effect, which can be inspected by the *currentscreen* command. If you want to alter that screen, you specify a frequency, angle, and spot function and call the *setscreen* operator. Then you pass a gray value to the interpreter (using either *setgray* or *image*), and it adjusts the size of the cells accordingly. Since every PostScript device has default values for frequency, angle, and spot function, all you need to do in the most basic setup is tell it the gray value: *.5 setgray* results in a fifty-percent black area (remember, *.1 setgray* results in ninety-percent black, and *.9 setgray* yields ten percent). The gray levels are further modified by the *settransfer* function, about which more anon.

Theoretically, what comes out of the printer will have the gray value you specify with *setgray* (as modified by *settransfer*). There's a lot more to it, though. Theory and practice are rarely equivalent.

Laser Grays

In practice, PostScript has to create the impression of a photographic screen using black and white output pixels. You can't change the size of the output pixels on a laser printer, imagesetter, or display screen, so it uses several output pixels to make up each halftone cell. And that raises a host of issues, beginning with the trade-off between resolution, screen frequency, and number of gray levels. Figure 10.2 displays that trade-off.

A little arithmetic makes this trade-off clear. Suppose you are printing at 300 dots per inch, and you want a 75 line-per-inch screen frequency. Since there are 75 halftone cells per inch, and 300 output pixels per inch, each halftone cell will be made up of 16 output pixels— 4 square (with a 0-degree screen angle—more on angles below). You get 17 gray levels, including white and black.

If you go to a coarser 50-line screen, you get 37 gray levels (the cell matrix is 6-by-6). With a fine, 150-line screen, you get only 5 gray

Figure 10.2. The same image halftoned at 300 dpi, using 50-, 75-, and 150-line screens with a zero-degree screen angle.

levels—a 2-by-2 cell matrix. Again, all this is with a 0-degree screen angle. You can see representations of these different cell matrices in Figure 10.3.

When you go to higher resolution output, the arithmetic looks a lot better. At 1,270 dpi, you can get 127-line screen with 100 gray levels (a 10-by-10 cell matrix). At 2,540 dpi, you should be able to get the same frequency with 400 gray levels (a 20-by-20 matrix). The two graphs in Figure 10.4 display the trade-off.

But wait. PostScript is limited to 256 gray levels. While you could presumably get around that by modifying *setscreen* and *settransfer* several times in one page, that's hardly an effective solution if you are working with a single scanned image. This time the limitation is in PostScript itself, not the PostScript output device. At the same time, the eye is hardly capable of perceiving more than 256 gray levels, and offset presses are hardly capable of reproducing variations that fine.

DISCRETE CELL MATRICES

With that exception, and one other discussed at the end of the chapter, all the other limitations on PostScript screens result from limitations of the output device. There are questions of reproduction as well—offset printing imposes its own restrictions—but for now let's look at the constraints imposed by digital imaging devices like laser printers, laser imagesetters, and (for Display PostScript) display monitors.

To begin with, the frequency and angle you request usually aren't what you actually get, especially on low-resolution devices. There's a simple reason for this: constraints on how many repeatable cell patterns there are at a given frequency or angle and output resolution.

The key word here is repeatable. One of PostScript's real strengths is its ability to produce seamless gray screens, in which each halftone cell uses the exact same matrix as its neighbor. Each adjacent cell must "tile" seamlessly with its neighbors. At any given angle or frequency,

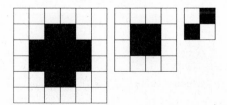

Figure 10.3. Representative drawings showing the halftone cell matrices for 300 dpi digital halftones at 50, 75, and 150 cells per inch with a zero-degree screen angle.

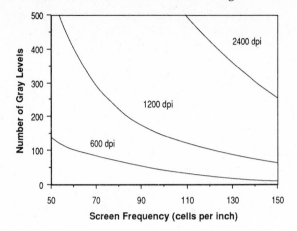

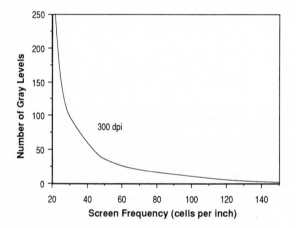

Figure 10.4. These graphs illustrate the tradeoff between output resolution, screen frequency, and number of gray levels with digital halftones. The axes are modified in the second chart to display the tradeoff at 300 dpi.

especially at low resolutions, there are only so many matrix patterns that will repeat seamlessly.

The following program, written by Bill Woodruff, gives a printed representation of the cell matrices you get with different angles and frequencies on a 300 dpi PostScript device. Download it a few times, changing the angle and frequency, to see how PostScript halftone cells work. You can see the results of such a series in Figure 10.5. Most important, notice that every time you change the angle or frequency by an increment, the cell shape doesn't necessarily change.

The numbers for the pixels relate to the order in which the PostScript interpreter goes through the pixels when applying a screen. We'll come back to that in the section on spot functions.

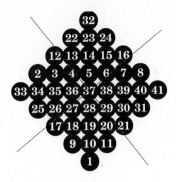

Figure 10.5. This output
from LookAtHalftoneCells
shows the representations of
halftone cell matrices at 300
dpi. From left, they
represent frequencies of 51,
52, 53, and 54 cells per
inch, all at 39 degrees.
Notice the discrete jumps;
52 and 53 are the same,
even though a different
frequency was specified.

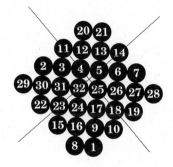
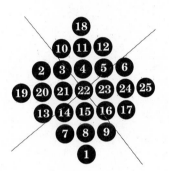

```
%!PS-Adobe1.0
%% Title: LookAtHalftoneCells
%% Creator: Bill Woodruff


/cs { dup stringwidth pop -2 div 0 rmoveto show} def


/msg {
     fn 14 scalefont setfont
     0 340 moveto
     (Plot of Halftone Cells and Order of Spot Function Action) cs
     currentpoint 30 sub exch neg exch moveto
     (Frequency = ) show f =string cvs show ( ... ) show
     (Angle = ) show a =string cvs show
     ( ... )  show (Number of Pixels = ) show
     p =string cvs show
} def
```

```
/p 0 def

/pscreen {        % def
gsave
      2 copy
      /a exch def
      /f exch def
      gsave
            { /p dup load 1 add def 1 } setscreen
      grestore

      /rad 20 def
      /pf dpi f div rad mul def

      a rotate
      gsave
            p 100 idiv dup 1 gt
            { 1.5 exch div dup scale } { pop }
            ifelse

            p -1 1
            {
            /n exch def
            pf mul exch pf mul exch
            gsave
                  translate 0 0 moveto
                  gsave newpath 0 0 rad 0 360 arc fill grestore
                  a neg rotate 0 -8 rmoveto
                  1 setgray
                  n =string cvs cs
            grestore
            }
            for
      grestore
      0 0 moveto
      .5 setgray .72 setlinewidth
      0 200 rlineto 0 -400 rlineto
      0 0 moveto
      200 0 rlineto -400 0 rlineto
      stroke
```

```
grestore
} def % /pscreen

306 390 translate 0 0 moveto

/fn /NewCenturySchlbk-Bold findfont def

fn 24 scalefont setfont

/dpi 72 0 dtransform dup mul exch dup mul add sqrt def

% put screen frequency and angle here
120 135 pscreen

msg

showpage
```

As you can see from the sample output, there are constraints on what cell matrices will work to provide a repeatable pattern of halftone cells, especially on lower-resolution devices. When you request a given angle and frequency, the PostScript interpreter does the best it can given the resolution of the output device, approximating the angle and frequency as closely as possible.

So while PostScript can theoretically provide any angle and frequency, in the real world of PostScript output, frequency/angle combinations are only available in discrete steps, constrained by the possible cell matrices. If you use a coarse frequency, there are more pixels in the cell, hence more possible cell shapes, and more available angles. Likewise, with higher-resolution output, there are more cell matrices possible, so there are more possible frequency/angle combinations.

All this means that PostScript output devices don't necessarily give you the screen frequency or angle you request, especially on lower-resolution devices. It's still a problem on high-resolution devices, however, especially with color separations. As Pat Wood and Herb Paynter point out in their chapters on color (chapters 11, 12, and 14), accurate frequencies and angles are essential to avoid moiré patterns.

The program by Henry Bortman that follows returns the actual screen frequencies and number of gray levels that a given output device will produce when you request a range of angles and frequencies. You

can modify the frequency and angle range before downloading, and
you will have to modify the resolution if you are not using a 300 dpi
printer. As it stands, the program takes about five minutes to complete
on an Apple LaserWriter Plus.

```
%!PS-Adobe
%Title: CountPixels.ps
%Creator: Henry Bortman


% The definition of the procedure actfreq uses 300 as the resolution.
% If you use this routine on an output device with a different
% resolution, you will have to change this number.


initgraphics grestoreall


%--------- procedure definitions


/inch {72 mul} def
/xdf {exch def} def
/st 80 string def


/pnum { st cvs print } def


/boxpath { 0 1 lineto 1 1 lineto 1 0 lineto closepath } def


/newspot {  % def
     dup mul exch dup mul add 1.0 exch sub
     /counter counter 1 add def
} def


/setUpScreen { freq angle /newspot load setscreen } def


/actfreq {
     300 counter sqrt div
} def % change for different dpi


/writeMessage {
% angle is the nominal angle
% actfreq is the actual frequency
% counter is the actual number of pixels
```

```
        angle pnum ( ) print
        actfreq pnum ( ) print
        counter pnum (\n) print flush
} def

% begin main program

1 inch 5 inch translate
0 0 moveto
currentpoint
.1 inch .1 inch scale
boxpath

33 1 50     % set nominal freq range: start, increment, end
{ /freq xdf
    (\n) print flush
    (nominal frequency:  ) print freq pnum
    (\n) print flush (\n) print flush
        0 1 45     % set angle range: start, increment, end
        {       %for
        /angle xdf
        /counter 0 def
        gsave
                setUpScreen .7 setgray fill
        grestore
        writeMessage
        } for
} for
```

The program goes through all the screen frequencies in the specified range, and all the specified angles for all those frequencies, and returns the actual frequency and the number of pixels per cell for each frequency/angle combination. You will need something like JustText or Lasertalk to use it—a program that captures data returned from the printer—or you will need to modify the program so it prints rather than returning the data.

The data come back in the following format. This is just a sample of what could potentially be a lot of information, depending on the range of angles and frequencies you request. The ellipses show where we cut for brevity's sake. You can massage this data to print a chart using various word processor and spreadsheet tools.

The first column is the requested angle; the second is the true frequency; the third is the number of pixels per cell.

```
nominal frequency:  33

0       33.3333     81
1       33.3333     81
2       33.3333     81
3       33.3333     81
4       33.1295     82
5       33.1295     82
.

.

43      35.3553     72
44      35.3553     72
45      35.3553     72
.

.

nominal frequency:  38

0       37.5        64
1       37.5        64
2       37.5        64
3       37.5        64
4       37.2104     65
5       37.2104     65
.

.

nominal frequency:  53

0       50.0        36
1       50.0        36
2       50.0        36
3       50.0        36
4       50.0        36
5       50.0        36
6       49.3197     37
.

.

15      58.8348     26
```

16	55.7086	29
.		
.		
36	51.4496	34
37	51.4496	34
38	60.0	25
39	53.033	32
.		
.		
45	53.033	32

This program is short and easy to key in, but it doesn't return the true angle (which is trickier) or print a chart of the results for you. The following program by Tom Bernard does both, though it is not as comprehensive; it prints only a couple of frequencies at a time. It takes a different approach to determining the true frequency, and calculates the angle using the method commented within the program.

```
%!PS-Adobe
%%Title: anglechart
%%Creator: Tom Bernard, Bersearch Information Services

(\n%%[ anglechart 880225 ]%%\n)= flush

/inch {72 mul} bind def

/fonttsize 10 def
/helbold /Helvetica-Bold findfont fonttsize scalefont def
/hel /Helvetica findfont fonttsize scalefont def

/cvsstr 30 string def

/frequency1 60 def
/frequency2 50 def

% "trueangle" and "truefrequency" calculate the true angle
% and true frequency from "truedx" and "truedy". "truedx"
% and "truedy" are the "dx" and "dy" between two adjacent
% pixels in cell coordinates.

% Adjacent pixels are not always calculated in sequence.
```

```
% If three pixels (1,2,3) are adjacent on the same line, then
% dx(1,2) = dx(2,3) and dy(1,2) = dy(2,3).


% The routine "findtruedelta" is called by "sccmmfunction"
% for each pixel until "truedx" and "truedy" are determined.
% "findtruedelta" calculates "dx" and "dy" for this pixel and
% the last pixel. "dx" and "dy" are then compared with "olddx"
% and "olddy". If both match, then "truedx" is set to "dx"
% and "truedy" is set to "dy". If the match is false, then
% "olddy" is set to "dy" and "olddx" is set to "dx".

/ifmatchtrue {      %def
      /truedx dx def
      /truedy dy def
      /dofindtruedelta false def      % we got it-don't waste time
} bind def

/ifmatchfalse {
      /olddx dx def
      /olddy dy def
      /oldx x def
      /oldy y def
} bind def



/findtruedelta { %def
      /dx x oldx sub def
      /dy y oldy sub def

      dx olddx eq
      dy olddy eq
      and
            /ifmatchtrue load
            /ifmatchfalse load
      ifelse
} bind def      % /findtruedelta

/sccmmfunction {
      /y exch def
      /x exch def
```

```
        /pixelcount pixelcount 1 add def
        dofindtruedelta /findtruedelta load if
        x y userspotfunction
} bind def


currentscreen /userspotfunction exch def pop pop        % get spot function


%  Determine device pixel resolution.
/resmatrix matrix defaultmatrix def
/resolution
        72 0 resmatrix dtransform
        dup mul exch dup mul add sqrt
def


% Definition of "resolution" adapted from "findresolution";
% "PostScript Language Tutorial and Cookbook", Adobe Systems Inc.,
% Addison-Wesley Publishing Company, 1985, p 191


/ifnolimitcheck { % bind def
        /trueangle
                360     truedy truedx atan     sub
                round cvi 360 mod
        def


        /truefrequency
                resolution
                2
                truedy dup mul
                truedx dup mul
                add sqrt
                div
                div
                10 mul round 10 div
        def
} bind def  % /ifnolimitcheck


/angledata {        % def
        /olddx 10 def       % by initializing these with
        /olddy 10 def       % values well outside the
        /oldx 10 def        % cell coordinates, we won't
```

```
        /oldy 10 def        % be tripped up by false values.
        /dofindtruedelta true def
        /nolimitcheck true def
        /pixelcount 0 def
        frequency rotation /sccmmfunction load setscreen

        % now that "sccmmfunction" has determined "pixelcount"
        % and "truedx" and "truedy", we can determine some
        % data about the screen; that is, only if
        % "setscreen" did not generate "limitcheck".

        nolimitcheck /ifnolimitcheck load if
} bind def  % /angledata


/sethb {helbold setfont} bind def


/showangle % bind def
{       % assumes current point for this line
        % set by calling routine

        /rotation exch def

        rotation = flush

        /frequency frequency1 def
        angledata

        gsave
                rotation showvaltab
                0.25 inch 0 rmoveto
                rotation trueangle eq
                frequency truefrequency eq
                and
                        /sethb load
                if

                trueangle showvaltab
                truefrequency showvaltab
        grestore

        /frequency frequency2 def
```

```
        angledata

        gsave
                rotation trueangle eq
                frequency truefrequency eq
                and
                        /sethb load
                if

                2 inch 0 rmoveto
                trueangle showvaltab
                truefrequency showvaltab
        grestore

        0 fonttsize neg rmoveto
} bind def  % /showangle

/cvsstr 30 string def

/showvaltab {
        cvsstr cvs
        dup stringwidth pop neg     0
        rmoveto show
        0.5 inch 0 rmoveto
} bind def


/showcr {
        show currentpoint exch pop
        fonttsize sub left exch moveto
} def

/left 1.25 inch def

%%EndProlog

hel setfont

left 10 inch moveto

(A:   Requested angle in degrees.) showcr
```

```
(B:   Actual angle in degrees for requested frequency of 60 dpi.) showcr
(C:   Actual frequency in dots/inch for requested frequency of 60 dpi.) showcr
(D:   Actual angle in degrees for requested frequency of 50 dpi.) showcr
(E:   Actual frequency in dots/inch for requested frequency of 50 dpi.) showcr


helbold setfont


1.25 inch 8.5 inch moveto
(A) showvaltab


0.25 inch 0 rmoveto
(B) showvaltab
(C) showvaltab


0.25 inch 0 rmoveto
(D) showvaltab
(E) showvaltab


4.75 inch 8.5 inch moveto
(A) showvaltab


0.25 inch 0 rmoveto
(B) showvaltab
(C) showvaltab


0.25 inch 0 rmoveto
(D) showvaltab
(E) showvaltab


hel setfont


1.25 inch 8 inch moveto
0 1 45 /showangle load  for


4.75 inch 8 inch moveto
46 1 90 /showangle load  for


showpage
```

You can see the output from this program in Figure 10.6. Either one of these programs will show you that there are limitations on the frequency/angle combinations available on PostScript devices.

As these two programs make clear, even on the LaserWriter (and most other 300 dpi PostScript printers) the default frequency/angle combination isn't really available. The default is nominally 60/45, and

A: Requested angle in degrees.
B: Actual angle in degrees for requested frequency of 60 dpi.
C: Actual frequency in dots/inch for requested frequency of 60 dpi.
D: Actual angle in degrees for requested frequency of 50 dpi.
E: Actual frequency in dots/inch for requested frequency of 50 dpi.

Figure 10.6. This output from anglechart shows the requested versus actual screen frequencies for a 300 dpi PostScript printer at 50 and 60 cells per inch with zero through 90 degree screen angles. Bold type marks the combinations where requested frequency and angle match actual frequency and angle.

A	B	C	D	E	A	B	C	D	E
0	**0**	**60.0**	**0**	**50.0**	46	53	60.0	45	53.0
1	0	60.0	0	50.0	47	53	60.0	45	53.0
2	0	60.0	0	50.0	48	53	60.0	45	53.0
3	0	60.0	0	50.0	49	53	60.0	51	46.9
4	0	60.0	0	50.0	50	53	60.0	51	46.9
5	0	60.0	0	60.0	51	53	60.0	51	46.9
6	11	58.8	11	58.8	52	53	60.0	51	46.9
7	11	58.8	11	58.8	53	**53**	**60.0**	51	46.9
8	11	58.8	11	58.8	54	53	60.0	51	46.9
9	11	58.8	11	58.8	55	53	60.0	59	51.4
10	11	58.8	11	58.8	56	53	60.0	59	51.4
11	11	58.8	11	58.8	57	53	60.0	59	51.4
12	11	58.8	11	58.8	58	53	60.0	59	51.4
13	11	58.8	11	58.8	59	53	60.0	59	51.4
14	11	58.8	11	58.8	60	53	60.0	59	51.4
15	11	58.8	18	47.4	61	63	67.1	59	51.4
16	11	58.8	18	47.4	62	63	67.1	59	51.4
17	11	58.8	18	47.4	63	63	67.1	59	51.4
18	22	55.7	18	47.4	64	63	67.1	59	51.4
19	22	55.7	18	47.4	65	68	55.7	59	51.4
20	22	55.7	18	47.4	66	68	55.7	68	55.7
21	22	55.7	18	47.4	67	68	55.7	72	47.4
22	22	55.7	18	47.4	68	68	55.7	72	47.4
23	22	55.7	18	47.4	69	68	55.7	72	47.4
24	22	55.7	22	55.7	70	68	55.7	72	47.4
25	22	55.7	31	51.4	71	68	55.7	72	47.4
26	27	67.1	31	51.4	72	68	55.7	72	47.4
27	27	67.1	31	51.4	73	79	58.8	72	47.4
28	27	67.1	31	51.4	74	79	58.8	72	47.4
29	27	67.1	31	51.4	75	79	58.8	81	49.3
30	37	60.0	31	51.4	76	79	58.8	81	49.3
31	37	60.0	31	51.4	77	79	58.8	81	49.3
32	37	60.0	31	51.4	78	79	58.8	81	49.3
33	37	60.0	31	51.4	79	79	58.8	81	49.3
34	37	60.0	31	51.4	80	79	58.8	81	49.3
35	37	60.0	31	51.4	81	79	58.8	81	49.3
36	37	60.0	39	46.9	82	79	58.8	81	49.3
37	**37**	**60.0**	39	46.9	83	79	58.8	81	49.3
38	37	60.0	39	46.9	84	79	58.8	81	49.3
39	37	60.0	39	46.9	85	90	60.0	81	49.3
40	37	60.0	39	46.9	86	90	60.0	90	50.0
41	37	60.0	39	46.9	87	90	60.0	90	50.0
42	37	60.0	45	53.0	88	90	60.0	90	50.0
43	37	60.0	45	53.0	89	90	60.0	90	50.0
44	37	60.0	45	53.0	90	**90**	**60.0**	**90**	**50.0**
45	45	53.0	45	53.0					

since 60 fits neatly into 300, you'd expect a nice 5-by-5 halftone cell (as suggested in the green book). As it turns out, because of the 45-degree screen angle, you get a 53-line screen with 32 pixels per cell (33 gray levels). Try the 60/45 combination with the LookAtHalftoneCell program above, and you'll count 32 dots in the output.

Grays and Densities

Okay, so you don't necessarily get the frequency or angle you requested. But do you get the gray level you request? Does .5 setgray yield a fifty-percent tint? Again, not necessarily. Several factors affect the darkness of your printed output, most being dependent on your output device.

Before we discuss those factors, though, let's talk about PostScript's methods for setting the gray level. No matter what your choices are for *setscreen*, you need to specify a gray level for the screen you've chosen. There are two PostScript operators for the purpose: *setgray* and *image*. These operators are well covered in the red and blue books, and *image* is well handled in the green book. But here's a quick explanation for those who aren't blessed with those volumes.

setgray is the simpler of the two operators. It takes only one argument, a number between zero and one. .1 setgray results (theoretically) in a ninety-percent screen, and .8 setgray provides a twenty-percent screen. You use *setgray* to specify a gray level for objects and their fills. It's almost too simple to require an example, but for those who haven't done it:

```
%!PS-Adobe
/boxpath {   %def
     100 100 moveto
     0 100 rlineto
     100 0 rlineto
     0 -100 rlineto
     closepath
} def %boxpath
boxpath
.4 setgray
fill
showpage
```

This one hundred–point square gets a sixty-percent gray fill. That's really all there is to *setgray*, though we'll discuss more about the actual grays that result further on.

The *image* operator is more complex and interesting. It's used primarily to print scanned images in which each sample point has a gray value. (A 300 dpi scanner "samples" an image every 1/300th-inch). You can also use *image* with your own data rather than using a scanned image. Instead of providing a uniform gray fill, *image* goes through each sample point in a string of data, and repeatedly applies the screen requested by *setscreen* according to the gray level specified for each sample point. The gray level changes for each sample point.

There are five arguments to *image*: the height and the width of the image (number of sample points vertically and horizontally); the number of bits per sample (how much gray information the scanner captures); the image matrix (the relationship between the position of the sample points and the position of their resulting halftone cells); and the data acquisition procedure (the method for reading the string of data).

Here's a simple program for imaging a string of hexadecimal data. The easiest way to get the hex data is to scan an image with a scanner capable of capturing gray levels for each sample point, and saving the image as an EPS file (the following program is a slight modification of an EPS export from ImageStudio). Then you can open the image with a text editor and move the data into your sample program (on the Macintosh, you may have to change the "Type" of the EPS file to TEXT before you can open it with your text editor). The alternative is to key in the data or write a program that will generate it for you.

This program will not work as is, since it only includes portions of the sample data:

```
%!PS-Adobe-2.0 EPSF-1.2
%%Creator:ImageStudio/Steve Roth
%%Title: DogsEye.ps
%%BoundingBox:0 0 90 87
%%This program images a set of sample data that is 72 samples
%%wide and 68 samples high.

%%EndComments
/width 72 def      %Number of sample points horizontal
/height 68 def     %Number of sample points vertical
```

```
/pixwidth 90 def  %Output size horizontal
/pixheight 87 def %Output size vertical
/picstr width string def %Convert width to string and save in picstr
/dopic {     %def
gsave
      width height 8     % First three arguments to image
      [width 0 0 height neg 0 height]     % image matrix
      {currentfile picstr readhexstring pop} % data acquisition
      image
grestore
}def %dopic
pixwidth pixheight scale      %size the image
dopic

%     Start of sample data
0000000000000000000000000000000000000000000000000000000000000000

.

Sample Data Here

.

00000000000000000031303031313334353638383636353333131303030303031
2E2B2D2F2F2F2D2E31302E2E31383C3A383A3A3B3B3B3A393B3C3B3A3C3E3E00

.

Sample Data Here

.

0000000000000000
%     End of Sample Data
showpage
```

The problem with this program is the size of the files you end up working with. It's easy to get into 200k+ files with scanned images saved in PostScript. Saving in binary format, which some scanning software will let you do, reduces file size by about fifty percent (note that you will need to use a *readstring* rather than *readhexstring* for binary data). Few text editors handle that big a file with much aplomb, and downloading takes a long time.

Here's a program by Tom Bernard that lets you download all the hex data once and store it in virtual memory (VM), then call it repeatedly with your imaging program, which is handy when you're mucking around with PostScript's halftoning operators.

There are some limitations with this program, based on how much VM you have. In my experience, anything over about 100k of data will result in a VM error and a printer reset (this on a version 23 LaserWriter; other printers handle more), so the program's primary utility is in working with small sample images and modifying *setscreen* and *settransfer* for various effects.

Also be aware that this approach doesn't conform to document structuring conventions. It's merely for the purpose of testing and engineering. Within these constraints, there's a big speed difference with large samples, which is important when you're printing an image over and over trying to get things right.

```
%!PS-Adobe
%% CreateHalftoneArray
%%Creator: Tom Bernard
%%EndComments:

% first escape save-restore context
% if the system password has been changed, then change 0
% to your password.

serverdict begin 0 exitserver

/inch {72 mul} def

/width 72 def      % # of sample points horizontal--from scan file
/height 68 def     % # of sample points vertical--from scan file
/bps 8 def  % bits per sample

% define array to hold n 1024 byte hexstrings and string to receive
% data temporarily.
/sac 0 def  % string array count
/picstr 256 string def  % string for temp storage of hex data
/picstrlength picstr length def

% define array to receive hex data
/pictarray
          width height mul bps mul 8 div
          picstrlength div 1 add cvi
     array
```

```
def

% define separate strings for each element of array
0 1 pictarray length 1 sub
{       % for
        pictarray exch picstrlength string put
} for         % index = 0 to pictarraylength-1 step 1

% "storestrpictarray" copies readhexstring result into
% pictarray sac get
/storestrpictarray {
        pictarray sac get exch 0 exch putinterval
} def

/readpictarrayfromfile { %def
      { %loop
              currentfile picstr readhexstring
              % returns substring actually read
              % and boolean, normally true,
              % false if EOF before filling string
              {
                      storestrpictarray        % true proc
                      /sac sac 1 add def
              }
              {
                      storestrpictarray        % false proc
                      exit
              }
              ifelse
      } loop
} def %readpictarrayfromfile

% readpictarrayfromfile is followed
% by the hex data.
readpictarrayfromfile
```

Place the hex data for the image after readpictarrayfromfile, and download the whole thing. From then on, all the hex data is in the printer's memory, ready to be used. To use the data stored in VM, you can use a program like the following:

```
%!PS-Adobe
%% CallHalftoneArray
%% Creator: Tom Bernard
%% EndComments:

currentscreen /defaultspotfunction exch def        % save current spot function
pop pop        % toss angle and frequency

/sac -1 def        % scan array count

/dopic { %def
    gsave
    % put settransfer here
    width height 8                        % first three arguments to image
    [width 0 0 height neg 0 height]       % image matrix
    {  /sac sac 1 add def                 % data acquisition
    pictarray sac get}
    image
    showpage
    grestore
}def %dopic


% now to modify the image...

66 45 { defaultspotfunction } setscreen     % modify as you wish

36 36 translate    % move up and over 1/2 inch

/scalesize 1 def  % set scaling

%scale height and width by scalesize
width scalesize mul height scalesize mul scale

dopic
```

The primary difference between this and DogsEye.PS above is in the data acquisition argument to image. Rather than reading the data from currentfile, it reads it from pictarray, which we set up using Create-HalftoneArray. The whole difference is that you only have to download the data once.

BACK TO GRAYS

Now that we've talked about methods for specifying gray levels in PostScript, let's go back to the real world: When you specify a gray level, is that what actually comes out of the printer? The answer, as I said above, is "not necessarily." Again, the output device is the constraining factor.

For laser output, the first thing to consider is dot gain. Laser printers use toner, which they bond onto the paper, and the toner spreads a little when it's bonded. The result is what printers call "dot gain," and has the most effect in light gray areas. A LaserWriter, for instance, is hard-pressed to produce less than a twenty-percent tint using *setgray* or *image* (you can do better if you start mucking around with the device pixels themselves). Bright papers designed for lasers can bring that to about ten percent. Figure 10.7 shows the actual gray that results from an Apple LaserWriter with plain copier paper compared to the gray requested.

The opposite problem, of course, is the blacks. The LaserWriter can push ninety-percent gray when it's got a good cartridge in it, and some of the "write-white" engines, like the Ricoh engine used in the AST TurboLaser and Texas Instruments OmniLaser, push ninety-five percent. A ten-percent screen on the LaserWriter looks very different from the same thing on a Texas Instruments OmniLaser, not to mention one of the Linotronic Imagesetters.

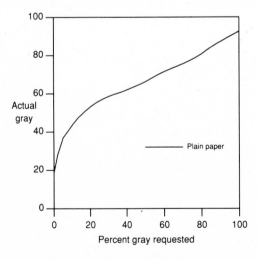

Figure 10.7. This graph illustrates the requested versus actual gray output on an Apple LaserWriter with plain copier paper. Courtesy, *PostScript Language Journal*.

REFLECTANCE, APPEARANCE, AND DENSITY

To explain these differences more fully, let's talk about how the eye perceives gray, and how that relates to the grays you request in PostScript. The key concept here is the relation between reflectance and density. Reflectance is essentially the same thing as coverage (actually its inverse). If the halftone cells of a given area black out half that area, it has a fifty percent reflectance. If twenty-five percent is blacked out, it has a seventy-five-percent reflectance. (Is PostScript's seeming reversal in using *setgray* starting to make sense now?)

While reflectance and coverage are inversely proportional, reflectance and *apparent* gray have a more complex relationship, due to the sensitivity curve of the human eye. If you look at an even transition from zero reflectance (one hundred-percent black) to full reflectance (pure white), it appears to have too much black and fade suddenly to white. Twenty-five-percent gray doesn't appear to be half as dark as fifty percent.

Because of this sensitivity curve, printers use another method of measuring grays, called density. For those who are interested, the relationship of reflectance to density is as follows:

$$\text{density} = \log_{10}\left(\frac{1}{\text{reflectance}}\right)$$

So a chart comparing screen percentages to density looks like this:

Screen	Density
0	0
50	.3
90	1
99	2

In practice, even on an offset press, you aren't likely to get better than a density of 1.9. On a laser printer, 1.5 is quite good. And even the whitest paper will have a density of .1 or .2. It's the facts of life.

Figure 10.8 shows the density/screen percent relationship graphically. The eye is more sensitive to dark areas, and the result is that those areas tend to dominate in a smooth transition from zero to one-hundred-percent black. The ultimate goal is to create a smooth transition of *density*—apparent gray—from black to white, not a smooth transition of screen percentage. Which brings us back to PostScript.

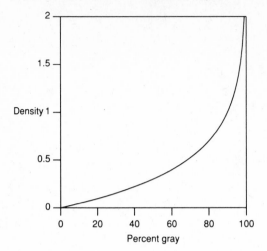

Figure 10.8. This graph illustrates the relationship between density and reflectance. Courtesy, PostScript Language Journal.

USING SETTRANSFER

From the above discussion of grays, densities, and the realities of laser output, it's obvious there's a need for some overriding operator that controls how a device images grays, without the need to go through a whole program changing the *setgray* and *image* values. That meta-operator is *settransfer*. Its job is to map the grays requested with *setgray* and *image* to a set of grays that PostScript uses for imaging.

   settransfer can be used for simple things like producing negatives, or in the second procedure following, by Bill Woodruff, to convert all the values between .25 and .75 to .5, while passing all the others through unaltered:

```
{ 1 exch sub } settransfer
{ dup .25 ge 1 index .75 le and { pop .5 } if } settransfer
```

   But the more interesting uses come when you start correcting the gray curve for the output device you're using. The following bit of code, for instance, adapted from Pat Wood's work in *The PostScript Language Journal*, maps the grays to provide a more even density transition on the Apple LaserWriter at its default frequency. The same method can be used for complex posterization (stairstepping the gray values for special effects) or for gamma correction in color separation work.

```
/transarray [ %def
   0  0  0  0  0  0  0  0  1  1  1  2  2  3  3  3
   4  4  5  5  5  6  6  6  7  7  8  8  8  9  9 10
  10 10 11 11 12 12 12 13 13 14 14 14 15 15 15 16
  16 17 17 17 18 18 20 20 20 22 22 24 24 24 26 26
  26 28 28 31 31 31 34 34 37 37 37 40 40 42 42 42
  44 44 46 46 46 48 48 48 49 49 51 51 51 52 52 54
  54 54 55 55 57 57 57 59 59 60 60 60 62 62 62 63
  63 65 65 65 66 66 68 68 68 69 69 71 71 71 72 72
  72 72 72 73 73 73 74 74 75 75 75 76 76 77 77 77
  78 78 78 78 78 79 79 79 80 80 81 81 81 82 82 83
  83 83 83 83 84 84 84 85 85 85 85 85 86 86 86 87
  87 87 87 87 88 88 88 88 88 89 89 89 89 89 90 90
  90 90 90 91 91 91 91 91 92 92 92 92 92 93 93 93
  93 93 94 94 94 94 94 94 95 95 95 95 95 96 96 96
  96 96 97 97 97 97 97 97 97 97 97 97 98 98 98 98
  98 98 98 98 98 98 99 99 99 99 99 100 100 100 100 100
] def % transarray
{
     255 mul cvi % multiply gray x 256 and make integer
     transarray exch get    % look up gray value in array
     100 div    % return gray setting to 0-1 range
} settransfer
```

The array consists of 256 values, one for each of 256 gray values. You could just as easily use 50, 100, or 200 values. The important thing is the gray scale mapping. Let's say the requested gray scale is .5. The transfer function multiplies it by 255 and converts it to an integer, yielding 127. It looks up the 127th value in the array (72), and divides it by 100, resulting in .72 setgray when you request .5.

This array is designed to work on LaserWriters and other Canon CX-engine printers at their default frequency (nominally 60 lines per inch, actually 53). If you change the frequency, you will need to change the array as well, since dot gain is more pronounced at higher frequencies. With other devices you need a completely different array. Figure 10.9 shows two "fountains" going from 0- to 100-percent gray. In the first, *settransfer* is unaltered. The second shows the results with the transfer array above.

Bear in mind that the PostScript interpreter doesn't need to go through this array lookup every time it encounters a gray level. It goes

Figure 10.9. These two fountains were created using the image operator. In the bottom one, the transfer function is unmodified. The top uses a 256-element transfer array to modify the transition from black to white.

through the whole thing once, building the gray mapping as an internal structure that it can access very quickly.

Spot Function

There is still one aspect of PostScript gray-handling that I haven't discussed: the spot function. This little devil controls the shape of the halftone cells. It is, in one sense, the most valuable part of PostScript's halftoning machinery; and at the same time, it can be viewed as the weakest link, the one thing that keeps PostScript halftoning from competing with the quality of photographic halftoning. I'll get into the limitations of the halftoning machinery at the end of the chapter. First let's talk about how that machinery works.

For starters, here is Bill Woodruff's whimsical explanation of the elusive spot function, which I can't resist inserting here, titled "Turning Pixels On:"

Pixels are normally excitable and sensual—none of your techno-repression here, thank you. They love to get turned on and dark. As one pixel said: "My goal in life is to have intercourse with a PostScript interpreter until I turn gray."

The spot function is a bartender in a seedy little watering hole called The Halftone Cell where pixels go after work. The light is dim, the hooch strong, the music digital and loud. Pixels come here 'cause they know there's a good chance they'll get turned on.

Here's how the spot function works to decide which pixels in a halftone cell get turned on:

When you call *setscreen*, the address of each pixel in the cell is passed to the spot function. This is where the numbers in the LookAt-HalftoneCells program and its output come in (see above). The PostScript interpreter goes through the pixels in the order shown in that figure, takes the address for each pixel (the x,y coordinate in the cell), and (based on the spot function) leaves behind a value for that pixel between -1 and 1.

These values are relative values. If the spot function assigns one pixel a value of .25 and another has a value of -.25, the higher-numbered pixel will get turned on at a lower gray level. At higher gray levels, the the pixels with lower values are turned on.

At the moment of the actual call to fill or stroke a path, or to show text, the internal gray-producing structures are ready to go; they know the priority of the pixels in the cell. The intensity of gray (as mapped by the transfer function) is passed to the internal procedures that determine which pixels become immortal on the page.

That's the conceptual overview. For a more practical approach, here's a spot function created by Tom Bernard that creates triangular halftone cells, along with his explanation:

```
2 exch sub exch abs 2 mul sub 3 div
```

You use it like this:

```
/trianglefn { 2 exch sub exch abs 2 mul sub 3 div } def
60 45 trianglefn setscreen
```

The goal of this spot function is to create large triangles with dark grays, and small triangles with light grays. Take a look at Figure 10.10. The arrows within the triangle show the desired ranking of the pixels. Pixels close to the "bottom" of the cell are ranked higher, as are pixels close to the vertical line where x=0. We want high values for pixels where x is close to zero, and y is close to -1.

There are a couple of catches, though. The three endpoints must have the same priority ranking within the cell, yet the x contribution is only half that of the y contribution, and is either positive or negative. So we take the absolute value of x and double it to compensate.

We can use this technique to produce triangles with any ratio of base to height. In this case the y contribution to the priority value of the pixel is $1-y$. The x contribution is $1-2|x|$ (that's absolute value). Add them and you get $2-y-2|x|$, which will produce rankings between -1

(-1,1)   (1,1)

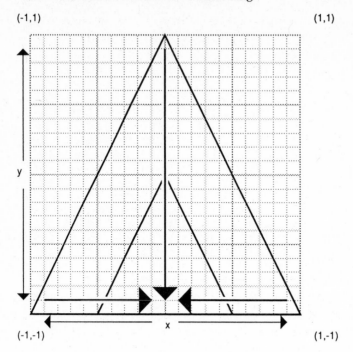

Figure 10.10. This
representation of a halftone
cell matrix shows the
relative x- and y-axis
contributions to Tom
Bernard's triangle spot
function.

(-1,-1)   (1,-1)

and 3. Divide the ranking value by 3 so the rankings are between 1
and −1 (actually, −.33 and 1, but the *relative* value of the pixels is
what counts, not the value itself), translate the formula into PostScript,
and you get the spot function above. It gives high priority to the pixels
at the bottom center, and less toward the upper corners.

This is a nice explanatory example, but not, perhaps, the most widely
used cell shape. PostScript devices all have default spot functions,
which are, of course, the ones you see the most. The default spot
function in earlier versions of PostScript was a straightforward dot
function:

```
{ dup mul exch dup mul add 1 exch sub }
```

This function builds a circular cell from the center (0,0) outward.
Adobe discovered that to produce better saturated grays when the gray
value is over fifty percent, it pays to start building in from the corners.
So they implemented an either/or default spot function, which assigns
pixel priorities differently depending on the gray level:

```
{ abs exch abs 2 copy add 1 gt { 1 sub dup mul exch 1 sub dup mul add 1
sub } { dup mul exch dup mul add 1 exch sub } ifelse }
```

If the gray value is less than fifty percent, this spot function simply uses the old spot function, building a circular dot out from the center. Greater than fifty, and it builds in from the corners. Figure 10.11 shows the output from the two spot functions at different gray levels with a 10-line, 0-degree screen. As you can see, the results can be surprising if you are using coarse screen frequencies. At finer frequencies, the results are generally superior to the old spot function.

Another commonly used halftone cell shape is the ellipse. For one example and an explanation of how and why it is used, see Pat Wood's chapter 12, "POSTSCRIPT Color Separations."

Spot functions can be hard to visualize, so here's a program, also by Tom Bernard, that shows you the pixel ranking both graphically and numerically. There are a couple of Tom's other spot functions embedded in here as well. You can see the results in Figure 10.12.

```
%!PS-Adobe-1.0
%%DocumentFonts: Helvetica Helvetica-Bold Times-Roman Times-Bold
%%Title: ShowTheCell 880224
%%Creator: Tom Bernard, Bersearch Information Services
%%Pages: 2
```

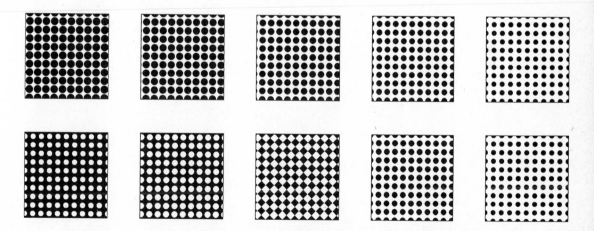

Figure 10.11. These boxes are all filled with 10 cell-per-inch screens at zero degrees. The requested grays are, from left to right, .3, .4, .5, .6, and .7. The top row shows the default spot function for older POSTSCRIPT interpreters (before version 38). The bottom row employs the new spot function and makes apparent its if/else nature with 50-percent breakpoint.

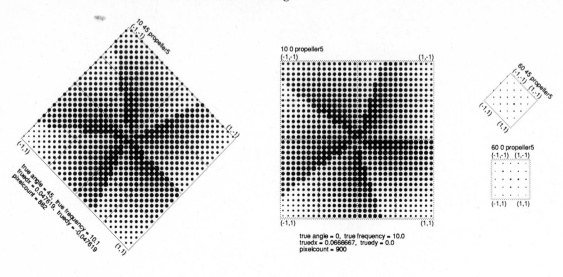

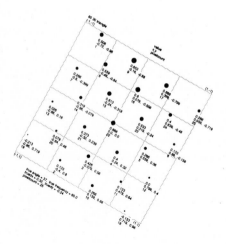

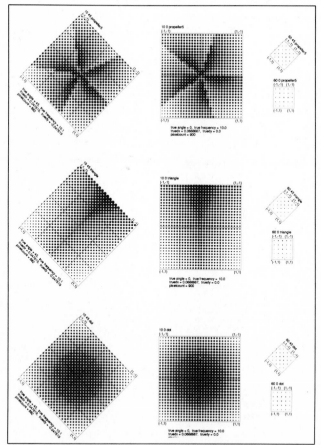

Figure 10.12. These images, which are output from showthecell, are in essence halftones of digital halftone cells. The larger the dot in the cell, the higher the ranking assigned to that device pixel by the given spot function.

```
%%EndComments

(%%[ ShowTheCell takes 12 minutes to produce output. ])=flush

/row1spot (propeller5) def
/row2spot (triangle) def
/row3spot (dot) def
/page2spot (triangle) def

% To use your own spot functions, replace the above strings
% with the names of your own functions and define your
% functions below. Be sure to bind your definitions for
% fastest run time.

% some spot functions

/dot {
     dup mul exch dup mul add 1.0 exch sub
} bind def

/triangle {
     2 exch sub exch abs 2 mul sub 3 div
} bind def

/propeller5 {
     /y exch def
     /x exch def

     /theta   y  x .001 add   atan  cvi def

     theta 72 mod  72 sub abs 72 div
     y y mul x x mul add 1 exch sub
     add
     2 div
} bind def

currentscreen
/defaultspotfunction exch def % get default spot function
pop pop     %  toss default angle & freq.
```

```
%   end spot function definitions

/inch {72 mul} bind def
/cvsstg 20 string def

% Define some frequency/angle combinations
/fr1045 {
      /frequency 10 def
      /rotation 45 def
} bind def

/fr6045 {
      /frequency 60 def
      /rotation 45 def
} bind def

/fr6030 {
      /frequency 60 def
      /rotation 30 def
} bind def

/fr10zero {
      /frequency 10 def
      /rotation 0 def
} bind def

/fr60zero {
      /frequency 60 def
      /rotation 0 def
} bind def

% See comments for the following in "anglechart"
/ifmatchtrue {
      /truedx dx def
      /truedy dy def
      /dofindtruedelta false def    % we got it - don't waste time
      pcstring print pixelcount = flush
} bind def

/ifmatchfalse {
```

```
        /olddx dx def
        /olddy dy def
        /oldx x def
        /oldy y def
} bind def


/findtruedelta {
        /dx    x oldx sub    def
        /dy    y oldy sub    def

        dx olddx eq
        dy olddy eq
        and
                /ifmatchtrue load
                /ifmatchfalse load
        ifelse
} bind def


% "label" is called from "sccdotfunction" if labeling of the pixels
% is required. "label" blanks the area under the label for easier
% reading. Then "label" labels the value of the pixel.


/roundcvs {
        1000 mul cvi 1000 div
        cvsstg cvs
} bind def


/showstring {        % () x y
        moveto
        gsave
                    0
                    ftsize 0.2 mul neg
            rmoveto
                dup stringwidth pop 2 cte div add
                    0
            rlineto
                    0
                    ftsize
            rlineto
                dup stringwidth pop 2 cte div add neg
```

```
                        0
            rlineto
            closepath
            1 setgray fill
        grestore
        show
} bind def      % /showstring


/showvalue {      % x y n
    roundcvs      % x y (n)
    3 1 roll      % (n) x y
    showstring
} bind def


/label {     % def
                pixelcount cvsstg cvs
                x -1 cte div add
                y .05 add ftsize 2 mul add
            showstring
                x -1 cte div add
                y .05 add ftsize add
                x
            showvalue

            commastring currentpoint showstring
            currentpoint y showvalue

                x -1 cte div add
                y .05 add
                pixelval
            showvalue

} bind def      % /label

/commastring (,  ) def

/sccdotfunction {      %def
    /y exch def
    /x exch def
```

```
/pixelcount pixelcount 1 add def

newpath
x y    userspotfunction /pixelval exch def
        x y
        pixelval m mul b add
        0 360
arc  fill

        frequency 60 ge
        resolution 300 le
        doshowlabel
and and
        /label load
if

    pixelval    % pass pixelval to screen machinery
} bind def  % /sccdotfunction

% See commenting on the following in "anglechart"

/sccmmfunction {
    /y exch def
    /x exch def

    /pixelcount pixelcount 1 add def

    dofindtruedelta   /findtruedelta load   if

    x y userspotfunction

    dup max gt {dup /max exch def} if
    dup min lt {dup /min exch def} if
} bind def

% Determine  device pixel resolution for later labeling decisions.
% See commenting on the following in "anglechart"

/resmatrix matrix def
```

```
/resolution
        72 0 resmatrix defaultmatrix dtransform
        dup mul exch dup mul add sqrt
def

% also determine if device coordinates run in the same directions
% or opposite directions as default user coordinates.

/xdir
        resmatrix 0 get
        dup abs div
def

/ydir
        resmatrix 3 get
        dup abs div
def

% "pmoveto" and "plineto" round x and y to the nearest device pixel,
% and then execute "moveto" or "lineto". This renders a better graph.

/pmoveto {
        transform round exch round exch itransform
        moveto
} bind def

/plineto {
        transform round exch round exch itransform
        lineto
} bind def

% ftmatrix will be used in font scaling

/ftmatrix matrix def

/ifctelinchge {
        -0.75 1 4 ftsize mul add moveto
        pcstring show pixelcount cvsstg cvs show

        -0.75 1 3 ftsize mul add moveto
```

```
        tdxstr show truedx cvsstg cvs show
        commastring show
        tdystr show truedy cvsstg cvs show

        -0.75 1 2 ftsize mul add moveto
        (true angle = ) show trueangle cvsstg cvs show
        commastring show
        (true frequency = ) show truefrequency cvsstg cvs show
} bind def

/ifdoshowlabel {
        /x 0 def
        /y
                -1 16 cte div sub
                ftsize 3 mul
                sub
        def

                x -1 cte div add
                y .05 add ftsize 2 mul add
        moveto (pixelcount) show

                x -1 cte div add
                y .05 add ftsize add
        moveto (x,y) show

                x -1 cte div add
                y .05 add
        moveto (value) show
} bind def

% This is the workhorse. "sccmmfunction" is called to
% determine the minimum and maximum cell pixel values.
% These are used to determine the straight-line
% relationship between the point radius and the pixel value.
% "sccmmfunction" also fetches the data needed to
% determine the true rotation.

% The minimum point radius is always 0.006 ; the maximum point
% radius is always 0.035 . Thus for
```

```
% radius = m (pixelvalue) + b
% 0.006 = m (min) + b
% 0.035 = m (max) + b
%
% "showthecell" solves for m and b from the above equations,
% draws the coordinates of the cell, then calls "sccdotfunction"
% to actually plot each pixel.

% The pixel values are labeled if frequency>=60 and resolution<=300
% and doshowlabel=true.

% "showthecell" expects the global variables "frequency" and
% "rotation" to be set before "showthecell" is called.

/showthecell {    % def
     % showthecell takes five arguments
     % from the stack:

     /doshowlabel exch def   % - boolean whether to show label
     /usf.stg exch def % - string rep of user's spot function
     /cte exch def      % - distance from center to edge
     /ty exch def       % - y centerpoint
     /tx exch def       % - x centerpoint

     /pixelcount 0 def       % initialize pixelcount

     /olddx 10 def     % by initializing these with
     /olddy 10 def     % values well outside the
     /oldx 10 def      % cell coordinates, we won't
     /oldy 10 def      % be tripped up by false values.
     /truedx 10 def
     /truedy 10 def
     /dofindtruedelta true def

     /userspotfunction
          usf.stg cvn load
     def   % - the spot function

     % compute minimum and maximum pixel values
```

```
/min  1  def        % this must precede "sccmmfunction" call
/max -1  def        % to obtain correct "min" and "max".


frequency rotation {sccmmfunction} setscreen


/minr 0.006 def
/maxr 0.035 def


% solve for m and b
/m
      max min ne
            {
                  maxr minr sub
                  max min sub
                  div
            }
            {0}     % Unlikely, but if a spot function specifies no
      ifelse        % priority (min=max) then all points will
def                 % be plotted with 0.035 radius. This avoids
                    % "undefinedresult" error.


/b
      maxr m max mul sub
def


% now that "sccmmfunction" has determined "pixelcount"
% and "truedx" and "truedy", we can determine some
% data about the screen.


/trueangle
      360     truedy truedx atan     sub
      round cvi 360 mod
def


/truefrequency
      resolution
                  2
                  truedy dup mul
                  truedx dup mul
                  add sqrt
```

```
            div
        div
        100 mul round 100 div    % rounded to 2 places
def

gsave
        tx ty translate    % to x and y of centerpoint

        cte xdir mul        % scale with respect to direction of
        cte ydir mul        % device coordinates
        scale

        trueangle rotate

        1 cte div    setlinewidth        % 1 linewidth in default space

        /ftsize 6 cte div def

        ftmatrix 0 ftsize xdir mul put
        ftmatrix 3 ftsize ydir mul put

        ftmatrix   5      % if font is flipped, it also
              ydir -0.5 mul 0.5 add    % must be shifted.
              ftsize mul
        put

        /Helvetica findfont      % 6 point Helvetica scaled in
        ftmatrix    % current coordinates, flipped
        makefont setfont  % as needed to be readable.

        .9 setgray

        60 45 /defaultspotfunction load setscreen

        cte 1 inch ge     % if cte >= 1 inch
        {     % draw 0.5 lines.
        gsave
              5 {
                    -1 -1 pmoveto
```

```
            -1 1 plineto
            stroke
            .5 0 translate
      } repeat
grestore


gsave
      5 {
            -1 -1 pmoveto
            1 -1 plineto
            stroke
            0 .5 translate
      } repeat
grestore
} if     % cte >= 1 inch

-1 -1 pmoveto
-1 1 plineto
1 1 plineto
1 -1 plineto
closepath stroke

0 setgray
1 1 moveto
((1,1)) rshow

1 -1 8 cte div neg add moveto
((1,-1)) rshow

-1 -1 8 cte div neg add moveto
((-1,-1)) show

-1 1 moveto
((-1,1)) show

-1 -1 ftsize 2.5 mul sub moveto
frequency cvsstg cvs show ( ) show
rotation cvsstg cvs show ( ) show
```

```
            usf.stg show

            % plot pixels
            /pixelcount 0 def        % reinit pixelcount
            frequency rotation /sccdotfunction load setscreen

            cte 1 inch ge
                    /ifctelinchge load
            if

            doshowlabel
                    /ifdoshowlabel load
            if
        grestore
} bind def   % showthecell

/pcstring (pixelcount = ) def
/tdxstr (truedx = ) def
/tdystr (truedy = ) def

/rshow {
        dup stringwidth pop neg 0
        rmoveto show
} bind def

/pagewidth 8.5 inch def
/pagelength 11 inch def

%%EndPrologue

%%Page: 1 1
%%PageFonts: Helvetica

% show rowlspot

fr1045
        2.25 inch    % center x
        pagelength 5 6 div mul  % center y
        1 inch       % distance from center to edge
        rowlspot     % string rep of spot function
```

```
        false % show label?
showthecell


fr10zero
        5.25 inch
        pagelength 5 6 div mul
        1 inch
        row1spot
        false
showthecell



fr6045
        7.25 inch
        pagelength 5 6 div mul 0.5 inch add
        .25 inch
        row1spot
        false
showthecell

fr60zero
        7.25 inch
        pagelength 5 6 div mul 0.5 inch sub
        .25 inch
        row1spot
        false
showthecell


% show row2spot

fr1045
        2.25 inch
        5.5 inch
        1 inch
        row2spot
        false
showthecell

fr10zero
        5.25 inch
```

```
        5.5 inch
        1 inch
        row2spot
        false
showthecell


fr6045
        7.25 inch
        6 inch
        .25 inch
        row2spot
        false
showthecell


fr60zero
        7.25 inch
        5 inch
        .25 inch
        row2spot
        false
showthecell


% show row3spot


fr1045
        2.25 inch
        pagelength 6 div
        1 inch
        row3spot
        false
showthecell



fr10zero
        5.25 inch
        pagelength 6 div
        1 inch
        row3spot
        false
showthecell
```

```
fr6045
      7.25 inch
      pagelength 6 div 0.5 inch add
      0.25 inch
      row3spot
      false
showthecell

fr60zero
      7.25 inch
      pagelength 6 div 0.5 inch sub
      0.25 inch
      row3spot
      false
showthecell

showpage

%%Page: 2 2
%%PageFonts: Helvetica

% show page2spot

fr6030
      4.25 inch    % center x
      8 inch       % center y
      1.75 inch    % distance from center to edge
      page2spot    % string rep of spot function
      true  % show label?
showthecell

fr60zero
      4.25 inch
      2.75 inch
      1.75 inch
      page2spot
      true
showthecell

showpage
```

This program can be a big help in creating spot functions, since it lets you see a visual representation of the pixel priority within the cell. It also encompasses most of the concepts we've discussed in this chapter. It prints the requested frequency and angle, the true frequency and angle, and the number of pixels in the cell.

Going further, it represents each pixel's ranking in the cell by changing the size (effectively halftoning a halftone cell). Alternately or concurrently, it labels the value of the pixel, and gives its coordinates and its priority for evaluation by the spot function (this last mimics the results of LookAtHalftoneCells). In short, it tells you everything there is to know about the halftone cell generated by given *setscreen* settings, and displays that information graphically.

Rotation Dependence, Cell Shape, and Irregular Cells

This program and its output also point out one of the key points about PostScript halftoning: the orientation of the halftone cells is device-dependent. The spot function operates in device space (as it must, since it is working on device pixels), while the rotation of the page is a function of user space.

Notice that when the triangle cell is rotated the cell itself rotates, not only the box in which it is contained. This has real implications when you print using the defaults on a Linotronic, in which case pages come out sideways. Sideways printing doesn't much matter when you are using the default 45-degree dot screen, but when you get into other shapes and frequencies, it definitely does. You may get a vertical linescreen on your laser printer, and a horizontal linescreen on the Lino. If you are using the triangle spot function at a coarse frequency to point left or right toward something on the page, you may find it pointing up or down instead when you print on a Linotronic.

Even with all this amazing halftone machinery, there is one thing that PostScript interpreters can't do with cell shapes which can be done with photographic screening, and it may be the biggest flaw in the whole scenario. Take a look at the comparison of photographic and PostScript halftones in Figure 10.13. Look closely where light areas border dark areas. Notice that the photographic halftone cells are not regularly shaped; they're pear-shaped, effectively. This results in very sharp edges and crisp halftones. The PostScript halftones don't share that effect.

Figure 10.13. The same halftone image is reproduced using traditional photographic equipment and using PostScript's halftoning machinery (Linotronic at 1270 dpi) at 85 cells per inch, 45 degrees. Note the clarity and crispness of the photographic halftone compared to the slight blurriness of the PostScript image.

The bad news is that PostScript simply can't create that type of irregularly shaped halftone cell. The halftoning machinery is set up to scan through the device pixels in a certain way, and it would need a different method—much more time-consuming—to allow for irregularly shaped dots based on adjacent light and dark areas. PostScript can't make one part of a cell light and another part dark. The result is not-quite-sharp halftones compared to their photographic counterparts.

You don't have this problem when you get past about a 150-line screen, but that is near the upper limit of what an offset press can reproduce (if you're going for Linotronic output, which is what you need for a 150-line screen, I have to assume you're printing offset). If you are going straight to film negatives off a high-resolution imagesetter, and the printer is prepared for very fine screens on press, you can get excellent results, in some cases surpassing photographic halftones. If the printer has to shoot film from paper positives, however, no matter what the imagesetting device, 150 lines is more than you can expect to reproduce faithfully.

Crispness is not much of a problem when you get into very coarse frequencies, since the coarse grains and resultant rough edges tend to mask the lack of irregularly-shaped dots. The same holds true when you use linescreens, posterizations, and other special effects, especially coarse ones. The eye will accept the image more readily since it is prepared for a less-than-representational image.

Finally, the lack of irregularly shaped cells is not as much of a problem with color separations as it is with black-and-white images. The high frequencies used for color seps, combined with the overlapping screens, serves to mitigate the blurriness that often results from POSTSCRIPT halftones.

Beyond Theory: Practice Makes Perfect

What I've tried to do in this chapter is go beyond the theory of POSTSCRIPT halftoning and talk about the reality of producing grays and halftoned images with POSTSCRIPT devices. As we've seen, the limitations and quirks of POSTSCRIPT halftoning are partially the result of POSTSCRIPT itself, and partially a result of its implementation on printing devices.

The other thing I've tried to do is put across some of the power and flexibility of POSTSCRIPT halftoning, and show some techniques for putting that power to work. As I said at the beginning of the chapter, this is a power you will be hard-pressed to find elsewhere, at least in so flexible a form, and it is one of the key advantages of using POSTSCRIPT to make marks immortal on paper.

Pat Wood

The PostScript language has two commands that deal specifically with color: *setrgbcolor* and *sethsbcolor*. These commands support the two most common color imaging models: red/green/blue (RGB) and hue/saturation/brightness (HSB), respectively. RGB is better known to most computer users, as color monitors use red, green, and blue pixels to simulate continuous colors.

Under the RGB color model, the primary colors of light are specified by values between zero and one; these colors are mixed to produce any color in the spectrum. Under the HSB model, the three parameters are specified by values between zero and one. The hue (colors) specifies a particular color, but not its intensity or brightness. The saturation specifies the intensity of the color (i.e., the amount of the color mixed in with a gray background); the brightness specifies the overall intensity of light.

The color value specifies a point on a "color circle" that starts at red (hue = 0), goes through green (hue = 1/3) and blue (hue = 2/3) back to red (hue = 1). The brightness in the HSB model is always the same as the current gray value. Thus bright red would be specified by 0 1 1 sethsbcolor and light green by .33333 .4 1.

In the RGB color model, a bright red would be specified as 1 0 0 setrgbcolor and a bright purple (blue plus red) as 1 0 1 setrgbcolor (actually the resulting color is more like magenta). You can define PostScript procedures that provide a color palette:

```
/red { 1 0 0 setrgbcolor } def
/green { 0 1 0 setrgbcolor } def
/blue { 0 0 1 setrgbcolor } def
/cyan { 0 1 1 setrgbcolor } def
/magenta { 1 0 1 setrgbcolor } def
/yellow { 1 1 0 setrgbcolor } def
/pink { 1 .8 .8 setrgbcolor } def
```

The last definition, pink, sets red on full intensity and green and blue at eighty percent. Since equal amounts of red, green, and blue make white light, pink produces eighty percent white plus twenty percent red (a light pink).

The following samples show different effects that can be achieved with colors. They all print as gray, of course, unless you have a color POSTSCRIPT printer. You can use them with the separation prologue, however, described in chapter 12, "POSTSCRIPT Color Separations."

This first example, shown in Plate 1, prints out ninety circles of differing colors. The first circle is printed with color zero in the HSB color model (red). Subsequent circles are printed with colors through green and blue back to red:

```
/colr 0 def
/inch { 72 mul } def
/circle {    % draws a circle
      newpath 0 360 arc stroke
} def


/spiro {    % draws lots of circles
      /ncircles exch def
      gsave
            ncircles {
                  colr 1 1 sethsbcolor
                  /colr 1 ncircles div colr add def
                  2 inch 0 1.5 inch circle
                  360 ncircles div rotate
            } repeat
      grestore
} def


4.25 inch 5.5 inch translate
90 spiro
showpage
```

This example, as shown in Plate 2a, prints a color fountain by painting lines of slightly varying colors next to each other:

```
/colr 0 def
/inch { 72 mul } def
```

```
/fountain {
      /height exch def
      /width exch def
      gsave
            width height scale
            /dx 1 width div def
            dx setlinewidth
            width {
                  colr 1 1 sethsbcolor
                  /colr 1 width div colr add def

                  0 0 moveto 0 1 lineto stroke

                  dx 0 translate
            } repeat
      grestore
} def

1 inch 1 inch translate
6 inch 1 inch fountain
showpage
```

This example, shown in Plate 2b, defines a procedure called color-show that uses *kshow* to set the current color to a random value before each character is shown:

```
% Insert call to separation prolog here ("cyan," "magenta," etc)

usertime srand    % set random number generator

/normalize 2 31 exp 1 sub def % 2^31 -1

% frand leaves a random number between 0 and 1 on the stack
/frand { rand normalize div } def

/colorshow {      % show chars in string with random colors
      { frand frand frand setrgbcolor } exch kshow
} def

% test this code
```

```
100 100 moveto
/Times-Roman findfont 72 scalefont setfont
(Random Colors!) colorshow
showpage
```

And last, as shown in Plate 3, a program by Tom Bernard prints eleven pages of color wheels showing hue, saturation, and brightness, one wheel for each level of brightness, in increments of .1 from 0 to 1:

```
%!PS-Adobe-1.0
%%DocumentFonts: Helvetica
%%Title: hsbColors
%%Creator: Tom Bernard, Bersearch Information Services
%%Pages: 11
%%EndComments


/inch {72 mul} def


/hel {/Helvetica findfont 10 scalefont setfont} def


/segment {
      newpath

      0 0
      saturation 2.5 inch mul 1 inch add
      hue 360 mul hue 360 mul 24 add
      arc

      0 0
      saturation 2.5 inch mul .75 inch add
      hue 360 mul 24 add hue 360 mul
      arcn

      closepath fill
} def


/bgtstg (brightness = 0.0) def


/huestgs [      %  These strings will be used by
```

```
            (hue = 0.0, red)  %  "labelpage".
            (hue = 0.333, green)
            (hue = 0.667, blue)
    ] def


    /labelpage {
            0 1 2 {      % hue tick    for    loop
                    dup   % we will use increment twice
                    gsave
                            120 mul     % place ticks at 120 degree inc.
                            rotate
                            3.5 inch 0 moveto
                            3.6 inch 0 lineto % draw this tick
                            stroke

                            3.7 inch 0 translate
                            -90 rotate
                            huestgs exch get dup
                            stringwidth pop 2 div neg     % center over tick.
                            0
                            moveto
                            show
                    grestore
            } for % hue tick for loop


            % saturation labels

            (saturation = 1.0) stringwidth pop 2 div neg
            3.6 inch
            moveto
            (saturation = 1.0) show

            (saturation = 0.0) stringwidth pop 2 div neg
            -5
            moveto
            (saturation = 0.0) show

            -.5 inch -4 inch    moveto      % brightness label
            bgtstg 13
            brightness (      ) cvs putinterval
```

```
      bgtstg show
} def

%%EndPrologue

hel

% This for loop prints 11 pages
0 .1 1.05 {   % brightness for loop

      % Insert call to separation prolog here ("cyan," "magenta," etc)
      % (prints 44 pages!)

      /brightness exch def
      gsave
            4.25 inch 5.75 inch translate
            labelpage
            0  .1  1.005  {    % saturation for loop
                  /saturation exch def
                  gsave
                        0  1 15 div  1.05  {     % hue for loop
                              /hue exch def
                              hue saturation brightness sethsbcolor
                              segment
                        } for % hue for loop
                  grestore
            } for % saturation for loop
      grestore
      showpage
} for % brightness    for    loop
%%Trailer
```

Output

This color manipulation is all very well and good, but what about
output? Color PostScript output devices are just emerging as this is
written; there won't be one commercially available for some months.

In a book called *Real World PostScript*, it hardly seems appropriate to talk about it. For the record, though, here is the state of color printers. (For real world stuff, read chapter 12 on color separations, which is possible and happening right now.)

Color printers have been around for a few years now. The most common types are dot-matrix, ink-jet, thermal-transfer, and laser. These printers usually work by laying down three or four colors, one at a time. The colors that are applied combine in different proportions to produce the illusion of continuous tones of color.

Color dot-matrix printers are usually ordinary dot-matrix printers with a multi-color option. This typically includes a special ribbon that has three colors on it and a special ribbon feed mechanism. The print head traverses the line once or twice for each color. Although most color dot-matrix printers can attain resolutions of over 200 dpi, this type of color printer is usually rather slow (five to ten minutes/page) because of the number of passes that must be made, particularly in a high-resolution graphics mode.

Color ink-jet printers work the same as color dot-matrix printers, except that the colors are applied by spraying ink onto the paper (some "bubble-jet" printers use solid inks that are vaporized and applied to the page). They must also make multiple passes for each line. Their resolution rivals dot-matrix printers, but they are much quieter and usually produce richer, more saturated colors. They are also more expensive than dot-matrix printers with similar features, resolution, and speed.

Color thermal-transfer printers also are similar to dot-matrix printers; however, they work by applying a waxy, colored substance from a ribbon to the paper. This is done by heating the ribbon wherever a color is wanted—the ribbon touches the paper, and the color is "transferred" to the paper. Thermal-transfer printers come in many forms. The least expensive look like dot-matrix printers with a strange-looking ribbon. The most expensive use a ribbon as wide as the paper and apply an entire line (or at least a single, horizontal, pixel-wide line) at a time.

The more expensive of the thermal-transfer printers are much faster than ink-jet or dot-matrix printers, on the order of a minute or two per page. These printers are also much more expensive than dot-matrix or ink-jet printers by a factor of four or more. Most thermal-transfer printers have resolutions of 240 or 300 dpi. The color PostScript printer manufactured by QMS uses a 300 dpi thermal-transfer print engine manufactured by Mitsubishi.

Color laser printers are still in the development stage. They can attain throughput of one page/minute or better at 300 dpi, but the printers, when available, will cost close to $30,000. Be prepared to dig deep.

Color separations are used by printers to reproduce color artwork (including photographs) in large quantities using four different colored inks: cyan, magenta, yellow, and black. Color separation has become a topic of interest to quite a few people these days. With the advent of high-resolution typesetters that can produce decent halftones, a new world has opened up for separators. Until recently, separations were done either photographically by hand or with expensive ($1 million–plus), specialized hardware. This chapter discusses the techniques used to produce quality color separations on a Linotype Linotronic 300.

Color Pigments

In order for you to understand the techniques behind computerized color separation, we first need to look at the basics of color printing.

There are three different types of color receptors in the human eye. Each responds to one of three broad, overlapping color ranges centered around red, green, and blue. A particular color will excite each type of cell in varying amounts. The brain combines these responses into the perception of a single color. Thus, the color purple actually excites the red and blue receptors in the eye, causing these signals to be sent to the brain and interpreted as purple. This explains why colored light can be mixed to produce other colors, and why equal combinations of red, green, and blue light appear white. Combining red, green, and blue allows us to simulate any color in the spectrum.

This leads us to the method in which color monitors and televisions work: phosphors that emit red, green, and blue light are placed in a matrix on the surface of the picture tube; individual dots are excited with differing amounts of energy to produce varying pinpoints of red, green, and blue. These dots are merged by the brain to produce the perception of continuous color tones.

This discussion is all well and good, but how does it apply to color printing? Well, producing color with red, green, and blue light is an additive process; colored light is added together to produce the impression of other colors. In color printing, you must deal with the opposite process: subtractive color. You start with a white page (one that reflects all colors equally) and subtract from the white the colors you don't want the eye to see. This is done by printing with inks that are the color opposites of red, green, and blue: cyan, magenta, and yellow, respectively. By "screening" these colors at different percentages and overlaying the screens, you can achieve the whole rainbow. (See Chapter 10, "Real World POSTSCRIPT Halftoning," for more on screens.)

Cyan pigment absorbs (filters) red, allowing green and blue light to pass through; thus, cyan subtracts red. Similarly, magenta and yellow subtract their complementary colors, green and blue. In order to print blue, cyan and magenta inks are printed on white paper, filtering red and green light, allowing blue light to pass through. In theory, combinations of cyan, yellow, and magenta in varying proportions can produce a full range of colors, just as combinations of red, green, and blue do. Equal screens (e.g., ten percent, fifty percent, etc.), of cyan, yellow, and magenta produce (theoretically) levels of gray. Solid (unscreened) amounts of the three colors when combined produce black.

The above discussion on subtractive color works fine in theory, but real pigments have impurities that cause the inks to absorb more than just one color. In practice, color pictures are printed with four colors instead of three. The fourth "color" is black, which is used to produce darker blacks and neutral grays. Use of black pigment also reduces the printing cost on large jobs by replacing some of the expensive color pigments with a less expensive black. I'll discuss the use of black in color printing in more detail later.

Halftone Screens in Color Printing

Halftoning is used to vary the percentage of ink on the page, and like halftoned black-and-white images, halftoned color images give the impression of continuous tone when printed with fine screens (see Steve Roth's chapter 10, "Real World POSTSCRIPT Halftoning," for more information on POSTSCRIPT's halftoning mechanism). When printing three or four halftones on top of each other; however, moiré patterns appear due to interference between the various halftone screens. If all the colors are printed using the same screen angle, objectionable moiré patterns will occur unless all four passes through the press are in perfect register (see Figure 12.1).

Since perfect register is unreasonable to expect, a different solution is used: each of the screens is rotated relative to the others, causing the moiré patterns to be very small. If the screen is fine enough, the patterns are almost impossible to see at a distance, much like halftone dots (see Figure 12.2).

The angles used for each screen vary, but the most often used angles are 0, 45, 15, and 75 degrees for yellow, black, cyan, and magenta, respectively. The reasons for choosing these angles are as follows: yellow is the least troublesome color from the standpoint of producing moirés, because it's the lightest color and its halftone pattern is the

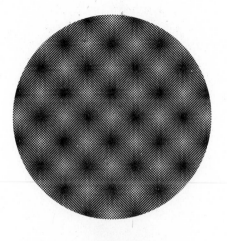

Figure 12.1. Moiré pattern from halftone screens with 3-degree offset.

Figure 12.2. Moiré pattern from halftone screens with 45-degree offset.

most difficult to distinguish, so it is printed at 0 degrees; black, the darkest, is printed at 45 degrees; cyan and magenta are printed at 30-degree offsets from black (the largest offset you can have when printing three colors), which gives them only a 15-degree offset from yellow.

Since cyan is also "dark," it is sometimes printed at 45 degrees with black at 15. Note that since halftones are usually composed of a grid of squares, there are only 90 degrees in which to distribute the four halftone screens, so 0 degrees is the same as 90, and 15 the same as 105, etc. You can print black, cyan, and magenta at angles other than 45, 15, and 75; however, you'd still want them offset from each other by 30 degrees. Placement of the yellow screen is less critical, and some printers even make the yellow screen the same angle as one of the other colors.

Before the advent of color separation systems, color separations were made by hand, by photographing a color original through filters and halftone screens (sheets of glass or plastic that are etched with a half-tone pattern). The screens were rotated to the specified angle for each photo. Printing plates were then made from the negatives. This manual method is still in use at some printing shops, but electronic scanners and separation systems have all but replaced it due to their speed and quality.

COLOR CORRECTION AND UNDERCOLOR REMOVAL

As previously mentioned, pigments used for commercial printing are impure and therefore aren't true cyan, yellow, and magenta, although yellow printer's ink is very close to pure yellow, and most color separation systems make the assumption that yellow ink is pure. Magenta printer's ink, however, appears contaminated with yellow—i.e., it absorbs some blue as well as green—and cyan ink appears contaminated with some magenta and a little yellow. These impure inks make color separation a more complex task than simply inverting the red, green, and blue intensities of the original.

In the manual method of color separation, filters are used to produce properly corrected separations. For example, the magenta separation is used as a partial filter when making the yellow separation, reducing the amount of yellow printed where magenta already is (since magenta contains some yellow, the idea is to remove some yellow under the magenta). This filtering process is called undercolor removal, as it removes colors "underneath" others.

In a computerized separation system, each pixel consists of some combination of cyan, yellow, and magenta. Simple algorithms can be used to remove magenta under cyan and yellow under magenta. Although inks vary slightly, the typical contamination amounts are thirty percent magenta in cyan and fifty percent yellow in magenta. This means that the amount of magenta printed at a pixel is reduced by thirty percent of the amount of cyan at that pixel, and the amount of yellow printed there is reduced by fifty percent of the amount of magenta.

Although a few critical applications may require more complex undercolor removal, this method is more than adequate for most commercial applications.

THE BLACK PRINTER

Most color separations made today are done as four colors: cyan, yellow, magenta, and black. The black printer is made for several reasons:

- Since printer's inks are not pure, combinations of solid cyan, yellow, and magenta don't produce black; they produce a muddy brown. To get good blacks, you have to use black ink

- For the same reason, grays can be off slightly when produced from cyan, yellow, and magenta instead of black

- The black printer gives the reproduction more contrast, allowing for greater detail rendition and dynamic range

- Black ink is less expensive than colored inks

- High-speed wet presses print all three or four colors at once without allowing the inks to dry in between applications. Large amounts of ink cannot be printed in one place (typically the coverage cannot be more than 240 to 260 percent when adding all the inks together). Thus, to get solid black, black ink must be used, and undercolor removal has to be performed on the other three colors

Black ink can be used wherever all three colors are used. For example, in an area where there is 30-percent cyan, 40-percent yellow, and 25-percent magenta, up to 25-percent black can be printed, reducing cyan, yellow, and magenta by a corresponding amount. This is another form of undercolor removal. Full removal of the black printer like this is not common, as registration becomes critical. (If this area is next to a pure magenta area, then the magenta percentage will immediately go from zero to one hundred. At this boundary, if the registration isn't perfect, a thin, white line could appear.) Usually, up to fifty percent of the black is removed from the other colors.

In traditional separation methods, producing the black printer was not easy. Several steps were performed not only to remove the black, but also to insure that black would not be printed in highlight areas and to insure proper balance of grays. In computerized systems, removal of black is simpler, as the intensities of the other three colors are individually correctable. Black can be safely printed in highlight areas without danger of "muddying'" the picture.

Contrast Enhancement/Reduction

One important feature of any black-and-white or color system is the ability to change the contrast of the print. For example, when performing undercolor removal of the black printer, the black must be "boosted" in darker areas because of an effect known as additive failure. Additive failure is simply the inability of overlapping inks to print as dark as they should. 50-percent black plus fifty percent of the other three colors should produce black; however, they produce only about 85-percent gray.

There are many causes of additive failure. The most common are the way the halftone cells overlap (50-percent black plus fifty percent of the other three colors will still leave some white space peeking through, since the screens are rotated and therefore don't overlap perfectly) and the fact that light reflects off the internal surfaces of the ink (and therefore isn't necessarily filtered by all four inks). Additive failure occurs when any two inks are printed over each other; however, it is most noticeable in dark grays and blacks that come out lighter than they should. Increasing the contrast of the black printer in darker areas fixes this.

Another problem is dot gain, or the tendency of the halftone spots to increase in size during each photographic step in the manufacture of a printing plate (negative to positive, positive to negative, negative to plate) and the tendency of ink to spread when it hits the paper. This causes an image to get darker (or colors more saturated) when printed. Again, the contrast can be adjusted to correct this.

Sometimes the contrast of a particular color must be changed to enhance the print. For example, yellow is often enhanced to produce lustrous golds and better skin tones.

Typically, the dynamic range or density of the original (the difference between the lightest and darkest parts) is greater than can be reproduced on a printing press (sometimes as much as two and a half times); thus the dynamic range must be compressed. However, brightness is not a linear function. Our eyes perceive brightness as a log function of the amount of light reflected, so dynamic range compression must be based on a log function of the percent reflection of an image.

Most low-end color scanners (and some of the higher-end ones) produce linear data, and often they do not properly compress the dynamic range of the original. Since each device operates differently, the contrast must be enhanced differently for each one. Similarly, if the scanner produces eight bits of data per color and the filmmaking device cannot produce 256 grays, the density must be compressed based on a log scale. Some scanners can produce twelve bits of data per color, which also must be compressed into the number of grays available.

Sharpness Enhancement/Reduction

Digital image processing techniques can be used to enhance or reduce the sharpness of a scanned image. A process called convolvment is used to change the sharpness of an image by accentuating (or reducing) intensity changes. Convolvment changes a pixel's value by adding to it the sum of its neighbors weighted by some factor. By varying the weighting factor, you can vary the amount of sharpness of the image (see Figure 12.3).

Sharpness enhancement has obvious advantages, but sharpness reduction also has much use in color printing. Facial close-ups often have reduced sharpness in one or more of the colors to smooth out the skin, and an unsharp black separation is sometimes used to "soften" a stark, contrasty image.

Color Separation on PostScript Devices

The advent of digital film recorders such as the Linotype Linotronic 300 Imagesetter allows electronic color separation to be done with typesetters for the first time. The Linotronic 300 has a resolution of 2,540 dots per inch, and can reproduce 256 grays with a halftone screen of 150 lines/inch. It can produce more than 200 grays with a screen

Figure 12.3. Sharpened and unsharpened halftones.

of 175 lines/inch. This device, with its high resolution, the ability to control output down to the pixel level, and high speed (4 seconds per inch at 1,270 dpi), is as well suited for digital color separation as any of the best separation systems on the market today.

In this section, I will discuss producing separations on PostScript devices, as these present a standard interface to the outside world for producing halftones, and allow us to look at an "idealized"' device. It should be noted that color separations can be produced on non-PostScript typesetters; however, since most do not have halftoning capabilities, you'd have to write a halftone dot generator to drive one of these devices.

SIMPLE COLOR SEPARATION OUTPUT

PostScript devices can produce decent color separations; however, they have some drawbacks due to the digital nature of their halftoning algorithm. It gives you control over the angle and screen frequency of the halftoning process (within the constraints discussed in chapter 10, on halftoning), allowing you to produce fairly high quality separations. Once the colors have been corrected and the black separation produced, four files can be sent to the printer.

Typically the data is sent over the AppleTalk connection, since the amount of data is large. An 8-by-10-inch separation at 150 lines/inch is about 1.8mb. With AppleTalk, the data can be sent in binary instead of hexadecimal, increasing throughput by a factor of two or more since there is no hex to binary conversion going on inside the PostScript interpreter.

The rotation angles for PostScript separations can be varied. The best results with a 120-line screen come from 0 degrees for yellow, 45 degrees for black, 15 degrees for cyan, and 75 degrees for magenta. The screen frequency can be as high as 250 to 300 lines/inch, but as the screen frequency goes up, problems with moiré patterns become acute due to fewer and fewer angles being available (see chapter 10 on half-toning for the problems of obtaining accurate frequencies and angles). The color plates were printed with a 150-line screen, but to reduce moiré patterns, angles of 0 , 15, 30, and 60 were used. (Often, changing the angles at a given screen frequency will change the patterns that are produced. If you're lucky, you can find a set of angles that doesn't produce moirés).

OTHER SPOT SHAPES

Elliptical dots are often used by printers to produce better middle tones (shades of gray between about twenty-five and seventy-five percent). They produce better middle tones than square or round dots due to the following effect: at 50-percent gray, the corners of the square dots all touch, producing what is known as an "optical jump" in the density; i.e., when the corners touch, the density changes faster than it should. The change in density between forty-nine and fifty-one percent appears more like a five percent jump in gray. Round dots have the same problem at around twenty-five percent. Elliptical dots have two jumps: one when the ends of the major axes touch, and one when the minor axes touch. By adjusting the ratio between these two axes of the dots, you can precisely control where these jumps will occur (typically at thirty and seventy percent). Since each of the jumps is produced by only two corners touching (as opposed to all four with square and round dots), the density jump appears to be smaller.

One major problem with elliptical dots is that they can accentuate moirés: between the two gray levels where the axes touch, the screen pattern is that of a lumpy line, and lines produce the worst moiré patterns of any screen. Even worse, the range between the two jumps is the middle tones where you're trying to reproduce the best results. Screen angles are therefore critical when using elliptical dots.

The following PostScript spot function produces elliptical dots that touch at approximately thirty percent and eighty percent gray:

```
{ 2 mul abs        % multiply y by 2
exch dup mul       % square x
add 3 div 2 mul    % normalize to 0-2
1 exch sub }       % -1 to 1
```

The procedure works by making the y axis contribute more to the total than the x axis. When the resulting number is normalized and subtracted from one, the y contribution causes pixels in areas where the magnitude of y is large (near 1 or -1) to have the smallest result, and these pixels are the first to be made white.

By varying the amount by which the y value is multiplied, you can change the densities where the jumps occur. (Remember to normalize the resulting number to the range zero to two so that when you subtract it from one you get a number in the range -1 to 1.)

GETTING THE DATA: SCANNERS

An integral part of color separation is the scanner, which obtains the RGB data for us to separate. There are many scanners that can produce RGB information from a variety of sources. Until recently most have been rather expensive, e.g., $30,000 to $50,000 for a scanner that could produce graphics-quality images. Now scanners in the $6,000 to $15,000 range are coming close to these graphics-quality scanners.

The Targa and Vista boards from AT&T can scan video images (frames) in RGB format into memory on the board. This data can then be passed to separation software. Similarly, the Howtek flatbed color scanner (as well as the Sharp and Imapro scanners, all of which are based on the same scanning engine made by Sharp) can scan flat art such as photographs at 300 dpi with 6 bits of information per color at each pixel (64 gray scales per color). The Barneyscan 35-mm slide scanner can scan color slides at up to 2,000 by 3,000 pixels, with 8 bits of information per color.

Note that when scanning color you end up with a lot of data—three times as much as black-and-white. With the Barneyscan at its highest resolution, the 2k-by-3k image is 6mb per color, or 18mb per image.

With the Howtek, approximately 7mb per color is required. Disk space gets sucked up really fast by these scanners.

Color Separations from PostScript Files

This section delves into the steps needed to produce spot-color (non-scanned color images where the color at a particular point is made up of separations defined by the current RGB setting, i.e., *currentrgbcolor*) from PostScript files, such as in the plates in this book.

COLOR FOUNTAINS

Color fountains are very simple to produce. For example, you can create one with three fountains that vary their intensities differently, for magenta, yellow, and cyan inks, respectively. Now here's the PostScript that produces these fountains:

```
% magenta fountain
/fountstring 256 string def
    0 1 255 { fountstring exch dup put } for

    432 60 scale
    256 1 8 [256 0 0 1 0 0]
    { fountstring } image
    showpage


    % yellow fountain
    /fountstring 256 string def
    0 1 255 {
            fountstring exch dup
            255 exch sub put
    } for

    432 60 scale
    256 1 8 [256 0 0 1 0 0]
    { fountstring } image
    showpage


    % cyan fountain
    /fountstring 256 string def
    0 1 127 {
```

```
        fountstring exch dup
        2 mul put
    } for


    128 1 255 {
        fountstring exch dup
        128 sub
        2 mul
        254 exch sub put
    } for


    432 60 scale
    256 1 8 [256 0 0 1 0 0]
    { fountstring } image
showpage
```

The first fountain is produced by passing a string of 255 numbers to the image operator. The first character in the string is set to 0 (the value, not the character), and each succeeding element of the string is set to one greater; so the string passed to image contains an even gradation from 0 to 255, producing a fountain that starts dark and gets light. The second fountain is the opposite of the first. By subtracting the number passed to the procedure by the *for* operator from 255, the fountstring array is filled with numbers that start at 255 and decrease to 0. This produces a fountain that starts light and gets darker.

The last fountain divides the array into two pieces. The first is filled with numbers from 0 to 254, increasing by 2; the second is filled with numbers from 254 to 0. This produces a fountain that starts dark, gets light in the middle, and then gets dark again.

By combining these three fountains, you get a constantly varying color scale. On the other hand, if you tried to use the same fountain for the three colors, you'd end up with a gray scale, as all three colors would be printed in equal quantities across the fountain. (Actually you'd end up with browns, not grays, due to impurities in the inks.) You can get six different color fountains by printing these fountains with different colors, e.g., print the first with cyan and the third with magenta.

Other fountains can be used to get different effects. You can make a fountain that has two "humps" instead of the one the third fountain has. Or you can program the third fountain to start light, get dark in the middle, and then get light again.

THREE-COLOR SEPARATIONS

PostScript has two operators that set the color to something other than gray: *setrgbcolor* (which sets the current color based upon red, green, and blue intensities) and *sethsbcolor* (which sets the current color based upon hue, saturation, and brightness). Quite a few programs produce PostScript files that use these operators (most use *setrgbcolor*), including Illustrator, Cricket Draw, AutoShade (used to shade AutoCAD files), and Zenographic. If we can figure out a way to interpret these two operators, we can then produce color separations. PostScript allows us to do this by defining operators of the same name in the user dictionary (the dictionary that is searched for commands before the system dictionary, where the actual commands are kept). For example:

```
/setrgbcolor { pop pop setgray } def
```

This causes the gray level to be determined from the amount of red given to subsequent uses of *setrgbcolor*. Note that you can always bypass the definitions in the user dictionary by explicitly pushing the system dictionary onto the dictionary stack:

```
systemdict begin
.3 .4 .5 setrgbcolor
end
```

With this in mind, let's look at a very simple-minded PostScript prolog for three-color separation:

```
/inch {72 mul} def
/color 1 def
/cyan {
      /color 3 def
      % set halftone screen angle to 30
      currentscreen exch pop 30 exch setscreen
      0 setgray
      gsave
            % print color along top of page
```

```
            systemdict begin 0 setgray end
            100 11.2 inch moveto
            /Times-Roman findfont
            10 scalefont setfont
            (CYAN) show
      grestore
} def
/magenta {
      /color 2 def
      % set halftone screen angle to 60
      currentscreen exch pop 60 exch setscreen
      0 setgray
      gsave
            % print color along top of page
            systemdict begin 0 setgray end
            200 11.2 inch moveto
            /Times-Roman findfont
            10 scalefont setfont
            (MAGENTA) show
      grestore
} def
/yellow {
      /color 1 def
      % set halftone screen angle to 0
      currentscreen exch pop 0 exch setscreen
      0 setgray
      gsave
            % print color along top of page
            systemdict begin 0 setgray end
            300 11.2 inch moveto
            /Times-Roman findfont
            10 scalefont setfont
            (YELLOW) show
      grestore
} def

userdict begin

% redefine sethsbcolor to convert to RGB
% and run our setrgbcolor on the result
```

```
/sethsbcolor {
      systemdict begin
            sethsbcolor
            currentrgbcolor
      end
      userdict begin setrgbcolor end
} def
/setrgbcolor {
      color 1 sub index
      setgray
      pop pop pop
} def
end
```

The first procedures defined are cyan, magenta, and yellow. These procedures set the halftone screen angles to different values for each color (each offset 30 degrees from the other two) and then write the color at the top of the page. (If you don't do this, you can end up not knowing which color a particular negative is for.)

In order to write above eleven inches you have to use the *setpage-param* operator, which is specific to the Linotronic typesetters. (Note that you really can't produce decent separations with a 300 dpi laser printer, so except for tests, I'm assuming that all output from these routines will go to an L100 or an L300.) The following code can be placed at the beginning of the separation program to increase the height of the page to the maximum:

```
% begin Linotronic specific stuff
% change page size to 8.5 x 11.7
statusdict /setpageparams known
{
      statusdict begin
      842 612 0 0 setpageparams
      end
} if
```

The first two parameters to *setpageparams* specify the width and length of the output page in points. The direction of the "width" is always the same with respect to the direction of paper travel (perpendicular). By default, the page orientation on the Linotronics with respect to paper travel is offset by 90 degrees from that of the Laser-Writer, meaning that pages on a Linotronic come out sideways. (The typesetter takes paper up to twelve inches in width, so the page is oriented with the y axis aligned along the width of the paper.) Thus the width parameter to *setpageparams* is actually the maximum y value of the imageable region, and the length parameter is the maximum x value. Note that although you can make the length more than 612, due to the maximum width of the film rolls, you can't make the width more than 842.

Also, assuming you're making negatives to contact-print plates, you'll have to produce right-reading, emulsion-side-down negatives on film:

```
/inch { 72 mul } def
8.5 inch 0 translate
-1 1 scale
{ 1 exch sub } settransfer
erasepage
```

We'll assume that both of these code fragments are prepended to the separation prologues discussed throughout this article.

Getting back to the separation prologue, the user dictionary is pushed onto the dictionary stack (just to be absolutely certain the new *setrgbcolor* and *sethsbcolor* are put there), and *sethsbcolor* and *setrgbcolor* are redefined.

The new *sethsbcolor* simply executes this operator out of the system dictionary, then executes *currentrgbcolor*, which gets the red, green, and blue values for the particular hue, saturation, and brightness values specified to *sethsbcolor*. The RGB values are then passed on to our own setrgbcolor procedure.

Our *setrgbcolor* procedure is quite simple: using the color variable's contents (set by one of the three color procedures) as an index, we set the gray value using one of the three values on the stack. Let's see if this works. If we assume that *setrgbcolor* is called with 1, 0, and 0 (red) on the stack, then cyan causes 1 to be passed to *setgray*, magenta causes 0 to be passed, and yellow causes 0 to be passed, producing an image with no cyan and solid magenta and yellow. This is correct, as magenta plus yellow produce red (the yellow filters out the blue in the magenta). If you run through other combinations, you'll see that the prologue produces theoretically-correct three-color separations.

To use the prologue, you specify which color you want separated and append the PostScript file to separate. For example:

```
/inch {72 mul} def
/color 1 def
/yellow {
      /color 3 def
      % set halftone screen angle to 30
. . .
      /setrgbcolor {
      color 1 sub index
      setgray
      pop pop pop
} def
end
yellow
0 1 0 setrgbcolor
1 inch 1 inch translate
0 0 moveto
1 inch 0 inch lineto
1 inch 1 inch lineto
0 inch 1 inch lineto
closepath
fill
showpage
```

This produces the yellow separation for a one-inch green square. Replacing the yellow with cyan or magenta will produce those separations instead.

COLOR CORRECTION

Now the problem is to perform color correction. In order to get decent grays and bright reds, you have to compensate for impurities in the inks. If we take the percentages given previously, thirty percent contamination of cyan by magenta and fifty percent contamination of magenta by yellow, we can write the undercolor removal into our prologue:

```
/inch {72 mul} def
/color 1 def
```

```
/UCRM .30 def   % percent of magenta UCR
/UCRY .50 def   % percent of yellow UCR

% the definitions for cyan, magenta,
% and yellow remain unchanged
. . .

userdict begin
/sethsbcolor {
    systemdict begin
        sethsbcolor
        currentrgbcolor
    end
    userdict begin setrgbcolor end
} def

/setrgbcolor {
    do_correct
    color 1 sub index
    setgray
    pop pop pop
} def

/do_correct {
    cvtrgbcym
    1 index UCRY mul sub 3 1 roll
    1 index UCRM mul sub 3 1 roll
    3 1 roll
    cvtrgbcym
} def

/cvtrgbcym {
    1 exch sub 3 1 roll
    1 exch sub 3 1 roll
    1 exch sub 3 1 roll
} def
end
```

The additions here are the procedures do_correct and cvtrgbcym. do_correct is called at the beginning of setrgbcolor, and it performs color correction based on the two variables UCRM and UCRY, which specify the amount of magenta to remove under cyan and the amount of yellow to remove under magenta, respectively.

When do_correct is called, the RGB information is on the stack. cvtrgbcym is called to convert this information into cyan, magenta, and yellow information. It simply subtracts each of the three values from one. Now the three numbers on the stack specify intensities for cyan, magenta, and yellow, respectively, with 0 meaning no color and 1 meaning solid color.

After cvtrgbcym returns, the amount of magenta is fetched (1 index) and is multiplied by the amount of yellow undercolor removal (UCRY mul). This quantity is subtracted from the actual amount of yellow to produce the corrected amount of yellow; then the three numbers are rolled so the same can be done for the magenta under cyan. Finally, cvtrgbcym is called again to convert the numbers back into RGB intensities. From here on everything works as before, with one of the three intensities being passed on to setgray depending on the color being separated.

BLACK UNDERCOLOR REMOVAL

One of the most important parts of good color separations is the production of a black plate, or printer. All high-quality color separations are produced in four colors, not three, where the fourth color is black. The use of black as a color allows you to produce grays that are closer to neutral, get more tonal range on the reproduction, and produce solid blacks. Three-color separations cannot produce good blacks, since solid combinations of cyan, yellow, and magenta result in a muddy brown color.

Black is printed at any point where the three other colors all print; a corresponding amount of the three colors is removed anywhere black is printed. So an image with its color set by .2 .3 .4 setrgbcolor can have black printed in it at up to sixty percent. (Recall that .2 .3 .4 setrgbcolor is equivalent to amounts of .8, .7, and .6 for cyan, magenta, and yellow, respectively.) Undercolor removal of black starts when the amounts of cyan, yellow, and magenta are all above fifty percent. Thus, if .2 .3 .4 setrgbcolor is used, the amount of black will be ten percent, and the amount of cyan, magenta, and yellow will be .7, .6, and .5, respectively, before color correction. At the very end, additive failure is compensated for by boosting the black.

The following prologue is the final version of the four-color separator:

```
/inch {72 mul} def
/color 0 def
/UCRB .5 def     % black UCR starts here
/UCRM .31 def    % percent of magenta UCR
/UCRY .48 def    % percent of yellow UCR


/cyan {
      /color 3 def
      % set halftone screen angle to 15
      currentscreen exch pop 15 exch setscreen
      0 setgray
      gsave
            % print color along top of page
            systemdict begin 0 setgray end
            100 11.2 inch moveto
            /Times-Roman findfont
            10 scalefont setfont
            (CYAN) show
      grestore
} def


/magenta {
      /color 2 def
      % set halftone screen angle to 75
      currentscreen exch pop 75 exch setscreen
      0 setgray
      gsave
            % print color along top of page
            systemdict begin 0 setgray end
            200 11.2 inch moveto
            /Times-Roman findfont
            10 scalefont setfont
            (MAGENTA) show
      grestore
} def


/yellow {
```

```
    /color 1 def
    % set halftone screen angle to 0
    currentscreen exch pop 0 exch setscreen
    0 setgray
    gsave
            % print color along top of page
            systemdict begin 0 setgray end
            300 11.2 inch moveto
            /Times-Roman findfont
            10 scalefont setfont
            (YELLOW) show
        grestore
} def


/black {
    /color 0 def
    % set halftone screen angle to 45
    currentscreen exch pop 45 exch setscreen
    0 setgray
    gsave
            % print color along top of page
            systemdict begin 0 setgray end
            400 11.2 inch moveto
            /Times-Roman findfont
            10 scalefont setfont
            (BLACK) show
        grestore
} def


userdict begin
/setgray {
    color 0 eq {     % black
    systemdict begin setgray end
    }
    {      % not black
        pop
        systemdict begin 1 setgray end
    } ifelse
} def
```

```
/sethsbcolor {
      systemdict begin
      sethsbcolor
      currentrgbcolor
      end
      userdict begin setrgbcolor end
} def

/setrgbcolor {
      color 0 eq {      % black
            do_ucrblack
            systemdict begin
            setgray
            pop pop pop
      }
      {
            do_ucrblack pop
            do_correct
            color 1 sub index
            systemdict begin
            setgray
            end
            pop pop pop
      } ifelse
} def

/do_correct {
      cvtrgbcym
      1 index UCRY mul sub 3 1 roll
      1 index UCRM mul sub 3 1 roll
      3 1 roll
      cvtrgbcym
} def

      /do_ucrblack {
      cvtrgbcym
      % get minimum color value
      min 3 index min
      /mincolor exch def
      pop pop
```

```
        % determine black UCR from
        % minimum color and UCRB
        /ucramt mincolor UCRB sub
        % clamp to zero
        dup 0 lt { pop 0 } if def

        % subtract black UCR from colors
        ucramt sub 3 1 roll
        ucramt sub 3 1 roll
        ucramt sub 3 1 roll
        cvtrgbcym
        % handle additive failure
        ucramt 1.25 mul
        % invert for setgray
        1 exch sub
} def


/cvtrgbcym {
        1 exch sub 3 1 roll
        1 exch sub 3 1 roll
        1 exch sub 3 1 roll
} def


/min {
        % min of top two on stack

        % push 0 or 1
        2 copy lt {1} {0} ifelse

        % grab min number
        index
} def
end
```

As you can see, several procedures have been added to handle the black. We redefine setgray so that gray areas are printed only when the color is black (i.e., setgray's operation isn't affected by the color separation). We redefine setrgbcolor so that when the color is black, the value returned by do_ucrblack is used for printing, and when the color is something else, the value returned by do_ucrblack is popped and the appropriate RGB color (properly corrected and black removed) is used.

do_ucrblack is the focal point of this program. It starts out by converting the RGB to cyan, magenta, and yellow, then it gets the minimum of the three. UCRB is subtracted from the minimum, and if the amount is less than zero, ucramt is set to zero so that no black undercolor removal is performed. If the amount is greater than zero, ucramt is set to that number. Then ucramt is subtracted from the three colors, and the colors are converted back to RGB. Finally, ucramt is increased by twenty-five percent to compensate for additive failure. This value is left on the stack (on top of the RGB values) so that now we have red, green, blue, and black on the stack. At this point, setrgbcolor either uses the black or pops it, corrects the colors, and uses one of them. You can use this prolog to separate screens, line art, and text.

Halftone Screens

You may have noticed that the screen angles in the previous prologues changed from 0, 30, and 60 to 0, 15, 45, and 75. I've found that the best set of angles varies for different screen frequencies and output resolutions. At 1,270 dpi, 120-line screens reproduce well with angles of 0, 15, 45, and 75 for yellow, cyan, black, and magenta, respectively. At 2,540 dpi, 150-line screens reproduce well with angles of 0, 15, 30, and 60 for cyan, black, magenta, and yellow, respectively.

One problem I've noticed is that the Linotronic 100 isn't quite good enough for producing color separations. Although good separations can be produced at 1,270 dpi at both 90 and 120 lines, the paper feed mechanism of the 100 jitters a little, causing very light striations perpendicular to the direction of paper travel. The Linotronic 300 also has this problem, but the striations are much less noticeable, and except in rare circumstances the problem isn't serious. The L300 also appears to produce crisper halftone spots, even at 1,270 dpi.

You can also speed up halftoning of scanned images by rotating the page ninety degrees. Normally the x axis is parallel to the slow scan direction. When producing a halftone, POSTSCRIPT must perform more work to generate the spots. By rotating the page by ninety degrees, you align the x axis with the fast scan direction, allowing for faster halftoning. Note that this will have little effect on the time required to print text, line art, or filled graphics.

Given the PostScript routines in this chapter, any spot-color PostScript file (i.e., any using *setrgbcolor* or *sethsbcolor*) can be separated into four colors. That means files from programs such as AutoShade (a shading program for AutoCAD), Zenographics (a color presentation system), and Illustrator all can be separated with relative ease.

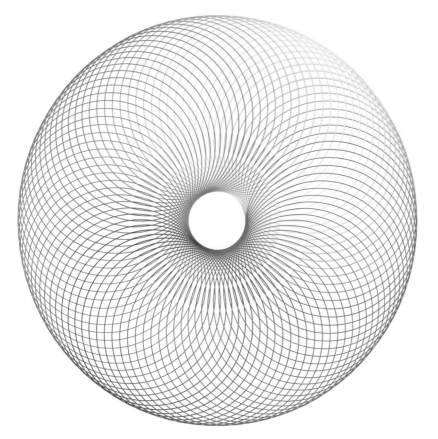

Plate 1. Output from spiro (see Chapter 11), separated with the prolog in Chapter 12.

Plate 2a. Output from fountain (see Chapter 11), separated with the prolog in Chapter 12.

Random Colors!

Plate 2b. Output from the random color generator (see Chapter 11), separated with the prolog in Chapter 12.

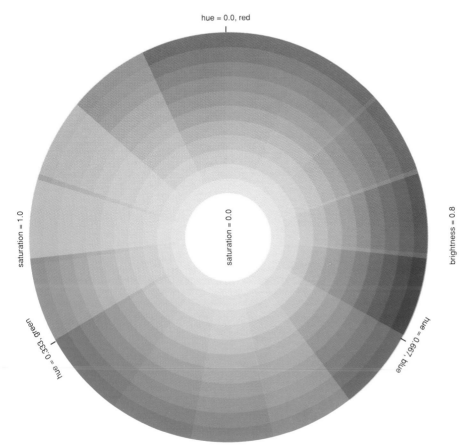

hue = 0.0, red

saturation = 1.0

saturation = 0.0

brightness = 0.8

hue = 0.333, green

hue = 0.667, blue

Plate 3. Output from hsbcolors (see Chapter 11), separated with the prolog in Chapter 12.

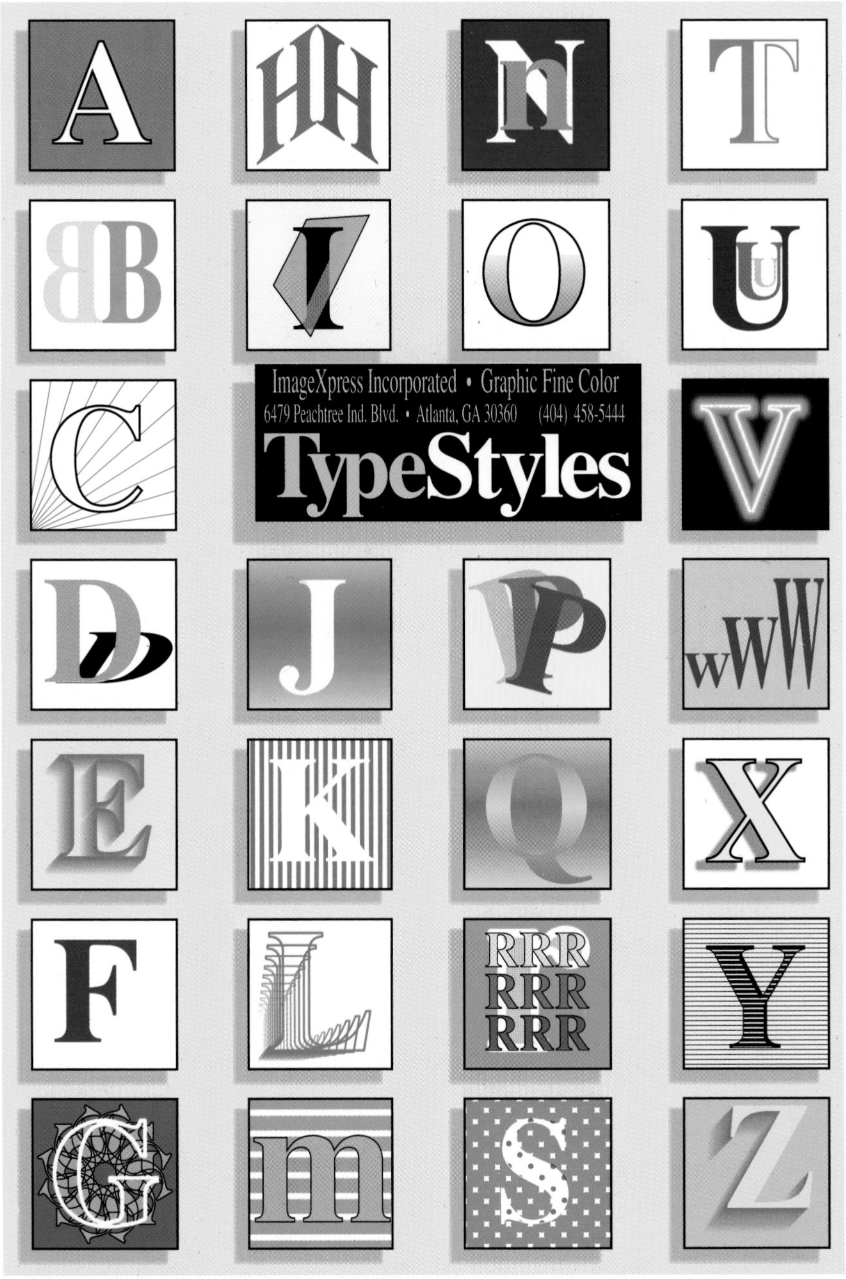

Special Thanks to: Herb Paynter-President and Creative Director, ImageXpress, Incorporated • Gordon Wilkinson-Director of Research and Development-Walk Thru the Bible Ministries
Very Special Thanks to: John Warnock and the entire ADOBE Systems team, for developing their versatile and powerful PostScript page description language.

Technical Information: All PostScript code was generated on a 5 megabyte Macintosh 2 computer, proofed on a PS Jet Plus laser printer, and finished separation films were output at medium resolution (1270) on Walk Thru the Bible s Linotype L-300 laser typesetter and Raster Image Processor at a litho screen ruling of 150 lines per inch (Black-45°, Cyan-105°, Magenta-75°, Yellow-90°)

Plate 4. The final color alphabet poster.

Part IV

Projects from the Pros

13 / A Spread from *Graphic Perspective*   *Simon Tuckett*

In this chapter I will be covering the assembly of a double-page spread in my magazine, *Graphic Perspective*. In order that people can understand how my mind works, it is perhaps best to look first at my own technique for writing code.

As I mentioned in chapter 1, the first thing I do is design the publication on paper. The pencil sketches are usually rendered on little pieces of scrap paper in airports, restaurants, and coffee shops. The initial task is to define the repeating elements of any particular issue of *Graphic Perspective*, and how they will be varied throughout the issue.

Repetitive Elements

The use of repetitive elements in any layout assures reaffirmation of a design theme, while modifying those elements results in greater variety.

Take a look at the sample *Graphic Perspective* layout in Figure 13.1. On the spread we feature not only embossed folios as repetitive elements, but the very grid on which those folios are placed. Additionally, part of the headline has features that repeat from page to page. Subtitles, with the exception of the color (subtitles and heads appear in black on other pages in the issue) are the same throughout the issue. Obviously it becomes necessary to plan in advance that the color of the image is defined outside the program that describes the subtitles.

Procedure

As mentioned before, the first stage in the advance planning is developing the design on paper. This quite possibly could be the real reason why restaurants have paper napkins.

Then comes a rough global planning of the code structure. In the case of the example spread, I looked first at what things were to be repeating

Figure 13.1. A spread from *Graphic Perspective*.

Graphic Perspective: Volume 1, Issue 4: Page 4: January 1987

elements. The programs to effect them could go down in the header used for every page. Above them I would need the basic definitions for standard user interaction calls—programs to squeeze the whole spread onto a laser printed sheet, or (most importantly for POSTSCRIPT programming) the call to do manual feed on the laser printer. Also in that part of the

Figure 13.1 continued

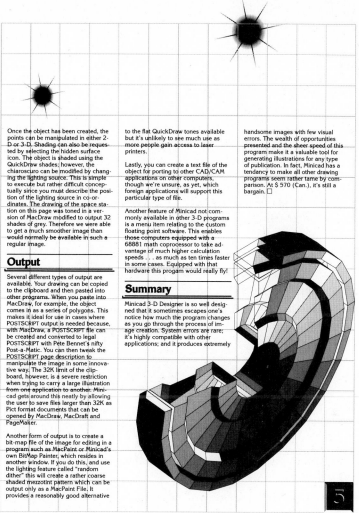

Once the object has been created, the points can be manipulated in either 2-D or 3-D. Shading can also be requested by selecting the hidden surface icon. The object is shaded using the QuickDraw shades; however, the chiaroscuro can be modified by changing the lighting source. This is simple to execute but difficult conceptually since you must describe the position of the lighting source in co-ordinates. The drawing of the space station on this page was toned in a version of MacDraw modified to output 32 shades of grey. Therefore we were able to get a much smoother image than would normally be available in such a regular image.

Output

Several different types of output are available. Your drawing can be copied to the clipboard and then pasted into other programs. When you paste into MacDraw, for example, the object comes in as a series of polygons. This makes it ideal for use in cases where POSTSCRIPT output is needed because, with MacDraw, a POSTSCRIPT file can be created and converted to legal POSTSCRIPT with Pete Bennet's nifty Post-a-Matic. You can then tweak the POSTSCRIPT page description to manipulate the image in some innovative way. The 32K limit of the clipboard, however, is a severe restriction when trying to carry a large illustration from one application to another. Minicad gets around this neatly by allowing the user to save files larger than 32K as Pict format documents that can be opened by MacDraw, MacDraft and PageMaker.

Another form of output is to create a bit-map file of the image for editing in a program such as MacPaint or Minicad's own BitMap Painter, which resides in another window. If you do this, and use the lighting feature called "random dither" this will create a rather coarse shaded mezzotint pattern which can be output only as a MacPaint File. It provides a reasonably good alternative

to the flat QuickDraw tones available but it's unlikely to see much use as more people gain access to laser printers.

Lastly, you can create a text file of the object for porting to other CAD/CAM applications on other computers, though we're unsure, as yet, which foreign applications will support this particular type of file.

Another feature of Minicad not commonly available in other 3-D programs is a menu item relating to the custom floating point software. This enables those computers equipped with a 68881 math coprocessor to take advantage of much higher calculation speeds . . . as much as ten times faster in some cases. Equipped with that hardware this progam would really fly!

Summary

Minicad 3-D Designer is so well designed that it sometimes escapes one's notice how much the program changes as you go through the process of image creation. System errors are rare; it's highly compatible with other applications; and it produces extremely

handsome images with few visual errors. The wealth of opportunities presented and the sheer speed of this program make it a valuable tool for generating illustrations for any type of publication. In fact, Minicad has a tendancy to make all other drawing programs seem rather tame by comparison. At $ 570 (Can.), it's still a bargain. □

For: Ashley House
By: GraphiComp Design — Ampersand Typographers
PostScript programs: GraphiComp Design · 1986

header would be the definition for doing full double-page spreads on the L300 typesetter. Further down the header would be a few programs for effects that might only be needed on a few pages.

The next step was deciding how the files would be structured, which has a lot to do with what software you're using. Layout work for the example spread was accomplished in JustText, which limited me to a file size of 32k. So all the illustration files were separate from the body of the layout; JustText pulled them all together at print time.

Artwork

The first part of the actual layout process was to prepare the artwork. Much of that work was done in MiniCad, the program that the review refers to.

THE SPACE STATION

The illustration of the Space Station was cut to the clipboard from Minicad, then pasted into MacDraw. To get a POSTSCRIPT file of the illustration I merely typed *Command-F* while clicking the *Okay* button in the print dialogue box. Instead of printing to the printer, the Apple LaserWriter driver sent the POSTSCRIPT output to disk.

Unfortunately, POSTSCRIPT is written with the routines in Laser Prep in mind and is illegible to most humans. So next came the tricky part. The POSTSCRIPT file on disk was processed using an application developed by Pete Bennet called Post-a-Matic. It was developed for just this task—converting MacDraw print files to pure POSTSCRIPT files.

Considering that Post-a-Matic was bound to have a very short life, the program never became very elaborate. Some six months after we started using it, Adobe Illustrator (and all the complexity of image that program was capable of) arrived. However, during the summer of 1986 MacDraw and Post-a-Matic were all we had. PaM did not convert circles, ovals, round-cornered rectangles, smoothed lines (and, hence, Bezier curves), or arrows. But, by modifying the MacDraw palette, we were able to get access to thirty-two shades of gray in our polygons.

Processing the space station illustration produced a 64k POSTSCRIPT file with the 0 0 point right in the center. There was a very sensible reason for this. I had a pretty clear idea where the center of the space station should be but no clue as to how large it should be. Here's how part of the file looked:

```
%!PS-Adobe-1.0
%%Title: New Tone Station
%%Creator: MacDraw1.9
%%CreationDate: Sunday, August 24, 1986
%%For: Simon
```

```
%%EndComments
%%Post-a-Matic:   Version 3.3z July 15, 1986
%%Converted by:   Peter Bennett
%%Inspiration by:  Simon Tuckett
%%Date Converted: 08/24/86 18:45:04
%%Length of X axis: 907   Y axis: 852

newpath
 282 -225 moveto
 395 -58 lineto
 427 -64 lineto
 304 -251 lineto
 282 -225 lineto
gsave
 0 setgray
  gsave 1 setgray stroke grestore


%%%%%%%%%%%%%%%%
%%and so on and so on
%%%%%%%%%%%%%%%%

newpath
 135  520 moveto
 160  502 lineto
 302  584 lineto
gsave
  gsave 1 setgray stroke grestore
grestore
newpath
 244  451 moveto
 202  278 lineto gsave 1 setgray stroke grestore
%%
%%
%% eof
```

This is typical of the PaM files that populated the first few issues of GP. Notice that there are no global scales, translates, or *gsave ... grestore* pairs at either end of the file. These things had to be in the layout document so I could tweak the artwork into position.

THE ELEVATED VIEW

The same thing happened for the illustration of the room. It was created in Minicad, copied to the clipboard, pasted into MacDraw, sent to a POSTSCRIPT file with *Command-F,* and processed in PaM. This time, though, the 0 0 point was in the lower left corner since that was the only certainty; the artwork had to start at that point on the grid if it was to add to the feeling of depth over the page.

THE STARBURSTS

Next, all those starbursts. They were created with custom POSTSCRIPT, since that was the only way to do it back then. You can do the same thing now with a drawing program like Illustrator or FreeHand, but you will find this routine executes faster and gives you more flexibility for changes in the future:

```
%!PS-Adobe-1.0
%%Title: Pete's Amazing Sunburst
%%Creator: Pete Bennett
%%CreationDate: 8/20/86 10:34 PM
%%EndComments


/circlefade {                  %% Requires 2 parameters:
                               %% Interior radius and exterior, in that order


  /exterior exch def           %% Radius of exterior circle
  /interior exch def           %% Radius of interior circle
  /gray 1 def                  % Starting gray scale (white)
  exterior interior sub        % Calculate bandwidth of fade area
%%.5 div                       % only if using .5 setlinewidth
  /width exch def              % Store it
  1 width div                  % Divide that into 1 for fade increment
                               % distance fade covers is number here

  /fade exch def               % Store it


  gsave                        % Save the current work so we don't screw it up
    1 setlinewidth             % Just if needed %% Need Linewidth match here
    gray setgray               % Start it as white

    newpath                    % Clear the path, we're coming thru
```

```
        0 0 interior 0 360 arc
     closepath
   gsave stroke grestore fill  % Draw and fill the inside circle

     width {fadetoblack} repeat % Draw all the other circles
   grestore              }      % And restore VM to original state
def


/fadetoblack  {              % The wonder routine
  /gray gray fade sub def    % Decrements gray value for fade
  gray setgray               % And sets it

  /interior interior 1 add def % Increments circle size %% Linewidth match

  newpath
    0 0 interior 0 360 arc
  closepath
  stroke     }               % Draws circle and strokes it with gray level
def


/TonePiece
{0 0 moveto 0 4 rlineto} def   % Now for defining the fading spikes


/DoFade
{gsave 1 setgray 1 setlinecap
1 -.01 0                        % start, increment, end
{newpath setgray TonePiece stroke 0 1 translate} for
grestore} def



/OneStar
{10 50 circlefade             % Smallest number should be first
gsave
2 setlinewidth 1 setgray
8 {0 7 translate DoFade 0 -7 translate -45 rotate} repeat
grestore} def


%%
%%
```

The Header

Writing the header for a publication is always one of the most enjoyable parts of cutting PostScript code. For one thing, it is very challenging. You can bet the header will be up on screen most of the time during the layout process as new mini-programs are added or modifications are made to existing effects:

```
%!Adobe-1.0
%%Title: GP Issue 4: Header
%%Creator: GraphiComp Design © 1986
%%CreationDate: Sunday, November 23, 1986
%%For: Simon Tuckett
%%Length of X axis: 1224   Y axis: 792
%%EndProlog
```

I broke the header into two areas. First came the standard code for all issues of the publication, followed by material needed for only this issue. The following sections describe the header and its parts for this spread.

MAXIMUM LINOTRONIC PAGE SIZE

The ResetImage program changes the imageable area on the L300 typesetter to a full eleven by seventeen inches. The development of this program was rather interesting:

```
/ResetImage
{statusdict        %% Mini program to reset L300 imageable area
begin              %%
830 1360 0 0       %% 1st number is paper width usage , 2nd is use of paper length
setpageparams      %% command to reset printer image area
end                %% Get out your money bags, this'll cost you!
70 20 translate    %% Image objects (crops) on page
}def               %% all Params changed to largest paper coverage
```

Naturally the L300 has a limit on page size, depending upon the resolution you have chosen. After I learned what code was used to change the page size, I chose the largest size I could imagine and kept reducing it. I kept doing this until I had a page size that the L300 would print. As it turned out, this area was slightly larger than required—11.5 by 18.75 inches. This allowed me to place such objects as crop marks, registration marks, and copyright slugs outside the 11-by-17 page area. Hence the need for a slight translate at the bottom of the definition to move the 0 0 point up into the imageable area (my standard 0 0 point is always in the lower left corner of the page).

LASERWRITER PROGRAMS

LWSqueezeOn shoved the whole image up to the top of the page, rotated right, and then scaled it down to sixty percent of its existing size so I could proof a whole double-page spread on one LaserWriter page. Many Apple Canada print advertisements were done in this way—proofed extensively with LWSqueezeOn and then output using ResetImage:

```
/LWSqueezeOn                %%Image the whole spread on a LaserWriter page
{ 0  792 translate
 -90 rotate 20 70 translate
.6   .6 scale } def
```

LWLeftPage did absolutely nothing. In fact it was only put there for housekeeping purposes so that it would match the following program.

LWRightPage shifted the whole imageable area over by one page. This was necessary for me to get a look at any of the full-size pages during production. By calling up either of these programs, I could see either side of the spread I was working on:

```
/LWLeftPage                %%Image the left page on LaserWriter
{0 0 translate } def
/LWRightPage               %%Image the right page on LaserWriter
{-612 0 translate } def
```

IMAGING LIMITS

There follow a couple of path definitions. The PageLimits program enabled me to use "PageLimits stroke" any time I wished to see the edges of the page. If I wanted a black page with white type, I could write BleedLimits 0 setgray fill and have the whole spread as a black background:

```
/BleedLimits {newpath      %%Permissable Bleed Limits of art
-8.5   801.5 moveto
-8.5 -8.5 lineto
```

```
1233.5 -8.5 lineto
1233.5  801.5 lineto closepath } def
```

```
/PageLimits                    %%Visible PageLimit for 11.0" x 17.00" area
{newpath
 0  792 moveto
 0  0 lineto
 1224  0 lineto
 1224  792 lineto closepath} def
```

REGISTRATION AND CROP MARKS

The crop marks program came next. Had I not just taken the code from a PaM file, it would have been much more condensed by my writing a program that generated the mark only once, followed by translates and rotates to get the other three on the page.

This was followed by the code describing a registration mark (called up and actually placed twice at the head of the layout):

```
/CropMarks {
0 setgray 1234  1 moveto 1269  1 lineto stroke
 1224 -9 moveto 1224 -19 lineto stroke
 1234  793 moveto 1269  793 lineto stroke
 1224  802 moveto 1224  812 lineto stroke
 1 -8 moveto 1 -18 lineto stroke
-10  1 moveto -45  1 lineto stroke
 0  802 moveto 0  812 lineto stroke
-11  793 moveto -46  793 lineto stroke } def
```

```
/RegiMark
{gsave 12 0 moveto 0 10 rlineto
12 14 moveto 0 10 rlineto
0 12 moveto 10 0 rlineto
14 12 moveto 10 0 rlineto
12 12 6 0 360 arc stroke grestore} def
```

FOLD LINES

The FoldLineImage, which came next, enabled me to get an idea of just where the gutter of the spread was. It placed a dashed line down the center of the spread. However, the definition that follows left little dashed lines outside the page area to show the offset printer where the gutter was without affecting the imaged area. This was used only on the final proofs and final art:

```
/FoldLineImage {gsave          %%Visible foldlines
0.5 setlinewidth [4 4] 4 setdash
newpath 612  -17 moveto 612  811 lineto stroke
grestore} def


/FoldLine
{gsave 0.5 setlinewidth
[4 4] 4 setdash                %%Final art foldlines
newpath 612  1 moveto
 612 -17 lineto stroke
 612  811 moveto
 612  793 lineto stroke grestore} def
```

L I N E R N O T E S

Just as records have liner notes, I always felt that layouts should have liner notes. The next definition is a description of the strings to be used on the liner notes which go up the side of the spread at either end of the image:

```
/LinerNotesA
{0 22 moveto
/Helvetica findfont 10 scalefont setfont
(For: Ashley House) show
0 11 moveto
(By: GraphiComp Design \320 )show
-0.385 0 rmoveto
(Ampersand )show
-0.126 0 rmoveto
(T)show
-0.385 0 rmoveto
(Typographers)show
0 0 moveto
(PostScript programs: GraphiComp Design )show
/Symbol findfont 10 scalefont setfont
(\343)show
/Helvetica findfont 10 scalefont setfont
```

```
(1986)show} def

/LinerStringA { (LeftTitleGoesHere) show} def
/LinerStringB { (RightTitleGoesHere) show} def

/LinerNotesB
{0 0 moveto
/Helvetica findfont 10 scalefont setfont
LinerStringA 612 0 moveto LinerStringB} def

/SetLinerNotesA {
gsave -15 10 translate
    90 rotate LinerNotesA
grestore
gsave
    1272 10 translate
90 rotate LinerNotesA
grestore} def
```

LinerStrings were the strings of type used in the names written across
the bottom of the spreads. They told the printer which spread we were
on. I know the choice of procedure name sounds a bit confusing, but
in actual practice it was quite transparent. Therefore LineNotesB was
the call to set the names of the spreads. Setting the liner notes themselves was a little more difficult. They needed no definition for the
strings because the copy for them never changed. They did require
rotation and translating into position, though, and the program Set-
LinerNotesA was the call to do that.

HANDFEED

Owing to the amount of proofing our spread for the magazine required,
I decided that I needed a one-word call to switch the LaserWriter to
manual feed. I am sure this saved me an enormous amount of paper,
as I was able to feed some sheets through the LaserWriter several times
to test little pieces of PostScript code:

```
/Handfeed {
statusdict                      %% Ok, this is the one for the LaserWriter
/manualfeed true put} def
```

Issue Header

After the section of the header that I used for every issue came the issue-specific header procedures. These procedures set up the page grid, folios, subheads, and other repetitive elements that I only used in this issue.

THE PAGE GRID

The issue was designed to reflect some of the things you could do with a partially visible grid over the entire spread. DoublePageVerts was the call to image vertical lines over the entire spread. Its sister definition, which follows, is a slightly different way of calling up the same effect, this time imaging two sets of horizontal lines over the double-page spread, one set on each page. This time the *repeat* operator was used rather than a counting *for* loop:

```
                                    %% Commence "This Issue" definitions


/DoublePageVerts
{gsave 37 23 translate              %% This is to produce the vertical lines
newpath 0 0 moveto
0 46 1150                           %%start increment end
{0 moveto 0 736 rlineto} for
stroke grestore} def


/DoublePageHors
{gsave 37 23 translate              %% This for the left horizontals
    17 {0 0 moveto 552 0 rlineto
    0 46 translate} repeat stroke
grestore


gsave 635 23 translate             %% This for the right horizontals
    17 {0 0 moveto 552 0 rlineto
    0 46 translate} repeat stroke
grestore} def
```

BUTTONS AND FOLIOS

To get the buttons onto the page required quite a lot of little definitions. First, in the definitions LeftFace, TopFace, RightFace, BotFace, and MainFace, I defined the paths for the folio button. The button was described as a path only, as there were several other things I wanted to do with these tile shapes in the issue. The definitions were followed by a call to combine the button in PageButton, with each face being set in a different color to effect a three-dimensional appearance:

```
/LeftFace                          %%Define Page Number Button face paths
{newpath 0  0 moveto 0  46 lineto
 4  42 lineto 4  4 lineto closepath} def


/TopFace
{newpath 4  42 moveto  0  46 lineto
 46  46 lineto 42  42 lineto closepath} def


/RightFace
{newpath 42  4 moveto 42  42 lineto
 46  46 lineto 46  0 lineto closepath} def


/BotFace
{newpath 0  0 moveto 4  4 lineto
 42  4 lineto 46  0 lineto closepath} def


/MainFace
{newpath 4  42 moveto 4  4 lineto
 42  4 lineto 42  42 lineto closepath} def          %%End def


/PageButton                    %% Create the button
     {1.415 setmiterlimit  .25 setlinewidth
     MainFace gsave .6 setgray fill grestore stroke
     BotFace gsave .1 setgray fill grestore stroke
     TopFace gsave .9 setgray fill grestore stroke
     LeftFace gsave .3 setgray fill grestore stroke
     RightFace gsave .8 setgray fill grestore stroke} def
```

LAYING DOWN THE PAGE NUMBERS

The next program in the header placed the page numbers on the page number button. The page number is defined as a two-figure number globally in order that it can accommodate a sixteen-page publication. For the single-figure numbers this was defeated and the number shifted slightly to center over the button

Notice how the actual page number was set several times; it is the order and the associated tones of that order that created the simple embossed effect. First a darker tone to the upper right of the center, then a light tone number to the lower left of the center and finally a mid-range tone in the center:

```
/PageNum {(1)show -2 0 rmoveto (2)show } def


/SetPageNum                     %%Set type on top
{/Korinna-Bold findfont 30 scalefont setfont
5 13 moveto 0.1 setgray PageNum
3 11 moveto 0.95 setgray PageNum
4 12 moveto 0.8 setgray PageNum} def
```

PINSTRIPED CHARACTERS

The next program, pinstripe, is one that my friend Pete Bennett wrote for me. The need for tighter code in this case was readily apparent. Essentially I needed some code that would set the headline and sub-heads with three duplicate characters, all offset from each other and in different tones.

The lowest one, at the extreme lower left, was to be set in white, then came one in black, higher and slightly to the right. This was to be followed by the final character set on the top in white. What I also needed (and this was where I needed Pete's assistance) was to be able to adjust the spacing of the type as I wished, both globally and between individual characters:

```
/pinstripe                      %%Procedure for headline type
{/thestring exch def
    /kernit exch def
    gsave 0 0 rmoveto 0 setgray
       {pop pop kernit 0 rmoveto}
       thestring kshow
    grestore
    gsave 2 2 rmoveto 1 setgray
       {pop pop kernit 0 rmoveto}
       thestring kshow
    grestore
    gsave 3 3 rmoveto 0 setgray
       {pop pop kernit 0 rmoveto}
```

```
    thestring kshow
  grestore
  thestring stringwidth pop 0 rmoveto
} def
```

One of my requirements for this mini program was that I would be able to modify it for similar use elsewhere. When we get to the actual layout, you will see how this program was actually used.

BARS FOR SUBHEADS

The bars for the subtitles were a relatively simple part of the process. They are rule lines placed on top of each other in much the same way the type has been set in pinstripe. They were positioned in order that the subtitles could easily be set inside them with just two translates. 2ColSubTitleBars was merely a modification of the single-column bar routine:

```
/SubtitleBars
{gsave
    gsave 1.5 setlinewidth
       0 0 moveto -3 0 moveto -3 -3 lineto
       171 0 rlineto stroke
       0 0 moveto 165 0 rlineto stroke
    grestore
    gsave 0 22 translate
       1 setlinewidth 0 0 moveto
       165 0 rlineto stroke
    grestore
grestore} def


/2ColSubtitleBars
{gsave
    gsave 1.5 setlinewidth
       0 0 moveto -3 0 moveto -3 -3 lineto
       356 0 rlineto stroke
       0 0 moveto 350 0 rlineto stroke
    grestore
    gsave 0 22 translate
       1 setlinewidth
       0 0 moveto 350 0 rlineto stroke
```

```
     grestore
grestore} def
```

GETTING AROUND

This was a nifty little program that Pete wrote enabling me to move anywhere on the double-page spread. Well, not quite anywhere. But writing two numbers would allow me to translate to the lower left corner of that grid box on the double-page grid we'd set up. While working on this issue I had a printed grid in front of me with the grid numbers penciled in, so I could quickly reference which grid lines I would move art to while doing the layout:

```
%% example of use:  1 1 movetobox
%%(Moves to the first box on the left hand page)
%% example of use:  13 13 movetobox
%%(Moves to the first box on the right hand page)


/movetobox {
    /V exch def /H exch def   %% Get the H and V box number
    V 1 sub 46 mul 23 add
    /V exch def               %% (V - 1) * 46 + 23
    H 1 sub 46 mul            %% (H - 1) * 46
    H 13 lt {37} {83} ifelse  %% If H is less than 13 then add 37
                              %% to compensate on left page
  add /H exch def             %% Otherwise add 83
  H V translate               %% Then moveto the H and V coordinate
} def                         %% translate can be changed to moveto there

%%
%%
%%
```

The Layout

The layout itself was accomplished in JustText, so much of what follows is heavily integrated with JustText coding. "{ps}" starts the POSTSCRIPT code, QQ ends it and moves back into JustText coding. The document you see is not the entire one. It's primarily the POSTSCRIPT parts, though as you can see from how frequently we zip in and out of POSTSCRIPT, the two are heavily intertwined.

DOCUMENT HEADERS

The headers of my JustText documents always include standard house-keeping calls—requests to the printer to do various things, as well as prepackaged definitions for things that appear on the page. At the head of this spread were two calls asking JustText to include a couple of POSTSCRIPT files from disk. They featured the hierarchical file search path that JustText must follow through the folders (proving once again to everybody that I have really silly names for my hard drives):

```
{inBuggles:GP:Issue 4:00 Issue 4 GP Header}
{inBuggles:GP:Issue 4:04005 PS-Stars}
```

The first, naturally, is the header call; the second is the file that contains the definition for producing a star. Both were discussed above.

GLOBAL PAGE TASKS

Now we're into the POSTSCRIPT for the layout itself. First came the global page tasks, also discussed above. If I needed to initiate them, I had merely to kill the two percent symbols and they were in operation:

```
{ps}
%%Handfeed
%%LWSqueezeOn
%%{1 exch sub }settransfer                          %% Stuck this in to save toner!
%%LWLeftPage
%%LWRightPage
%%ResetImage
%%Use ONLY for  L300
/LinerStringA {
     (Graphic Perspective: Volume 1, Issue 4: Page 4: January 1987) show
} def
/LinerStringB { (Graphic Perspective: Volume 1, Issue 4: Page 5: January 1987) show} def
gsave SetLinerNotesA grestore
gsave 34 -17 translate LinerNotesB grestore
%%set one on left
gsave 0.5 setlinewidth CropMarks grestore
%%gsave FoldLineImage grestore
%%Kill 'Image' on final art
gsave FoldLine grestore
gsave BleedLimits 0.5 setlinewidth
```

```
gsave 0 setgray fill grestore stroke
%%This for black B/G
grestore
%%gsave PageLimits 0.5 setlinewidth stroke grestore
gsave newpath 0.5 setlinewidth -43 397 translate RegiMark grestore
gsave newpath 0.5 setlinewidth 1244 397 translate RegiMark grestore
```

The third procedure, {1 exch sub }settransfer, is interesting. Not wishing to kill an entire toner cartridge while proofing one black double-page spread over and over again, I put this little line of code at the head so that the printer would produce a negative version of the entire page. It was quite effective and I am certain it saved me an awful lot of toner.

The LinerStrings are specified correctly at this stage so that we can identify the page from the printout. Then come the calls to set the LinerNotes up the side. This part could have been left in the header, seeing as the notes appear on every page. But there were occasions when I wished to move them around. The same goes for the registration marks.

HOW MANY STARS CAN YOU FIT IN A LINO?

The little block of code that follows was the call to image the stars on the page. We had a problem here. When I initially designed the spread I had several more stars on the page. The first time I ran a medium-resolution proof of the spread on the L300, it wouldn't print. After a few quizzical moments I decided to kill all the stars (I'd used similar techniques before, as you can tell). The starless spread printed with no problem. I next killed the *showpage* at the tail of the file and then ran the spread again with all the stars. Error city.

I reran the spread, editing out a star each time. The file ran without errors after two stars had disappeared. As you can see, the stars were moved into position and then rotated. A scale was applied and then the procedure initiated:

```
gsave 100 325 translate  12 rotate .5 .5 scale OneStar grestore
gsave 350 150 translate  12 rotate .6 .6 scale OneStar grestore
%%gsave 350 750 translate  12 rotate .75 .75 scale OneStar grestore
gsave 700 650 translate  12 rotate .4 .4 scale OneStar grestore
gsave 1020 747 translate  12 rotate .6 .6 scale OneStar grestore
%%gsave 1120 100 translate  12 rotate .65 .65 scale OneStar grestore
```

PLACING THE GRID

The line of code that follows the stars placed the grid on the page after having given it a (rather critical) gray level. Owing to output and offset printing deficiencies I'm not sure that it made all that much difference, but assigning a level of seventy-two percent gray as opposed to eighty percent certainly made me feel better. Following this, the page numbers were assigned and positioned. Notice that there is a translate after the PageButton in order that the number would be centered over it:

```
gsave 0.28 setgray DoublePageVerts DoublePageHors grestore

/PageNum {(4)show} def
gsave 37 23 translate PageButton 8 0 translate SetPageNum grestore
/PageNum {(5)show} def
gsave 1141 23 translate PageButton 9 0 translate SetPageNum grestore
```

PLACING THE HEADLINE

The M path was the outline of the large initial capital in the title (which, when duplicated, also served as a rather large drop cap for the body copy). The code for that path was followed by the path information for the center of the M:

```
/Mpath
{ newpath 0 1 moveto                             %%M path
 0 157 lineto 34 157 lineto 81 86 lineto
128 157 lineto 162 157 lineto 162 1 lineto
0 1 lineto 23 81 moveto 23 12 lineto
69 12 lineto 23 81 lineto} def

/MCentrePath {newpath 23 81 moveto
69 12 lineto 23 12 lineto 23 81 lineto
closepath} def


gsave 50 578 translate 1 1 scale                     %%Top left one
    gsave MCentrePath clip -6 -6 translate newpath Mpath
        gsave 0.5 setgray fill grestore stroke
    grestore
    gsave
        newpath Mpath gsave 0.9 setgray fill grestore stroke
```

```
        grestore
grestore

gsave 132 464 translate 1 1 scale
%%Lower right one
    gsave MCentrePath clip -6 -6 translate newpath Mpath
        gsave 0.5 setgray fill grestore stroke
    grestore
    gsave newpath Mpath
      gsave 0.9 setgray fill grestore stroke
    grestore
grestore
```

Once again this code came from some MacDraw to Post-a-Matic code. It was then immediately used in the little group of procedures that follow. First the central path is clipped and the M is imaged to the lower left by six points. This is filled and stroked, and then the same thing is done in the normal position for the M, but to give an impression of depth, the overall tone for the M face is lightened. The program was then run again to set a duplicate of the M offset from the one underneath.

PLACING THE SUBHEADS

pinstripe was then redefined so that we could set the title. The code that actually set the title follows. Having the kerning program already in place accounts for the brevity of the commands. The 72-point type in this case required that, for the first few characters, two points were removed between each pair, then four points for the last characters:

```
/pinstripe
{/thestring exch def
    /kernit exch def
    gsave 0 0 rmoveto 1 setgray {pop pop kernit 0 rmoveto} thestring kshow grestore
    gsave 2 2 rmoveto 0 setgray {pop pop kernit 0 rmoveto} thestring kshow grestore
    gsave 3 3 rmoveto 1 setgray {pop pop kernit 0 rmoveto} thestring kshow grestore
    thestring stringwidth pop 0 rmoveto
  } def

gsave
/Korinna-Bold findfont 72 scalefont setfont 1 1 scale 215 640 moveto
```

```
-2 (inicad ) pinstripe
-4 (3-D) pinstripe
grestore


1 setgray                 %% Initiate type color
QQ    % Back  to JustText
```

The call to initiate the body copy color merely reaffirmed that it would be in white. Most things had been specified that way until this point, but I thought it better to actually spell it out just in case any accidents had happened above and the color had not been changed back to white. The two Qs take us back into JustText coding for the body copy.

BODY COPY

Next comes the JustText code to set the body copy. We started out by defining the font, point size, and leading. Then came the column definitions, some of which had been turned into notes because they were not being used. It is always good to have them specified together; then they can be copied to subsequent pages. Then came a call to set type ragged right and the request to jump into the first column. A jump down 140 points was compounded by a six-pica indent to move around the "drop cap" of the second M. The font was restated, and then we start setting text:

```
{f31}{p9}{110}
{noc1,743,47,40,212}
{c1,743,231,40,396}
{c2,743,415,40,580}
{c3,743,645,40,810}
{c4,743,829,40,994}
{noc6,743,1013,40,1178}


{rr}{cj1}{a140}{i16}
{f31}inicad 3-D Designer from Diehl Graphsoft offers tremendous creative
flexibility when it comes to creating elaborate objects. In the last
issue of GP, we looked at some of the ways to create simple objects and
manipulate them. There are also numerous ways to translate the image you
have in {xi}your head at the start of the session, onto the screen.
Sessions are long though . . . because 3-D drawings have a lot more
```

information, you can almost assume a three-fold increase in the time
spent manipulating an object in three, rather than two
dimensions.{ql}{al0}

{a30}   % Move down 30 points in JustText

SETTING SUBTITLES

The next part of interest in the file was the call to set a subtitle. It is a
copy of the headline type call with a scale applied to it. Final positioning of all subtitles was done at the end of the layout. As there was no
way of tying POSTSCRIPT code dynamically to JustText layouts, the
translate was a specific call to a point on the page, guided by the x,y
coordinate of the previous line of JustText–set type:

```
{ps}   %%Start PS coding
gsave
415 565 translate                          %% Next Baseline
0 14 translate SubtitleBars 0 5 translate
/Korinna-Bold findfont 72 scalefont setfont
0 0 moveto .22 .22 scale
-1 (Space Station) pinstripe
grestore
QQ    % Back to JustText
```

{f31}Cylindrical objects can

... and so on and so on until we get to the end of the JustText coding for the page...

At $ 570 (Can.), it's still a {-}bargain. {p7}{lw0.5}{oq}{p9}{ql}{al0}

```
{ps}  % Into PostScript again
0 setgray                           %% Cancel type tone
gsave
 997  250 translate
 0 rotate
 .25  .25 scale
0 setgray
1 setlinewidth
```

```
QQ      %JustText...

{inBuggles:GP:Issue 4:04-05 PS-Space Station}

{ps}  % PostScript...
grestore
QQ  %JustText
{inBuggles:GP:Issue 4:04-05 PS-Room}
```

The only other piece of handwritten code on the page was a very simple translate and scale before calling in the Space Station code. The code calling in the Room art had no need of positioning information as that was already in the Room code document. It was a small enough file that it could have its own window on screen as I was laying out the document. In later months I streamlined the whole process and ensured that all illustrative POSTSCRIPT files came in without positioning information. This helped when I came to use the same artwork in other jobs, as they were completely stand-alone files with naught but a *gsave* at the head and a *grestore* at the tail. Translates and scales were done right on the layout.

Clean-up and Flip Check

So much for the code. The layout for this particular spread went remarkably smoothly. The artwork in most cases needed nothing but scaling and positioning information. Then the text was set to run around everything.

I did find, however, that it was prudent to run a "flip check" on the spread to see whether there were any missing *gsave . . . grestore*s. Flip checks usually consist of translating the whole spread across the imageable area and then flipping it back with a *1-1* scale command. The result should be an inverted version of the page (referred to in the "biz" as wrong reading). It is this little procedure that invariably uncovers any inconsistencies with the *saves* and *restores* in the document. This may not be all that important when the page is being run normally. It is important, however, when you are flipping and inverting the image to produce negatives on film.

I learned this from experience. The cover to our second issue was to look quite different from the way it actually appeared. Unfortunately one of the two color plates was missing a rather important *grestore*.

The problem did not appear until the image was flipped—which took place while I was out of town. Upon my return the printer called to say that something was inconsistent. We had to radically edit the black ink negative just to get the magazine out. Hence the need for flip checks. They save on surprises, which are fine for birthdays but not so good when you're under deadline.

Bathroom Graffitti

The definition for the page number buttons is repeated here under a different name so I can change the gray values assigned to the tile faces. This was done for a spread at the back of the issue that would be using the page tiles all over the spread in a seemingly haphazard arrangement, some of them running under type (Figure 13.2). Hence the need for really light tones on the tile. PageTileSides was exactly the same definition with the MainFace missing. This was so that I could put some graffiti on the bathroom tiles on the last page:

```
/PageTile    %% Create bathroom tiles
{     % def
      1.415 setmiterlimit  .25 setlinewidth
      MainFace .9 setgray gsave fill grestore stroke
      BotFace .7 setgray gsave fill grestore stroke
      TopFace .95 setgray gsave fill grestore stroke
      LeftFace .8 setgray gsave fill grestore stroke
      RightFace .85 setgray gsave fill grestore stroke
} def      %/PageTile


/PageTileSides     %% Create different bathroom tiles
{     % def
      1.415 setmiterlimit  .25 setlinewidth
      BotFace .7 setgray gsave fill grestore stroke
      TopFace .95 setgray gsave fill grestore stroke
      LeftFace .8 setgray gsave fill grestore stroke
      RightFace .85 setgray gsave fill grestore stroke
} def      %/PageTileSides


/PageTileMask     % Create mask to cover these
{     % def
      1.415 setmiterlimit  1 setlinewidth
```

Figure 13.2. Simon Tuckett's bathroom graffitti page.

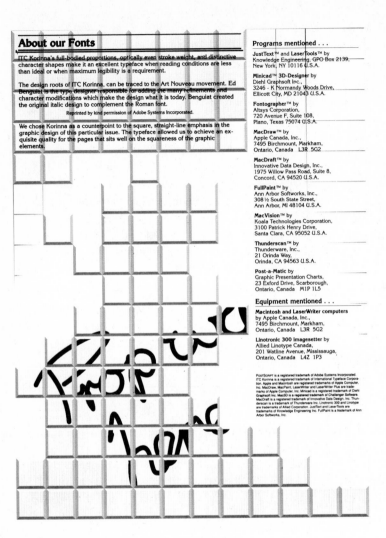

About our Fonts

ITC Korinna's full-bodied proportions, optically even stroke weight, and distinctive character shapes make it an excellent typeface when reading conditions are less than ideal or when maximum legibility is a requirement.

The design roots of ITC Korinna, can be traced to the Art Nouveau movement. Ed Benguiat is the type designer responsible for adding the many refinements and character modifications which make the design what it is today. Benguiat created the original italic design to complement the Roman font.

Reprinted by kind permission of Adobe Systems Incorporated.

We chose Korinna as a counterpoint to the square, straight-line emphasis in the graphic design of this particular issue. The typeface allowed us to achieve an exquisite quality for the pages that sits well on the squareness of the graphic elements.

Programs mentioned . . .

JustText™ and **LaserTools™** by Knowledge Engineering, GPO Box 2139, New York, NY 10116 U.S.A.

Minicad™ 3D-Designer by Diehl Graphsoft Inc., 3246 - K Normandy Woods Drive, Ellicott City, MD 21043 U.S.A.

Fontographer™ by Altsys Corporation, 720 Avenue F, Suite 108, Plano, Texas 75074 U.S.A.

MacDraw™ by Apple Canada, Inc., 7495 Birchmount, Markham, Ontario, Canada L3R 5G2

MacDraft™ by Innovative Data Design, Inc., 1975 Willow Pass Road, Suite 8, Concord, CA 94520 U.S.A.

FullPaint™ by Ann Arbor Softworks, Inc., 308 ½ South State Street, Ann Arbor, MI 48104 U.S.A.

MacVision™ by Koala Technologies Corporation, 3100 Patrick Henry Drive, Santa Clara, CA 95052 U.S.A.

Thunderscan™ by Thunderware, Inc., 21 Orinda Way, Orinda, CA 94563 U.S.A.

Post-a-Matic by Graphic Presentation Charts, 23 Exford Drive, Scarborough, Ontario, Canada M1P 1L5

Equipment mentioned . . .

Macintosh and LaserWriter computers by Apple Canada, Inc., 7495 Birchmount, Markham, Ontario, Canada L3R 5G2

Linotronic 300 imagesetter by Allied Linotype Canada, 201 Watline Avenue, Mississauga, Ontario, Canada L4Z 1P3

PostScript is a registered trademark of Adobe Systems Incorporated. ITC Korinna is a registered trademark of International Typeface Corporation. Apple and Macintosh are registered trademarks of Apple Computer, Inc. MacDraw, MacPaint, LaserWriter and LaserWriter Plus are trademarks of Apple Computer, Inc. Minicad is a registered trademark of Diehl Graphsoft Inc. Mac3D is a registered trademark of Challenger Software. MacDraft is a registered trademark of Innovative Data Design, Inc. Thunderscan is a trademark of Thunderware Inc. Linotronic 300 and Linotype are trademarks of Allied Corporation. JustText and LaserTools are trademarks of Knowledge Engineering Inc. FullPaint is a trademark of Ann Arbor Softworks, Inc.

For: Ashley House
By: GraphiComp Design — Ampersand Typographers
PostScript programs: GraphiComp Design ©1986

Graphic Perspective: Volume 1, Issue 4: Inside Back Cover: January 1987

```
newpath 0 0 moveto
0 46 lineto
46 46 lineto
46 0 lineto closepath
```

```
     gsave 1 setgray fill grestore .9 setgray stroke
} def      % /PageTileMask
```

I had hoped to place the tiles on the last page and then place a path on top of them that looked like thick scrawling type. To do this I had intended to clip the path using all the main faces of the tiles on the last page so that the type would appear to be imaged only on the top faces, as it would appear in any normal bathroom.

Unfortunately I was forgetting just how long it takes the printer to clip such paths, and after many a long wait I decided to take a more expedient route. First lay down all the bathroom tiles (no need for sticky cement here!), then place my graffiti over the top of them.

Now the scrawl was appearing in the tile gutters (everyone knows that grout doesn't take graffitti). To remove it, I repeated the program to lay down all the tiles but this time used the PageTileSides program instead of the PageTile program. This effectively wiped out all the marks in the tile gutters. I wonder if any janitors are aware of this technique for removing graffiti?

Depth, Translucence, Shading, and Reflectance

The title of this section embodies four of my favorite design effects, all of which I manage to use in just about every issue of *Graphic Perspective*—if not on every spread. The effects are difficult to achieve using traditional methods, and though they aren't trivial in POSTSCRIPT, they can be done without the man hours that airbrushing requires.

So herewith, some examples of how I've gone about achieving these effects.

DEPTH AS A DESIGN ELEMENT

In the issue of *Graphic Perspective* that I discuss elsewhere in this chapter the folios appeared in the lower left- and lower right-hand corners as buttons upon which the page number was "embossed." The embossing is an example of something I feel is a very important element of graphic design, and one I use often: three-dimensional layouts. I'm not talking about those layouts that pop up from the center as you turn the page, but rather pages that have visual depth, with elements that appear to be floating above other elements.

PostScript lends itself very well to this procedure. In an opaque system like PostScript, many of the techniques for achieving visual depth are already taken care of. Objects already overlay other objects, so that all most people need work on are such additional effects as perspective, translucence, and the interplay between light sources and the objects on which they shed light.

Techniques for achieving perspective vary widely. Most illustrations can be made to look as though they were rendered using perspective simply by defining vanishing points in the original drawing application and running all lines toward them. But what about type? There is no automatic method of achieving a perspective effect in PostScript typesetting.

The following piece of code shows how I achieved a perspective effect for an article headline (see Figure 13.3). Even if you don't have Garamond for your printer you can see what's happening by using any bold serif PostScript typeface and sending the file:

```
/basefont /Garamond-Bold findfont def


/SetExpo {   %def
        0 0 moveto
        basefont [130 0 56 108 0 0] makefont setfont
        (E) show
        16 0 rmoveto
        basefont [130 0 10 108 0 0] makefont setfont
        (X) show
        17 0 rmoveto
        basefont [130 0 -20 108 0 0] makefont setfont
        (P) show
```

Figure 13.3. A feeling of depth is created by skewing and placing each character individually and then placing a drop shadow behind them.

```
      15 0 rmoveto
      basefont [130 0 -46 108 0 0] makefont setfont
      (O) show
} def      % SetExpo


/SetMacWorld {      %def
      0 0 moveto
      basefont [50 0 25 41 0 0] makefont setfont
      (M) show
      1 0 rmoveto
      basefont [50 0 18 41 0 0] makefont setfont
      (A) show
      -2 0 rmoveto
      basefont [50 0 11 41 0 0] makefont setfont
      (C) show
      3 0 rmoveto
      basefont [50 0 3 41 0 0] makefont setfont
      (W) show
      0 0 rmoveto
      basefont [50 0 -3 41 0 0] makefont setfont
      (O) show
      1 0 rmoveto
      basefont [50 0 -11 41 0 0] makefont setfont
      (R) show
      3 0 rmoveto
      basefont [50 0 -17 41 0 0] makefont setfont
      (L) show
      1 0 rmoveto
      basefont [50 0 -25 41 0 0] makefont setfont
      (D) show
} def %SetMacworld


gsave %%Define shadow
      41 600 translate -4 -4 translate
      gsave
            0 setgray
            SetExpo
      grestore
```

```
    gsave
            53 80 translate -2 -2 translate
            0 setgray
            SetMacWorld
    grestore
grestore    %end of Shadow


gsave 41 600 translate   %Define front face
    gsave 1 setgray
            SetExpo
    grestore


    gsave
            53 80 translate 1 setgray
            SetMacWorld
    grestore
grestore    %%end of title
```

Two definitions, SetExpo and SetMacWorld, describe the words in the title. For each character in the title, there is first a *moveto*, then the new shear is described using the *makefont* operator, and finally the character is defined and placed. These definitions are then used in the placement of the shadow, followed by the definition for the front face of the title. If you are rendering this yourself, make sure that it is placed against a medium-gray background.

Alternatively, you could strip the image in, having defined an origin point and made use of the *scale* command, shearing each letter multiple times and showing a slice of each iteration through a progressively moving window. This technique, however, has the particular effect of rendering the resolution of the printing device totally useless. Each iteration results in some "stairstepping," unless, of course, you are using increments that match the output resolution of the printer, i.e., 2540 windows every inch when using an L300 in high-res mode. If your artwork is anything other than the simplest image, it could be very time-consuming.

The only place where this technique becomes useful is in the imaging of distorted halftones (you'll find Adobe's code for that purpose on the Colophon disks). The halftone screen hides any aberrations created by the windowing, and one can image the artwork in far fewer strips.

TRANSLUCENCE

Many effects depend on the illusion of translucence. I say illusion because you can't really see through the objects. POSTSCRIPT uses a non-transparent ink principle (the object on top obscures the object below), so you have to create the impression of transparency when overlaying objects.

There are several ways of achieving a visual translucence. All of them have to do with a form of clipping. In a drawing application you can easily achieve a translucent effect by placing tones progressively on top of one another, taking care that the outline of the central tone fits exactly over the area where the tones intersect. My discussion of the *Graphic Perspective* logo in chapter 1 is a good example.

Shading and Reflectance

Perhaps one of the most popular forms of shading in POSTSCRIPT is the graduated shade, or fountain: stepping and incrementing toned lines or fills by either translating or scaling until a desired tonal value is reached. The PrintZip program in the blue book describes the procedure and, for most of us, it took little innovation or modification to produce graduated tones rather than type. The important thing to remember is that the tones should increment in single-point increments to get maximum speed efficiency while retaining a high level of image quality from the L300 typesetter.

In a very good example of how one can modify existing POSTSCRIPT code for other applications, other effects were attempted using the simple PrintZip *for* loop as a base. Suddenly, with a small of amount of modification, the very same code was being used to give the impression of shading and reflectance. Throw in a small highlight up at the top and a little depth to the upper left and we have an image that would be extremely difficult to achieve at the drafting table. Not impossible, merely expensive. Here's how the program looks in the modified form:

```
%!
gsave
100 100 translate

/PrintLine  %% define line procedure
{0 0 moveto 250 0 rlineto } def      %% length of line
```

```
/FadeBG      %% Definition for Background tone
{0 .01 1    %% "for" loop #1
{newpath setgray PrintLine stroke 0 -1 translate} for
} def


/String
{/Helvetica-Oblique findfont 48 scalefont setfont
(COMPUTE)show} def



/PrintTypeDepth   %% Definition for type depth
{/Helvetica-Oblique findfont 48 scalefont setfont 0 setgray
0 .125 1    %% "for" loop #2. basically the PrintZip program
{setgray 0 0 moveto String -.25 -.25 translate} for
} def


/Sheen       %% Definition for Sheen
{/Helvetica-Oblique findfont 48 scalefont setfont
2 2 moveto -2 -2 rmoveto
(COMPUTE)true charpath  %% Find the type's outline
clip  %% Clip it
gsave
    1 setgray fill    %% Fill front face of type with white
grestore
gsave 0 -4 translate 0 setgray      %% Move origin slightly below type baseline
    0 .03 1     %% "for" loop #3
    {newpath setgray PrintLine stroke 0 1 translate} for
grestore
```

Figure 13.4. Custom PostScript fountains (from the days when that was the only way to get fountains) give the impression of reflectance.

```
} def

gsave
     0 70 translate 0 setgray       %% Position background
     FadeBG       %% Set it
grestore

gsave  PrintTypeDepth  Sheen grestore

grestore
```

The *for* loop appears three times. The first loop increments the painting of a line from black to white, moving down each time in single-point increments. This creates the background. The second loop steps the setting of the word COMPUTE from black through to white, moving down and left .125 points each time. In the third version of the loop, the same original line is set, but this time inside the character outlines of the front face of the type, and moving upwards from black at the bottom to white at the top (see Figure 13.4).

For another example of depth and shading, check out the preceding section on Bathroom Graffiti.

Herb Paynter

As I sit at my keyboard ready to write a blow-by-blow description of the ABCs Poster (circa 1986, shown on Plate 4), I am conscious of the fact that more programmers will be reading this book than designers and lithographers.

Though this poster accomplished my goal of producing a very complex, purely PostScript color separation, I must confess that the project itself wore out what few endorphins I have left in my brain. If I had been actively involved with computer software for the last fifteen years, perhaps generating code would be a lot more intuitive (and no doubt a lot quicker). But, alas, I haven't . . . and it isn't! I am a designer and lithographer, not a programmer. For the last twenty-five years I have been involved in the preparation and production of printed materials. I was producing color separations when many of those reading this were throwing food from their high chairs. At the same time I am envious of those who can write code with such ease.

The major drawback to the serious development of color separation applications is a lack of understanding of the not-so-obvious basics of lithography. Producing a "separation" from a properly prepared PostScript file is not that earth-shattering. I mean, we're talking about splitting Red/Green/Blue and converting the values into Cyan/Yellow/Magenta/Black . . . big deal! The real magic is in the proper utilization of color "traps," and the correct choice of screen angles and frequencies. More on these issues shortly.

A lack of experiential depth has caused many applications, boasting separation capability to produce printing negatives that either don't fit on press or that produce obnoxious moiré patterns, or both. So rather than simply go through the code from a cold start, I think it best to mention a few of the basics of color separation and a couple of insights into the art of composing film (stripping).

Hang in there programmers! First we'll take a brief look at litho as seen through the eyes of an engraver. Those who have ventured into this chapter from the design/litho world will hold a distinct advantage over the computer techies, because you probably have some experience in pre-press requirements and terminology. I'll ask you to bear with me as I draw some rather poor analogies, and, in turn, I will attempt to walk you through the POSTSCRIPT code in a nonthreatening manner. I think that you will find the POSTSCRIPT page description language to be capable of handling your work from the design table through the stripping table.

Color Separations

Color separation is the process of dividing color artwork into three component colors: cyan (commonly called blue, but looks more like baby blue); magenta (known as red but looks more like a mellowed-down hot pink); and yellow. These are the three secondary colors on the color wheel, opposite the primary red, green, and blue, respectively. Typically a piece of artwork is placed either on a lithographic scanner or a camera, and filtered through the three primary color filters to produce three separate litho negatives. Black is added for contrast. When cyan, magenta, and yellow inks are printed, one on top of the other, the illusion of a "full-color picture" is produced. With the addition of a carefully produced black "printer" (printing terminology for each color's film in a separation), the separation can produce a reasonable facsimile of the original picture.

Though the process of "separating" our colors is quite different in POSTSCRIPT than in the traditional photographic method, many of the basic principles need to be understood to produce successful separation files.

FREQUENCY VS. LINES PER INCH

This is one of my favorite topics. Frequency is the rough equivalent of lines per inch. I say rough because POSTSCRIPT doesn't respond to a literal call for 133-line screen. For example, if you ask for 133 lines per inch, you will get 128, or something close.

In some ways this is insignificant. After all, printing presses can't read. Besides that, if they can hold a 133-line screen (print the full range of tones at a selected frequency of 133 halftone cells per linear inch without clogging up the darkest—shadow—tones), they should be able to handle 128. Incidentally, it takes some pretty sophisticated measurements to tell the difference between 128 and 133. The human eye simply can't perceive it.

But on the other hand, can you imagine the dynamic effects you could generate if you could combine PostScript graphic effects with a photographic separation from a litho scanner? Unfortunately, while the actual "frequency" of screens generated on a Hell scanner is not exactly 133, it is not PostScript's 128 either. Any mismatch in screens causes moiré patterns. The two types of separations can be combined on the stripping table, but the resulting trap (more on traps below) will show a pattern resembling cross-stitching.

ROSETTES VS. MOIRÉS

Rosettes are the visual dot clusters created by the proper angling of screens of similar line count. Moirés are the disturbing visual patterns created when rows of dots intersect each other at more (or less) than thirty-degree angles. The rule is as solid as granite: thirty degrees—no more, no less.

There is another way to produce a moiré. And as luck would have it, we get to tangle with this one more than the angular one. A moiré can be caused by two different frequencies of screens. That is, when a 133-line screen is overlaid by a screen of a different line count, say 134. Obviously you won't purposely request two different frequencies. You won't have to! PostScript will probably do it for you. It actually happens automatically every time you rotate a screen. This is undoubtedly one of the most challenging issues to face developers, and it has to do with the relationship between frequency and angles.

There is a significant change in actual line-per-inch measurement as the PostScript screens are rotated. This means that you face the possibility that your four negatives will have four different line counts. Even though the difference is sometimes a mere fraction of a line, remember, any mismatch in screens causes moiré patterns. Some of us are working feverishly to determine the correct combination of angles and frequencies, and though I find that frequency/angle options are few, there are several (ironically, the most frequently specified) that do work fine.

For more on the vagaries of PostScript screen frequencies and angles, and some code to work with those vagaries, see chapter 10, "Real World PostScript Halftoning."

TRAPS

The term trap has little to do with animals or football in this context. A trap is the overlapping of one color into another. Successive impressions (one for each color ink used) may not—and probably won't—align perfectly on press. Basically, a trap is the enlarging of one or the other color surface areas for the purpose of causing a slight overlapping of the two colors. This overlapping assures the proper fit on press, even if the sheet does bounce slightly between impression cylinders. Of course, the real question is which to enlarge. The answer is logical. Since cyan is a "darker" color than magenta, then magenta gets the call.

How do we print our "rim" of magenta to be overlapped by the cyan circle? In the stripping department, we would shrink the knockout mask on the magenta printer, allowing a small rim of red to be "trapped" or overprinted by the cyan circle. In POSTSCRIPT, we will start by creating the magenta square and overlapping the square with a cyan circle. That's normal. But here comes the trick. First, fill the circle with cyan and stroke it with both cyan and magenta. Then create a second circle (directly on top of the first) and fill it with cyan. A one-point thick stroke equates to a half-point trap and is sufficient for most printing requirements.

Traps make allowances for the multitude of gremlins who live in printing plants. There isn't a printing press known to man that can print tight registration without the proper traps. Take this one to the bank: you *must* include traps in your separations if you want to play in the big league.

To presume that I can relate the complexities of stripping procedures in this chapter is both a silly proposition and an insult to the litho trade. Whipping up Blender Hollandaise from your Betty Crocker cookbook won't make you a gourmet chef. This cursory illustration of a trap hardly addresses the issue of stripping procedures. For that, I suggest you contact your local engraver and take a (litho) stripper to lunch.

Needless to say, unless software publishers learn the basics of litho prep requirements, or have the insight to put an engraver on staff as an advisor, POSTSCRIPT separations will be viewed by the printing/engraving community as little more than a novelty.

Starting at the Beginning

POSTSCRIPT is a very colorful and capable page description language, but to get the most out of it you must understand the basic rules of the game. We will start with a few of the most obvious ones as they apply to the poster.

If you are beginning a file to be downloaded to a PostScript printer, there are only a couple of mandatory things that you *must* perform. One of these is the placement of %! at the very beginning of the file and showpage at the very end. The first notifies the printer that a PostScript file is coming (i.e., no Laser Prep file needed), and the last tells the printer to print the file. I don't want to admit how many times I have written a rather complex file, waited ten minutes for the download to be completed, and had nothing come out of the LaserWriter! Before I discovered that I simply hadn't finished my file with a showpage, I had rewritten most of the code. Don't laugh, it will happen to you!

Another thing PostScript allows you to do is work in your own language. For example, using the line: /in { 72 mul } def enables me to specify places and positions on the page in coordinates I am highly familiar with. The line of code merely has the printer convert inches to points. You should also gain a healthy respect for the two words gsave and grestore; they might just save your life (or at least your sanity). Look at the simple definition that follows:

```
/LetterBox{
        0 0 moveto
        1 in 0 rlineto
        0 1 in rlineto
        -1 in 0 rlineto
        closepath
} def
```

The LetterBox path is built and the routine ends with *closepath*. When we invoke LetterBox, we will start with a 144 144 moveto and follow with a LetterBox *gsave* before we fill the path. Now we call back our graphics state to stroke the line. Since the *fill* command automatically resets the graphics state, it is imperative that we recall our currentpoint location so that we stroke the same path that we filled.

Have you ever wondered how large discount stores handle massive quantities of materials? They employ a warehouse inventory coding system that specifies each product by a simple name/number combination. This item is probably well stocked in the warehouse, and as needed, each item is delivered to a specified location in the store.

This is a pretty good idea as far as I'm concerned. After all, can you imagine a department store that keeps every item in stock out on the main floor? Moving around would be awkward, to say the least! (You can appreciate this even more if you have a teenager living in your house.)

In many ways, the PostScript "housekeeping" method of organizing things is like our department store. We can describe, in full detail, a very complex object, tag the definition, and put the object in our file's "warehouse" (much like the inventory code at our department store). Now every time we want one of these objects to appear at a specific place, we just identify the desired "delivery point" and call for the object. Thus, 144 288 LetterBox is a call back to our warehouse requesting that one LetterBox be delivered and constructed at the intersection of 2-inch Avenue and 4-inch Street, N.E.

Since everything in PostScript consists of opaque layers of tone/color information, we'll start our page description at the bottom layer. First we construct a background. This is nothing more than a large filled rectangle:

```
/BackgroundBox{
      0 0 moveto
      6.5 in 0 rlineto
      0 8.5 in rlineto
      -6.5 in 0 rlineto
      closepath
} def
```

The background in the poster (see Plate 4) is a cream color, but we'll get to the color breakdown later. For the moment, we'll concentrate on constructing the elements of our page in simple black-and-white.

The next element in our layered stack are the shadows cast by the letter boxes. Since the shadows are approximately the same size as the letter boxes themselves, we can use the generic LetterBox element for both shadows and letter boxes. To invoke it, I simply call for LetterBox, and the specified LetterBox will appear. The shade or tone is then applied.

PostScript's ability to include one definition within a more complex definition, as long as the first appears as a complete definition first, is a strong point. Once the definitions are established I am ready to call for these elements and place them at the desired locations on the page. Keep in mind that when we call for our LetterBox (since we drew it so that the "basepoint" of the LetterBox is at the lower left corner), we will be locating the lower-left corner of this LetterBox at a specific intersection on the page.

I choose to keep all my definitions at the beginning of the file, though there is no hard, fast rule about this. As long as a definition precedes the call for that definition, all is legal. I am simply one who likes to keep all my socks on the same side of the same drawer (and all the black ones separate from the blue ones). It's easier to find things that way. As you will see in the actual code for this file, PostScript files can be wordy; Thus, good housekeeping is the first rule of order.

Comments

It's also a good idea to make judicious use of the commenting ability to keep pockets of code well defined. This is done simply by inserting a % to the right of the line of code, followed by a very human explanation of what that line of code is doing. A comment may include several lines of explanation as long as each line of comment is preceded by a %. I find this is very helpful when trouble-shooting a file or trying to grasp the full ramifications of a concat call.

No job can be endured without a little levity, and PostScript has its share, particularly when creating names of definitions. Note the definition of BOWF on page 271. Since, to me, definitions should correlate with their names, I chose to remember the routine as the one that delivers a Black Outline and a White Fill. The tag seemed appropriate. Of course, I could have named it LampShade or any other combination of letters and numbers, and it would have performed the same function. The only restriction on definition names is that they be limited to one word.

Though most of the basic definitions are located in the "header" (that portion of the file that precedes the actual program), small variations of each definition may be defined and redefined within the program itself. There is no actual limit to the size of your header. The file discussed here has a pretty healthy one. Once all our definitions have been completed, we can move on to the actual program.

DEFINITIONS

As I said, I prefer to have all my definitions up at the head of the file, so I can simply call them further down. This modular approach makes for a structured, organized approach to building pages.

The following calls are all defined in code near the head of the document.

```
%statusdict begin negativeprint true def end
```

This makes the file print negative. Comment-out (place a % in front of) this line when printing out this file on a laser printer.

Following is abbreviated code to determine the correct angle and frequency of each color. The words Poster, Seps, and Angle (along with the appropriate angle) will appear at the beginning of each color's file:

```
/Poster {currentscreen /p exch def   } def      %Get spot function
/Seps { pop pop 150 } def      %Toss frequency & angle, set freq to 150
/Angle {/p load setscreen } def      %Assign angle (set for each color)
```

A small formula that translates points to inches.

```
/in {72 mul } def
```

Definitions for the locations of various "intersections" on the page. C stands for column and R stands for row:

```
/C1 {1 in } def
/C2 {2.5 in  } def
/C3 {4 in } def
/C4 {5.5 in } def
/R1 { .4 in translate } def
/R2 { 1.6 in translate } def
/R3 { 2.8 in translate } def
/R4 { 4 in translate } def
/R5 { 5.2 in translate } def
/R6 { 6.4 in translate } def
/R7 { 7.6 in translate } def
```

NudgeNE is the distance, common to all letters, from the shadow to the letter itself:

```
/NudgeNE { 6 6 translate } def
```

OutLine is a one-point-thick black outline:

```
/OutLine { 1 setlinewidth 0 setgray stroke } def
```

This self-explanatory code just makes the file appear more "human" and easier to navigate:

```
/White {1 setgray} def
/WhiteFill {1 setgray fill }def
```

Here's our famous routine that draws a black outline around an object filled with white:

```
/BOWF {gsave WhiteFill grestore OutLine } def
```

A one-inch-by-one-inch square path. Note that we have neither stroked (outlined) nor filled this path at this point. This will happen as we encounter each letter's characteristics:

```
/LetterBox{
       0 0 moveto
       1 in 0 rlineto
       0 1 in rlineto
       -1 in 0 rlineto
       closepath
} def
```

The overall background panel:

```
/BackgroundBox{
       0 0 moveto
       6.5 in 0 rlineto
       0 8.5 in rlineto
       -6.5 in 0 rlineto
       closepath
} def
```

A clipping region (or mask) used to filter the *fill* command for the letter T:

```
/HalfLetterBox {
     newpath
     0 0 moveto
     0 1 in rlineto
     .5 in 0 rlineto
     0 -1 in  rlineto
     closepath
} def
```

The (Color)BoxShadow routine stages a series of overprinting lines that decrease in thickness as they increase in value. If you visualize this as a topographical map, you'll sort of get the idea. The illusion created is that of a soft-edged shadow. This routine must be used in combination with, and behind, a path description such as LetterBox above:

```
/CBoxShadow   {
1 setlinejoin   LetterBox
gsave
     3 setlinewidth .90 setgray stroke
grestore
gsave
     2 setlinewidth .87 setgray stroke
grestore
gsave
     1 setlinewidth .84 setgray stroke
grestore
     .81 setgray  fill
} def
```

In similar fashion to LetterBox, this routine will create the large panel for our title block:

```
/TitleBox {
     0 0 moveto
     2.66 in 0 rlineto
     0 1.05 in rlineto
     -2.66 in 0 rlineto
```

```
      closepath
} def
```

Similar to BoxShadow above, the (Color)TitleBlockShadow routine will build the shadows behind our title block. Since each color has its own tint values, we itemize them accordingly:

```
/BlackTitleBlockShadow {
      1 setlinejoin 1 setlinewidth
      3 setlinewidth .95 setgray TitleBox stroke
      2 setlinewidth .93 setgray TitleBox stroke
      TitleBox .90 setgray fill
} def
```

Using the basic Title(Color)Box routine, we assign the appropriate color fills for each color.

```
/TitleBlackBox { TitleBox 0 setgray fill } def
```

This piece of code creates a series of lines that radiate from a common basepoint and are separated by a specified angle. Note that the user determines both the starting and ending angles (0 angle is at three o'clock).

```
/Rays {
      0 setgray .4 setlinewidth
      0       % Determine starting angle
      8       % Determine degree interval
      90      % Determine ending angle
      {
      gsave rotate
            newpath 0 0  moveto      % Determine starting position
            1.5 in 0 lineto stroke   % Determine line length
      grestore
      } for
} def
```

A centered line:

```
/lineto {
      newpath  0 10 moveto 1 setlinewidth
```

```
        .65 in 0 rmoveto -.65 in 0 rlineto stroke
} def
```

A vignette routine (also known as a fountain or fade) based on stepped, gray-shaded lines:

```
/SingleLineVignette  {
gsave
        1.5 .5 scale
        .1  .01  .9  {setgray lineto  0  1 translate } for
grestore
} def
```

Another centered line, but offset vertically to start at the middle of the box:

```
/Line {
        newpath   0 78 moveto
        .75 in 0 rmoveto
        -.75 in 0 rlineto stroke
} def
```

Similar to SingleLineVignette but written to build two vignettes, one graduating up from the middle of the box, and one graduating down:

```
/LineVignette {
gsave
        1.5 .5 scale .
        9  -.01 .1 {setgray Line 0 1 translate} for
grestore
gsave
        1.5 .5 scale .
        9 -.01 .1 {setgray Line 0 -1 translate } for
grestore
} def
```

The same routine as above with the direction of the line progression reversed:

```
/RevLineVignette {
gsave
        1.5 .5 scale  .1  .01 .9  {setgray Line  01 translate } for
```

```
grestore
gsave
        1.5 .5 scale .1 .01 .9  {setgray Line 0 -1 translate } for
grestore
}def
```

The thick bars utilized in the letter m, created for the various colors:

```
/CHorizontalBars { .9 setgray HorizontalBars } def
```

Shortened versions of Times-Bold and Times-Roman findfont:

```
/TR { /Times-Roman findfont } def
/TRB { /Times-Bold findfont } def
```

A shortened version of scalefont setfont:

```
/SS { scalefont setfont } def
```

This word encapsulates all the jargon necessary to set up the letters in the poster. Instead of rattling off /Times-Bold findfont 72 scalefont setfont every time we want a letter in our alphabet, we will simply ask for CapLetter :

```
/CapLetter {TRB 72 SS} def
```

A shortened version of true charpath:

```
/TC { true charpath } def
```

DLetter contains the character information needed for the letter D:

```
/DLetter {CapLetter 5 13 moveto (D) show } def
```

WLetters contains the character information needed for all sizes of the letter W:

```
/WLetters {
      TRB 24 SS 0 10 moveto (W) show
      TRB 48 SS 19 10 moveto .6 1.03 scale (W) show
      CapLetter 74 10 moveto .6 1.03 scale (W) show
} def
```

The character information needed for the Z, large size "G," and small size G:

```
/ZLetter   {CapLetter newpath 5 5 moveto (Z) show } def
/GLetter { CapLetter (G) } def
/SmallGLetter {TRB 36 SS (G) } def
```

White 2-point-thick outline of the Large G:

```
/KOG {
       -28 -24  moveto White
       GLetter 2 setlinewidth TC stroke
grestore } def
```

(color)GLetterEffect gives the tints of each color (see prefix) needed for the ''rotating G'' effect:

```
/KGLetterEffect {
       /Koshow {TC stroke} def
       /circleofKGs {
            30 30 360
            {gsave
                   rotate 0 0 moveto SmallGLetter Koshow
            grestore
            }
            for
       }def
       gsave .5 setlinewidth 36 36 translate circleofKGs KOG
} def
```

A special trapezoid shape to be used for the translucent panel in the letter I:

```
/WindowPane {
       newpath 30 63 moveto
       -17  -32 rlineto
       19  -25 rlineto
       30  59 rlineto
       closepath
}def
```

The clipping region used to filter the tinted version of the letter I:

```
/WindowPaneMask {
      newpath 30 63 moveto
      -17  -32 rlineto
      14   -16 rlineto
      30   59 rlineto
      closepath clip
} def
```

A register mark made up of a horizontal line through a small circle, with all lines stroked on 1/10-point thickness:

```
/HorRegistermark {
      newpath -.125 in 0 in moveto
      .125 in 0 in lineto .1 setlinewidth stroke
      newpath 0 in 0 in .05 in 0 360 arc stroke
} def
```

The same register mark with a vertical line instead of horizontal:

```
/VertRegistermark {
      newpath 0 in .125 in moveto
      0 in -.125 in lineto .1 setlinewidth stroke
      newpath 0 in 0 in .05 in 0 360 arc stroke
} def
```

This routine places the register marks at the appropriate positions on the page:

```
/CenterMarks {
      gsave
            3.875 in 9 in translate VertRegistermark  % Top CenterMark
      grestore
      gsave
            3.875 in -.5 in translate VertRegistermark      % BottomCenterMark
      grestore
      gsave
            .5 in 4.675 in translate HorRegistermark  % Left CenterMark
      grestore
      gsave
            7.375 in 4.675 in translate HorRegistermark     % Right CenterMark
      grestore
```

```
}def
save
```

Note that at the end of the definitions we placed a *save* command. This means that we are taking a snapshot of these definitions so we can recall all of them at the beginning of each new file, rather than rewriting them (the command *showpage* at the end of each file purges all information from the printed file).

The Program

At this point we will begin our task of implementing our individual letter designs. Since we know that each letter will be placed against a common-sized background element, we will begin each letter's description with a call for (Color)BoxShadow (except for the Black printer, since our shadows are made of cyan, magenta, and yellow only) and then ask for NudgeNE to move the currentpoint up and to the right to begin the LetterBox routine.

Rather than explaining every step in the following code twice, I refer you to the comments.

```
%!
serverdict begin 0 exitserver

statusdict begin negativeprint true def
0 setjobtimeout
end


[ -1 0 0 1 1 1 ] concat
-594 0 translate
.78 .78 scale


%%%%%%% Coordinates %%%%%%%%%%%%%


/Poster {currentscreen /p exch def   } def
/Seps { pop pop 150 } def
/Angle {/p load setscreen } def
```

```
/in {72 mul } def
/C1 {1 in } def
/C2 {2.5 in  } def
/C3 {4 in } def
/C4 {5.5 in } def
/R1 { .4 in translate } def
/R2 { 1.6 in translate } def
/R3 { 2.8 in translate } def
/R4 { 4 in translate } def
/R5 { 5.2 in translate } def
/R6 { 6.4 in translate } def
/R7 { 7.6 in translate } def
/NudgeNE { 6 6 translate } def
/OutLine { 1 setlinewidth 0 setgray stroke } def
/White {1 setgray} def
/WhiteFill {1 setgray fill }def
/BOWF {gsave WhiteFill grestore OutLine } def


%%%%%%%%%%  BoxRoutines %%%%%%%%%%%%%%


/LetterBox{
0 0 moveto
1 in 0 rlineto
0 1 in rlineto
-1 in 0 rlineto
closepath
} def


/TitleBox {
0 0 moveto
2.66 in 0 rlineto
0 1.05 in rlineto
-2.66 in 0 rlineto
closepath
} def


/BackgroundBox{
0 0 moveto
6.5 in 0 rlineto
0 8.5 in rlineto
```

```
-6.5 in 0 rlineto
closepath
} def


/HalfLetterBox { newpath 0 0 moveto
0 1 in rlineto
.5 in 0 rlineto
0 -1 in  rlineto
closepath} def


%%%%%%%%  Shadow Routines %%%%%%%%%


/CyanShadow {1 setlinejoin  LetterBox
gsave
     3 setlinewidth .90 setgray stroke
grestore
gsave
     2 setlinewidth .87 setgray stroke
grestore
gsave
     1 setlinewidth .84 setgray stroke
grestore
     .81 setgray  fill
} def


/MagShadow  {1 setlinejoin
gsave
     3 setlinewidth .95 setgray stroke
grestore
gsave
     2 setlinewidth .92 setgray stroke
grestore
gsave
     1 setlinewidth .89 setgray stroke
grestore
     .86 setgray  fill
} def


/YellShadow  {1 setlinejoin
gsave
```

```
        3 setlinewidth .70 setgray stroke
grestore
gsave
        2 setlinewidth .67 setgray stroke
grestore
gsave
        1 setlinewidth .63 setgray stroke
grestore
        .60 setgray   fill
} def


/CBoxShadow   {   LetterBox CyanShadow } def
/MBoxShadow   {   LetterBox MagShadow} def
/YBoxShadow   {   LetterBox YellShadow} def


/BlackTitleBlockShadow  { TitleBox CyanShadow } def
/MagTitleBlockShadow  { TitleBox MagShadow} def
/YelTitleBlockShadow  { TitleBox YellShadow} def



%%%%%%%  ColorTitleBlock Routines %%%%%%%


/TitleBlackBox { TitleBox  0 setgray fill } def


/TitleBlueBox  { TitleBox .6 setgray fill } def


/TitleMagBox   { TitleBox WhiteFill } def


/TitleYeloBox  { TitleBox WhiteFill } def


%%%%%%%%%%   Rays Routine %%%%%%%%%%%


/Rays { 0 setgray .4 setlinewidth
        0                                        % Determine starting angle
        8                                        % Determine degree interval
        90                                       % Determine ending angle
{ gsave rotate
 newpath 0 0  moveto            % Determine starting position
  1.5 in 0 lineto stroke           % Determine line length
```

```
grestore
} for } def


%%%%%%%%   LineVignette Routines %%%%%%%%


/SingleLine {
  newpath  0 10 moveto 1 setlinewidth
  .65 in 0 rmoveto -.65 in 0 rlineto stroke
} def


/SingleLineVignette  {
gsave
  1.5 .5 scale
  .1  .01  .9  {setgray SingleLine  0  1 translate } for
grestore
} def


/Line { newpath  0 78 moveto
.75 in 0 rmoveto  -.75 in 0 rlineto stroke} def


/LineVignette {
gsave
 1.5 .5 scale .9 -.01 .1 {setgray Line 0 1 translate} for
grestore
gsave
  1.5 .5 scale .9 -.01 .1 {setgray Line 0 -1 translate } for  grestore
}def


/RevLineVignette {
gsave
  1.5 .5 scale  .1  .01 .9  {setgray Line  0 1 translate } for
grestore
gsave
  1.5 .5 scale .1 .01 .9  {setgray Line 0 -1 translate } for  grestore
}def


%%%%%  HorizontalBars Routines  %%%%%%%%


/HorizontalBars { 7 setlinewidth newpath
0 10 72 { 0 exch moveto  72 0 rlineto } for  stroke } def
```

```
/CHorizontalBars { .9 setgray HorizontalBars } def


/MHorizontalBars { .7 setgray HorizontalBars } def


/YHorizontalBars {0 setgray HorizontalBars } def


%%%%%%%%%% Letter Routines %%%%%%%%%%%%


/TR { /Times-Roman findfont } def


/TRB { /Times-Bold findfont } def


/SS { scalefont setfont } def
/CapLetter {TRB 72 SS} def


/TC { true charpath } def


/DLetter {CapLetter 5 13 moveto (D) show } def


/WLetters { TRB 24 SS 0 10 moveto (W) show
  TRB 48 SS 19 10 moveto .6 1.03 scale (W) show
  CapLetter 74 10 moveto .6 1.03 scale (W) show } def


/ZLetter  {CapLetter newpath 5 5 moveto (Z) show } def



%%%%%%%%%% G Routines %%%%%%%%%%%%
/GLetter { CapLetter (G) } def


/SmallGLetter {TRB 36 SS (G) } def


/KOG { -28 -24  moveto White
GLetter 2 setlinewidth TC stroke
grestore } def


/KGLetterEffect {
/Koshow {TC stroke} def
/circleofKGs {30 30 360
   {gsave rotate 0 0 moveto SmallGLetter Koshow grestore }for }def
   gsave .5 setlinewidth 36 36 translate circleofKGs KOG } def
```

```
/CMGLetterEffect {
/CMoshow {TC .8 setgray fill } def
/circleofCMGs {30 30 360
  {gsave rotate 0 0 moveto SmallGLetter CMoshow grestore }for }def
  gsave .5 setlinewidth 36 36 translate circleofCMGs KOG } def


/YGLetterEffect {
/Yoshow {TC .5 setgray fill } def
/circleofYGs {30 30 360
  {gsave rotate 0 0 moveto SmallGLetter Yoshow grestore }for }def
gsave .5 setlinewidth 36 36 translate circleofYGs KOG } def


%%%%%  WindowPane Routines  %%%%%%


/WindowPane {
newpath 30 63 moveto
 -17  -32 rlineto
  19  -25 rlineto
  30  59 rlineto
 closepath  }def


/WindowPaneMask {
newpath 30 63 moveto
 -17  -32 rlineto
  14  -16 rlineto
  30  59 rlineto
 closepath clip } def


%%%%% CenterMarks %%%%%%%%%%


/HorRegistermark
  { newpath -.125 in 0 in moveto
  .125 in 0 in lineto .1 setlinewidth stroke
  newpath 0 in 0 in .05 in 0 in 360 arc stroke} def


/VertRegistermark
  { newpath 0 in .125 in moveto
   0 in -.125 in lineto .1 setlinewidth stroke
   newpath 0 in 0 in .05 in 0 in 360 arc stroke} def
```

```
/CenterMarks {
gsave
   3.875 in 9 in translate VertRegistermark
% Top CenterMark
grestore
gsave
   3.875 in -.5 in translate VertRegistermark
% BottomCenterMark
grestore
gsave
   .5 in 4.675 in translate HorRegistermark
% Left CenterMark
grestore
gsave
   7.375 in 4.675 in translate HorRegistermark
% Right CenterMark
grestore
}def


0 72 moveto currentpoint translate


save



%%%%%%  BLACK PRINTER  %%%%%%%%%
%% Poster (BLACK)        %Visual reminder of the color printer
Poster Seps  45 Angle       %Set angle to 45° for the black printer


%%%%%%%%%%  A  %%%%%%%%%%%%%%
gsave
     C1 R7 NudgeNE LetterBox  BOWF %Page coordinates, white box, black outline
     CapLetter 10 13 moveto (A) TC stroke     %Outline the "A"
grestore


%%%%%%%%%%  B  %%%%%%%%%%%%%%
gsave
     C1  R6 NudgeNE LetterBox  BOWF       %Page coordinates, white box, black outline
grestore
```

```
%%%%%%%%%%   C   %%%%%%%%%%%%%%%%%%
gsave
        C1 R5 NudgeNE LetterBox  BOWF        %Page coordinates, white box, black outline
        CapLetter 7 10 moveto (C) TC  stroke      %Outline the "C"
grestore


%%%%%%%%%%   D   %%%%%%%%%%%%%%%%%%
gsave
        C1 R4 NudgeNE LetterBox  BOWF        %Page coordinates, white box, black outline
gsave %Remember this coordinate
        [1 0 .7 1 0 0] concat 1 .5 scale 0 setgray fill %Skew, scale and set the color to black
        -.05 in  .175 in translate  DLetter %Jockey our position and paint the letter "D"
grestore    %Restore our last coordinate
        White DLetter        %Paint a white normal "D" on top of the black
                             % to "knock-out" a place for the colored letter
grestore


%%%%%%%%%%   E  %%%%%%%%%%%%%%%%%%
gsave
        C1 R3 NudgeNE LetterBox  BOWF        %Page coordinates, white box, black outline
grestore


%%%%%%%%%%   F   %%%%%%%%%%%%%%%%%%
gsave
        C1 R2 NudgeNE LetterBox   BOWF        %Page coordinates, white box, black outline
grestore


%%%%%%%%%%   G   %%%%%%%%%%%%%%%%%%
gsave
        C1 R1 NudgeNE LetterBox  BOWF        %Page coordinates, white box, black outline
KGLetterEffect    %Black version of "G" (see definitions)
grestore


%%%%%%%%%%   H   %%%%%%%%%%%%%%%%%%
gsave
        C2  R7 NudgeNE LetterBox BOWF %Page coordinates, white box, black outline
grestore


%%%%%%%%%%   I   %%%%%%%%%%%%%%%%%%
gsave
        C2  R6 NudgeNE  LetterBox  BOWF        %Coordinates, white box, black outline
```

```
     CapLetter 22 10 moveto  (I)  0 setgray  show      %Paint a solid black "I"
     WindowPane  clip  %Call our "WindowPane" routine for a mask
     CapLetter 22 10 moveto (I) .8 setgray show       %Filter a 20% "I" thru the mask
gsave %Remember these coordinates
     WindowPaneMask       %Call our WindowPaneMask routine
     CapLetter 22 10 moveto  (I)  0 setgray  show    %Filter a solid black "I" thru this mask
grestore   %Restore our coordinates
     WindowPane OutLine     %Paint a black outline around the first mask
grestore


%%%%%%%%%%  J  %%%%%%%%%%%%%%%%%%
gsave
     C2 R4 NudgeNE LetterBox  BOWF       %Page coordinates, white box, black outline
grestore


%%%%%%%%%%  K  %%%%%%%%%%%%%%%%%%
gsave
     C2 R3 NudgeNE LetterBox  BOWF       %Page coordinates, white box, black outline
grestore


%%%%%%%%%%  L  %%%%%%%%%%%%%%%%%%
gsave
     C2 R2 NudgeNE LetterBox  BOWF       %Page coordinates, white box, black outline
grestore


%%%%%%%%%%  M  %%%%%%%%%%%%%%%%%%
gsave
C2 R1 NudgeNE LetterBox  BOWF       %Page coordinates, white box, black outline
TRB 88 SS 0 13 moveto (m) .5 setlinewidth TC stroke   %Specify 88 pt "m" and paint it as an outline
grestore


%%%%%%%%%%  N  %%%%%%%%%%%%%%%%%%
gsave
     C3 R7 NudgeNE LetterBox  BOWF       %Page coordinates, white box, black outline
grestore


%%%%%%%%%%  O  %%%%%%%%%%%%%%%%%%
gsave
     C3 R6 NudgeNE LetterBox  BOWF       %Page coordinates, white box, black outline
     CapLetter 7 13 moveto (O)  TC  stroke     %Paint "O" as an outline
```

```
grestore


%%%%%%%%%%   P  %%%%%%%%%%%%%%%%%%
gsave
       C3 R4 NudgeNE LetterBox   BOWF       %Page coordinates, white box, black outline
grestore


%%%%%%%%%%   Q  %%%%%%%%%%%%%%%%%%
gsave
       C3 R3 NudgeNE LetterBox   BOWF       %Page coordinates, white box, black outline
grestore


%%%%%%%%%%   R  %%%%%%%%%%%%%%%%%%
gsave
       C3 R2 NudgeNE LetterBox   BOWF       %Page coordinates, white box, black outline
       TRB 120 SS 10 10 moveto (r) TC       %Specify 120 pt "r"
gsave       %Remember this character path
       .9 setgray fill    %Fill it with a 10% tint
grestore     %Restore 120 pt "r"
       White 4 setlinewidth stroke    %Paint the path with a 4 pt white outline
       TRB 24 SS 0 setgray       %Specify 24 pt Times Roman Bold
       10 9  moveto (RRR) TC        %Page coordinates, specify 3 "R"s
gsave      %Remember this character path
       WhiteFill    %Fill it with white
grestore     %Restore the character path
       .4 setlinewidth stroke  %Paint the path (still white) with .4 pt outline
       10 29 moveto (RRR) TC        %Page coordinates, specify 3 "R"s
gsave      %Remember this character path
       WhiteFill       %Fill it with white
grestore     %Restore the character path
       .4 setlinewidth stroke  %Paint the path (still white) with .4 pt outline
       10 49 moveto (RRR) TC        %Page coordinates, specify 3 "R"s
gsave      %Remember this character path
       WhiteFill    %Fill it with white
grestore     %Restore the character path
       .4 setlinewidth stroke  %Paint the path (still white) with .4 pt outline
grestore


%%%%%%%%%%   S  %%%%%%%%%%%%%%%%%%
gsave
       C3 R1 NudgeNE LetterBox   BOWF        %Page coordinates, white box, black outline
```

```
grestore


%%%%%%%%%   T  %%%%%%%%%%%%%%%%%
gsave
      C4 R7 NudgeNE LetterBox  BOWF        %Page coordinates, white box, black outline
grestore


%%%%%%%%%   U  %%%%%%%%%%%%%%%%%
gsave
      C4 R6 NudgeNE LetterBox  BOWF        %Page coordinates, white box, black outline
grestore


%%%%%%%%%   V  %%%%%%%%%%%%%%%%%
gsave
      C4 R5 NudgeNE LetterBox        %Page coordinates, box path
gsave       %Remember this path
     .05 setgray fill  %Fill it with 95% tint
grestore    %Restore this path
     OutLine      %Outline box
     CapLetter 8 10 moveto (V) TC  %Specify capitol "V" character path
     1 setlinejoin      %Specify rounded paths
     gsave 15 setlinewidth .1 setgray stroke grestore
     %Set the line width and paint it 90 % black
     gsave 14 setlinewidth .2 setgray stroke grestore
     %Set the line width and paint it 80 % black
     gsave 13 setlinewidth .3 setgray stroke grestore
     %Set the line width and paint it 70 % black
     gsave 12 setlinewidth .4 setgray stroke grestore
     %Set the line width and paint it 60 % black
     gsave 11 setlinewidth .5 setgray stroke grestore
     %Set the line width and paint it 50 % black
     gsave 10 setlinewidth .65 setgray stroke grestore
     %Set the line width and paint it 35 % black
     gsave 9 setlinewidth .8 setgray stroke grestore
     %Set the line width and paint it 20 % black
     gsave 8 setlinewidth .9 setgray stroke grestore
     %Set the line width and paint it 10 % black
     gsave 7 setlinewidth White stroke grestore
     %Set the line width and paint it white
grestore
```

```
%%%%%%%%%%  W  %%%%%%%%%%%%%%%%%%
gsave
      C4 R4 NudgeNE LetterBox  BOWF        %Page coordinates, white box, black outline
grestore


%%%%%%%%%%  X  %%%%%%%%%%%%%%%%%%
gsave
      C4 R3 NudgeNE LetterBox  BOWF        %Page coordinates, white box, black outline
      %Specify "X" character path, paint it black
      CapLetter 10 13 moveto (X) TC 0  setgray  stroke
grestore


%%%%%%%%%%  Y  %%%%%%%%%%%%%%%%%%
gsave
      C4 R2 NudgeNE LetterBox        %Page coordinates, box path
      gsave       %Remember path and original graphics state
          40 90 { exch pop abs 1 exch sub } setscreen   %Specify 40 line, vertical line screen
          .85 setgray fill  %Specify 15% tint (line screen equivalent)
      grestore     %Restore this path and graphics state
      OutLine CapLetter 10 10 moveto (Y) TC   %Specify "Y" as a character path
      gsave       %Remember this path
          clip       %Utilize it as a template
          gsave        %Remember the new graphics state
              0 setgray fill       %Paint the "Y" black
          grestore       %Restore the new graphics state
          newpath 8.5 8.5 moveto (Y) TC   %New coordinates, specify "Y" character path
          40 90 { exch pop abs 1 exch sub } setscreen   %Specify 40 line, vertical line screen
          .35 setgray fill  %Specify 65% tint (line screen equivalent)
      grestore     %Restore the original graphics state
      .4 setlinewidth stroke  %Set the line width and outline character path
grestore


%%%%%%%%%%  Z  %%%%%%%%%%%%%%%%%%
gsave
      C4 R1 NudgeNE LetterBox  OutLine     %Page coordinates, white box, black outline
grestore


%%%%%%%%%%  TitleBlackLetterBox  %%%%%%%%%%
gsave
      C2  R5      10 10 translate TitleBlackBox %Page coordinates, solid black box
```

```
grestore


%%%%%%%%%  TitleBlock Copy  %%%%%%%%%%%%%%%%%
gsave
      White        %Specify white
      2.755 in 6.2 in moveto .67 1.3 scale TR 13 SS   %Coordinates, specify condensed type
      (ImageXpress Incorporated  \267  Graphic Fine Color) show   %Enter type string
grestore
gsave
      White        %Specify white
      2.7 in 6.0 in moveto .5 1 scale TR 13 SS  %Coordinates, specify condensed type
      (6479 Peachtree Ind. Blvd.  \267  Atlanta, GA 30360)show    %Enter type string
      9.2 in 6.0 in moveto (  \267  \(404\)  458-5444)show      %New coordinates, type string
grestore
gsave
      2.68 in C4    moveto 1.17 1.13 scale TRB 40 SS White      %Coordinates, scale type to fit
                    (T) show    %This headline is carefully kerned
      -8 0 rmoveto (y) show    % letter by letter, for optimal visual
      -5 0 rmoveto (p) show    % style and is painted white
      -2 0 rmoveto (e) show
      -2 0 rmoveto (S) show
      -2 0 rmoveto (t) show
      -2 0 rmoveto (y) show
      -3 0 rmoveto (l) show
      -3 0 rmoveto (e) show
      -2 0 rmoveto (s) show
grestore



%%%%%%%%%  Tag Line Copy  %%%%%%%%%%%%%%%%%
gsave
      0 -.25 in translate .925 in  .35 in moveto       %Coordinates
      /Symbol findfont 5 SS (\343)show   %Print a bullet (ASKII call)
      TR 5 SS ( 1988 Copyright Herb Paynter
      --All Rights Reserved.)show
      %Specify type, text string

      TRB 5 SS .925 in  0.25 in moveto (Special Thanks to:   )show      %Bold type, text string, etc.


      TR 5 SS (Herb Paynter-President and Creative Director, ImageXpress, Incorporated
```

```
\267 Gordon Wilkinson, WTB Ministries)show

    TRB 5 SS .925 in .18 in moveto  (Very Special Thanks to:   )show

    TR 5 SS (John Warnock and the entire ADOBE Systems team, for developing their
    versatile and powerful PostScript page description language.)show

    TRB 5 SS .925 in .05 in moveto  (Technical Information:   )show

TR 5 SS (All PostScript code was generated on a 5 megabyte Macintosh 2 computer with a 40
megabyte internal drive, proofed on a PS Jet Plus laser printer, and fully composed press-ready
\(RRED negative\) separation films were)show

    .925 in -.03 in moveto (output at medium resolution  \(1270\)  on WTB's Linotype L-
300 laser typesetter and Raster Image Processor at a litho screen ruling of 150 lines per inch
    \(Black-45\312, Cyan-105\312, Magenta-75\312, Yellow-90\312\))show
grestore

CenterMarks %Paint registration marks on file

%%%%%%%%  Begin Color Marks %%%%%%%%

C3 -.65 in moveto /Helvetica-Bold findfont 12 SS %Coordinates, specify font and size
(BLACK) 0 setgray show  %Paint "BLACK" with black

showpage     %Image the black file

restore      %Restore definitions for cyan printer

%%%%%%%%%%%%%%%%%%%%%%%%%%%%%%%%%%%%%%%%%%%%%

%% Poster (CYAN)  %Visual reminder of the color printer
Poster Seps 105 Angle   %Set angle to 105° for the cyan printer

save

%%%%%%%%%%  THE PROGRAM  %%%%%%%%%%%%

%%%%%%%  BackgroundBox  %%%%%%%%%%%%%%
```

```
gsave
       .675 in .3 in translate BackgroundBox WhiteFill %Paint background white
grestore


%%%%%%%%%%  A  %%%%%%%%%%%%%%%%%%
gsave
       C1 R7 CBoxShadow NudgeNE LetterBox  .7 setgray  fill
       %Coordinates, Shadow, 30% filled box
       CapLetter 10 13 moveto (A)  White show    %Drop white "A" out of background
grestore


%%%%%%%%%%  B  %%%%%%%%%%%%%%%%%%
gsave
       C1 R6 CBoxShadow NudgeNE LetterBox  White  fill
       %Coordinates, Shadow, white box
       CapLetter 34.55 13 moveto .7 1 scale (B) .25 setgray show
        %Specify and scale"B", paint as 75%
       -44 0 rmoveto -1 1 scale (B) .75 setgray show   %Coordinate move, mirror, paint 25%
grestore


%%%%%%%%%%  C  %%%%%%%%%%%%%%%%%%

gsave
       C1 R5 CBoxShadow NudgeNE LetterBox  WhiteFill   %Page coordinates, white box
grestore


%%%%%%%%%%  D  %%%%%%%%%%%%%%%%%%
gsave
       C1 R4 CBoxShadow NudgeNE LetterBox  WhiteFill   %Page coordinates, white box
grestore


%%%%%%%%%%  E  %%%%%%%%%%%%%%%%%%

gsave
       C1 R3 CBoxShadow NudgeNE LetterBox  WhiteFill   %Page coordinates, white box
grestore


%%%%%%%%%%  F  %%%%%%%%%%%%%%%%%%
gsave
       C1 R2 CBoxShadow NudgeNE LetterBox  WhiteFill   %Page coordinates, white box
```

```
     CapLetter 10 13 moveto 0 setgray (F) show %Font call, move, paint "F" solid cyan
grestore


%%%%%%%%%%  G  %%%%%%%%%%%%%%%%%
gsave
     C1 R1 CBoxShadow NudgeNE LetterBox  %Page coordinates, box routine
     .3 setgray fill CMGLetterEffect      %70% cyan box, call "G" effect
grestore


%%%%%%%%%%  H  %%%%%%%%%%%%%%%%%
gsave
     C2 R7 CBoxShadow NudgeNE LetterBox  WhiteFill   %Page coordinates, white box
     /CHLetterShow {TRB 70 SS 7 -1.3 moveto (H) show } def %Left "H" letter definition and position
     gsave %Remember this coordinate
          [.6 .4 0 1 0 0] concat 0 setgray CHLetterShow   %Skew "H" and paint solid cyan
     grestore   %Restore our last coordinate
     /RCHLetterShow {TRB 70 SS -112 -94  moveto (H) show } def   %Rt "H" letter definition and position
     gsave      %Remember this coordinate
          -1 1 scale [.6 .4 0 -1 0 0] concat .8 setgray RCHLetterShow
          %Reverse skew "H", paint 20% cyan
     grestore   %Restore our last coordinate
grestore


%%%%%%%%%%  I  %%%%%%%%%%%%%%%%%
gsave
     C2 R6 CBoxShadow NudgeNE LetterBox         %Page coordinates
     .93 setgray fill       %7% cyan box
     CapLetter 22 10 moveto (I) show     %Font call, move, paint "I" solid cyan
     WindowPane  %Call our "WindowPane" routine
     gsave       %Remember this routine
          .6 setgray fill        %40% cyan tint
     grestore    %Restore our routine
     clip  %Now use these coordinates as a mask
     CapLetter 22 10 moveto .6 setgray (I) show      %And filter the"I" through the mask at 40% cyan
grestore


%%%%%%%%%%  J  %%%%%%%%%%%%%%%%%
gsave
     C2 R4 CBoxShadow NudgeNE gsave LetterBox  %Page coordinates, box routine
     clip RevLineVignette %Use as mask, for straight line vignette
```

```
        grestore
        CapLetter 15 13 moveto (J) White show      %Coordinates, "J" paints white
    grestore


%%%%%%%%%   K  %%%%%%%%%%%%%%%%%
    gsave
        C2 R3 CBoxShadow NudgeNE LetterBox WhiteFill     %Page coordinates, white box, black outline
    grestore


%%%%%%%%%   L  %%%%%%%%%%%%%%%%%
    gsave
        C2 R2 CBoxShadow NudgeNE LetterBox WhiteFill     %Page coordinates, white box
        /LLetter {TRB 32 SS .4 setlinewidth 4 4 moveto (L)      %"L" scaled to 32 point, .6 point outlined
        gsave        %Remember these specifications
            WhiteFill    %Paint "L" white
        grestore     %Recall our specifications
        TC   stroke } def  %Outline "L" in solid cyan
        .95 -.1 0 {setgray LLetter  -.1 -.1      %Define screening
        translate  1.1 1.1 scale } for      %Define incremental scaling
        0 0 moveto LLetter  0 setgray stroke      %Coordinates "L" solid cyan outline
    grestore


%%%%%%%%%   M  %%%%%%%%%%%%%%%%%
    gsave
        C2 R1 CBoxShadow NudgeNE LetterBox  %Page coordinates, call box routine
        gsave %Remember this routine
            WhiteFill    %Fill the box with white
        grestore     %Recall our routine
        clip CHorizontalBars    %Use it as a mask for the cyan horizontal bars
        TRB 88 SS 0 13 moveto (m) White show      %Call "m" and paint it white
    grestore


%%%%%%%%%   N  %%%%%%%%%%%%%%%%%
    gsave
        C3 R7 CBoxShadow NudgeNE LetterBox 0 setgray fill  %Page coordinates, white box
        CapLetter 10 13 moveto (N) White show    %Call "N" and paint it white
        -45 6 rmoveto (n) .4 setgray show   %Coordinates, call "n" and paint it 60% cyan
    grestore
```

```
%%%%%%%%%%  O  %%%%%%%%%%%%%%%%%%
gsave
        C3 R6 CBoxShadow NudgeNE LetterBox WhiteFill   %Coordinates, white box
grestore


%%%%%%%%%%  P  %%%%%%%%%%%%%%%%%%
gsave
        C3 R4 CBoxShadow NudgeNE LetterBox WhiteFill      %Coordinates, white box
        CapLetter 15 13 moveto currentpoint translate     %New coordinates
        gsave      %Remember these coordinates
             0 -2  rmoveto (P) 17 rotate .95 setgray show     %Call "P" rotate it to left, paint it 5% cyan
        grestore   %Restore to original coordinates
        gsave      %Remember these coordinates
        4 0 rmoveto (P)  4 rotate .7 setgray show %Call "P" rotate and paint 30% cyan
        grestore      %Recall the coordinates
        4 0 rmoveto (P) -15 rotate  .5 setgray show     %Call "P" rotate it right, paint it 50% cyan
grestore


%%%%%%%%%%  Q  %%%%%%%%%%%%%%%%%%
gsave
        C3 R3 CBoxShadow NudgeNE LetterBox WhiteFill      %Page coordinates white box
grestore


%%%%%%%%%%  R  %%%%%%%%%%%%%%%%%%
gsave
        C3 R2 CBoxShadow NudgeNE LetterBox  %Page coordinates, call box routine
        .5 setgray  fill %Paint box 50% cyan
        TRB 120 SS  %Scale font to 120 pt
        10 10 moveto (r) TC     %Coordinates, call "r"
        gsave      %Remember path
             WhiteFill        %Fill it with white
        grestore      %Recall path
        4 setlinewidth White stroke    %Paint 4 pt white outline
        TRB 24 SS   %Specify Times Roman 24 pt
        10 9 moveto  (RRR) TC  .8 setgray fill    %Page coordinates, paint 3 "R"s 20% cyan
        10 29 moveto (RRR)  TC  .15 setgray fill   %Page coordinates, paint 3 "R"s 85% cyan
        10 49 moveto (RRR)  TC  .8 setgray fill   %Page coordinates, paint 3 "R"s 20% cyan
grestore
```

```
%%%%%%%%%%   S   %%%%%%%%%%%%%%%%%%
gsave
      C3 R1 CBoxShadow NudgeNE LetterBox  %Page coordinates, call box routine
      10 45 {dup mul exch dup mul add 1 exch sub }    %Specify 10 lpi dot screen
      setscreen .1 setgray  fill    %Fill box with 90% cyan tint
      CapLetter 15 13 moveto  %Call capital letter routine, add coordinates
      White (S) show    %Paint "S" white
grestore


%%%%%%%%%%   T   %%%%%%%%%%%%%%%%%%
gsave
      C4 R7 CBoxShadow NudgeNE LetterBox WhiteFill    %Page coordinates, white box
      CapLetter 12.5 13 moveto (T) TC    %Coordinates, "T" character path
      gsave %Remember character path
            WhiteFill    %Fill path with white
      grestore    %Recall character path
      gsave        %...and remember it again
            clip HalfLetterBox .2 setgray fill  %Use path to filter vertical 80% cyan box
      grestore    %Recall character path again
      .2 setgray stroke %Outline it with 80% cyan
grestore


%%%%%%%%%%   U   %%%%%%%%%%%%%%%%%%
gsave
      C4 R6 CBoxShadow NudgeNE LetterBox WhiteFill    %Page coordinates, white box
      TRB 20 SS 34 30 moveto .8 setgray (U) show       %Scale "U", move position and paint 20% cyan
      TRB 40 SS 24 24 moveto .5 setgray (U) show       %Scale "U", move position and paint 50% cyan
      CapLetter 8 10 moveto 0 setgray (U) show  %Scale "U", move position and paint solid cyan
grestore


%%%%%%%%%%   V   %%%%%%%%%%%%%%%%%%
gsave
      C4 R5 CBoxShadow NudgeNE LetterBox  %Page coordinates, box path
      .6 setgray fill    %Fill box with 40% cyan
      CapLetter 8 10 moveto (V) TC  %Specify capitol "V" character path
      1 setlinejoin      %Specify rounded joints
      gsave 15 setlinewidth .12 setgray stroke grestore     %Set the line width and paint it 88% cyan
      gsave 14 setlinewidth .13 setgray stroke grestore     %Set the line width and paint it 87% cyan
      gsave 13 setlinewidth .14 setgray stroke grestore     %Set the line width and paint it 86% cyan
      gsave 5   setlinewidth .25 setgray stroke grestore     %Set the line width and paint it 75% cyan
```

```
        gsave 4    setlinewidth .38 setgray stroke grestore      %Set the line width and paint it 62% cyan
        gsave 3    setlinewidth .50 setgray stroke grestore      %Set the line width and paint it 50% cyan
        gsave 2    setlinewidth .70 setgray stroke grestore      %Set the line width and paint it 30% cyan
        gsave 1    setlinewidth White stroke grestore     %Set the line width and paint it white
grestore


%%%%%%%%%%  W  %%%%%%%%%%%%%%%%%%
gsave
  C4 R4 CBoxShadow NudgeNE LetterBox        %Page coordinates, box path
  .9 setgray fill .5 setgray WLetters       %10% cyan box, paint "WLetters" 50% cyan
grestore


%%%%%%%%%%  X  %%%%%%%%%%%%%%%%%%
gsave
        C4 R3 CBoxShadow NudgeNE LetterBox WhiteFill     %Page coordinates, white box
        CapLetter 6 10 moveto (X) TC 1 setlinejoin       %Coordinates, call "X" character path
        gsave       %Remember path
            5 setlinewidth .95  setgray stroke  %Set line width and paint path 5% cyan
        grestore      %Recall path again
        gsave       %Remember path again
            4 setlinewidth .85  setgray stroke  %Set line width and paint path 15% cyan
        grestore
        gsave
            3 setlinewidth .75  setgray stroke  %Set line width and paint path 25% cyan
        grestore
        gsave
            2 setlinewidth .65  setgray stroke  %Set line width and paint path 35% cyan
        grestore
        .65  setgray  fill 10 13 moveto (X) White show  %Fill path 35%, move, call "X" and paint white
grestore


%%%%%%%%%%  Y  %%%%%%%%%%%%%%%%%%
gsave
        C4 R2 CBoxShadow NudgeNE LetterBox .92 setgray fill    %Page coordinates, 8% cyan box
grestore


%%%%%%%%%%  Z  %%%%%%%%%%%%%%%%%%
gsave
  C4 R1 CBoxShadow NudgeNE LetterBox WhiteFill  %Page coordinates, white box
grestore
```

```
%%%%%%%%%%  BlackTitleBlockShadowLetterBox  %%%%%%%%%%%%%%%%%%
gsave
        C2 R5 BlackTitleBlockShadow        %Page coordinates, cyan shadow routine
        10 10 translate TitleBlueBox  %Page coordinates, 40% cyan box
grestore


%%%%%%%%%%  TitleBlock Copy  %%%%%%%%%%%%%%%%%%
gsave
        2.68 in C4    moveto 1.17 1.13 scale TRB 40 SS    %Coordinates, scale type to fit
        .6 setgray       (T) show      %This headline is carefully kerned
        -8 0 rmoveto (y) show   % letter by letter, for optimal visual
        -5 0 rmoveto (p) show   % style. "Type" is painted 40%
        -2 0 rmoveto (e) show   %cyan and "Styles" is painted white
        White
        -2 0 rmoveto (S) TC
        -2 0 rmoveto (t) TC
        -2 0 rmoveto (y) TC
        -3 0 rmoveto (l) TC
        -3 0 rmoveto (e) TC
        -2 0 rmoveto (s) TC
        gsave %Remember these character paths
            fill  %Paint them white
        grestore      %Recall the character paths
        .75 setlinewidth stroke        %Specify 3/4 pt outlines, paint white
grestore


CenterMarks      %Paint registration marks on file


%%%%%%%%%%%%%%%%%  Begin Color Marks %%%%%%%%%%%%%%%%


C3   -.65 in moveto  /Helvetica-Bold findfont 12 SS      %Coordinates, specify font and size
(BLACK) White show (CYAN) 0 setgray show  %Paint "CYAN" with cyan
showpage      %Image the cyan file
restore       %Restore definitions for magenta printer


%%%%%%%%%%%%%%%%%%%%%%%%%%%%%%%%%%%%%%%%%%%%%%%%%%%%%%


% Poster (MAGENTA)      %Visual reminder of the color printer
Poster Seps  75 Angle   %Set angle to 75° for the magenta printer
```

```
save


%%%%%%%%%%%   PROGRAM   %%%%%%%%%%%%



%%%%%%%%%%   BackgroundLetterBox   %%%%%%%%%
gsave
     .675 in .3 in translate BackgroundBox .92 setgray fill
     %Paint background 8% magenta
grestore


%%%%%%%%%%   A   %%%%%%%%%%%%%%%%%%%
gsave
     C1 R7 MBoxShadow NudgeNE LetterBox .6 setgray  fill
     %Coordinates, Shadow, 40% filled box
     CapLetter 10 13 moveto (A)  White show     %Drop white "A" out of background
grestore


%%%%%%%%%%   B   %%%%%%%%%%%%%%%%%%
gsave
     C1 R6 MBoxShadow NudgeNE LetterBox WhiteFill
     %Coordinates, Shadow, white box
grestore


%%%%%%%%%%   C   %%%%%%%%%%%%%%%%%%
gsave
     C1 R5 MBoxShadow NudgeNE LetterBox  %Coordinates, shadow
     gsave        %Remember box coordinates
         WhiteFill    %White box
     grestore     %Recall box coordinates
     clip -3 -3 translate Rays CapLetter %Use box path to filter "Rays" routine
     10 13 moveto (C) White show   %Coordinates, Paint "C" white
grestore


%%%%%%%%%%   D   %%%%%%%%%%%%%%%%%%
gsave
     C1 R4 MBoxShadow NudgeNE LetterBox White fill    %Page coordinates, white box
     CapLetter 5 13 moveto (D) .4 setgray show %Move, paint "D" 60% magenta
grestore
```

```
%%%%%%%%%%   E  %%%%%%%%%%%%%%%%%%
gsave
      C1 R3 MBoxShadow NudgeNE LetterBox .9 setgray   fill
      %Coordinates, paint box 10% magenta
      /ELetter { CapLetter 1.2 setlinewidth 5 7 moveto (E)   %"E" letter definition
      gsave WhiteFill grestore TC   stroke } def
      .9 -.05 .1 {setgray ELetter .5 .5 translate } for     %Define screen staging and "drift"
      0 0 moveto ELetter  0 setgray stroke       %Coordinates "E" solid magenta outline
grestore


%%%%%%%%%%   F  %%%%%%%%%%%%%%%%%%
gsave
      C1 R2 MBoxShadow NudgeNE LetterBox White   fill  %Page coordinates, white box
      CapLetter 10 13 moveto .3 setgray (F) show       %Font call, move, paint "F" 70% magenta
grestore


%%%%%%%%%%   G  %%%%%%%%%%%%%%%%%%
gsave
      C1 R1 MBoxShadow NudgeNE LetterBox  %Page coordinates, box routine
      .7 setgray fill CMGLetterEffect      %30% magenta box, call "G" effect
grestore


%%%%%%%%%%   H  %%%%%%%%%%%%%%%%%%
gsave
      C2 R7 MBoxShadow NudgeNE LetterBox WhiteFill     %Page coordinates, white box
      /MHLetterShow {TRB 70 SS 7 -1.3 moveto (H) show } def %Left "H" letter definition and position
      gsave %Remember this coordinate
           [.6 .4 0 1 0 0] concat .8 setgray MHLetterShow %Skew "H" and paint 20% magenta
      grestore     %Restore our last coordinate
      /RevMHLetterShow {TRB 70 SS -112 -94  moveto (H) show } def    %Rt "H" letter definition and position
      gsave        %Remember this coordinate
           -1 1 scale [.6 .4 0 -1 0 0] concat 0 setgray RevMHLetterShow %Rev skew "H", paint 20% magenta
      grestore     %Restore our last coordinate
grestore


%%%%%%%%%%   I  %%%%%%%%%%%%%%%%%%
gsave
      C2 R6 MBoxShadow NudgeNE LetterBox WhiteFill     %Page coordinates, white box
      CapLetter 22 10 Moveto (1) show
      WindowPane gsave  .9 setgray fill grestore       %Call "WindowPane" fill 10%
```

```
        clip  %Use as mask
        CapLetter 22 10 moveto .9 setgray (I) show      %Filter 10% "I" through mask
grestore


%%%%%%%%%%  J  %%%%%%%%%%%%%%%%%%
gsave
        C2 R4 MBoxShadow NudgeNE LetterBox WhiteFill    %Page coordinates, white box
grestore


%%%%%%%%%%  K  %%%%%%%%%%%%%%%%%%
gsave
        C2 R3 MBoxShadow NudgeNE LetterBox  %Page coordinates, box routine
        20 0 { exch pop abs 1 exch sub }    %Specify 20 line, horizontal screen
        setscreen .5 setgray fill     %Spec 50% tint (line screen)
        CapLetter 8.5 13 moveto (K) White show     %Paint "K" white
grestore


%%%%%%%%%%  L  %%%%%%%%%%%%%%%%%%
gsave
        C2 R2 MBoxShadow NudgeNE LetterBox WhiteFill
        %Coordinates, Shadow, white box
grestore


%%%%%%%%%%  M  %%%%%%%%%%%%%%%%%%
gsave
        C2 R1 MBoxShadow NudgeNE LetterBox        %Page coordinates, box routine
        gsave        %Remember box coordinates
            WhiteFill          %White box
        grestore     %Recall box coordinates
        clip MHorizontalBars TRB 88 SS     %Use it as a mask for the magenta bars
        0 13 moveto (m) .6 setgray show     %Call "m" and paint it 40% magenta
grestore


%%%%%%%%%%  N  %%%%%%%%%%%%%%%%%%
gsave
        C3 R7 MBoxShadow NudgeNE LetterBox .2 setgray fill     %Page coordinates, 80% magenta box
        CapLetter 10 13 moveto (N) White show     %Call "N" and paint it white
        -45 6 rmoveto (n) .9 setgray show    %Coordinates, paint "n" 10% magenta
grestore
```

```
%%%%%%%%%%  O  %%%%%%%%%%%%%%%%%%
gsave
      C3 R6 MBoxShadow NudgeNE LetterBox WhiteFill    %Coordinates, white box
      CapLetter 7 13 moveto (O) TC clip SingleLineVignette  %Call "O", use as a mask for vignette
grestore


%%%%%%%%%%  P  %%%%%%%%%%%%%%%%%%
gsave
      C3 R4 MBoxShadow NudgeNE LetterBox WhiteFill    %Coordinates, white box
      CapLetter 15 13 moveto currentpoint translate   %New coordinates
      gsave      %Remember these coordinates
            0 -2  rmoveto (P) 17 rotate .8 setgray show    %Call "P", rotate,  paint 20% magenta
      grestore   %Restore to original coordinates
      gsave      %Remember these coordinates
            4 0 rmoveto (P)  4 rotate   .5 setgray show    %Call "P", rotate, paint 50% magenta
      grestore   %Recall the coordinates
            4 0 rmoveto (P) -15 rotate .3 setgray show     %Call "P" rotate it right, paint it 70%
grestore


%%%%%%%%%%  Q  %%%%%%%%%%%%%%%%%%
gsave
      C3 R3 MBoxShadow NudgeNE       %Page coordinates, box routine
      gsave      %Remember box coordinates
LetterBox   clip RevLineVignette         %Use them as a mask for vignette
      grestore   %Recall box coordinates
      CapLetter 9 15 moveto (Q) TC %New coordinates, call"Q"
      clip LineVignette  %Use character path as mask for opposing vignettes
grestore
%%%%%%%%%%  R  %%%%%%%%%%%%%%%%%%
gsave
      C3 R2 MBoxShadow NudgeNE LetterBox  %Page coordinates, call box routine
      White fill      %Paint box white
      TRB 120 SS 10 10 moveto (r) TC      %Scale font to 120 pt, call "r"
      gsave %Remember path
            .8 setgray fill    %Fill it with 20% magenta
      grestore   %Recall path
      4 setlinewidth WhiteFill      %Paint 4 pt white outline
      TRB 24 SS  %Specify Times Roman 24 pt
      10 9 moveto  (RRR) TC .2 setgray fill    %Page coordinates, paint 3 "R"s 80%
      10 29 moveto (RRR) TC  .8 setgray fill       %Page coordinates, paint 3 "R"s 20%
```

```
          10 49 moveto (RRR)  TC  WhiteFill              %Page coordinates, paint 3 "R"s white
grestore


%%%%%%%%%%  S  %%%%%%%%%%%%%%%%%%
gsave
          C3 R1 MBoxShadow NudgeNE LetterBox  %Page coordinates, call box routine
          WhiteFill          %Fill box with white
          CapLetter 15 13 moveto  %Call capital letter routine, add coordinates
          10 45 {dup mul exch dup mul add 1 exch sub }     %Specify 10 lpi dot screen
          setscreen .9 setgray (S) show      %Fill character path with 10% magenta tint
grestore


%%%%%%%%%%  T  %%%%%%%%%%%%%%%%%%
gsave
          C4 R7 MBoxShadow NudgeNE LetterBox WhiteFill    %Page coordinates white box
grestore


%%%%%%%%%%  U  %%%%%%%%%%%%%%%%%%
gsave
          C4 R6 MBoxShadow NudgeNE LetterBox WhiteFill    %Page coordinates white box
          TRB 20 SS .8 setgray 34 30 moveto (U) show     %Scale "U", move position, paint 20% magenta
          TRB 40 SS .5 setgray 24 24 moveto (U) show     %Scale "U", move position, paint 50% magenta
          CapLetter  0 setgray 8 10 moveto (U) show      %Scale "U", move position, paint solid magenta
grestore


%%%%%%%%%%  V  %%%%%%%%%%%%%%%%%%
gsave
          C4 R5 MBoxShadow NudgeNE LetterBox  WhiteFill   %Page coordinates white box
grestore


%%%%%%%%%%  W  %%%%%%%%%%%%%%%%%%
gsave
          C4 R4 MBoxShadow NudgeNE LetterBox .82 setgray  fill       %Page coordinates 18% magenta fill
          0 setgray WLetters     %Paint "WLetters" solid magenta
grestore


%%%%%%%%%%  X  %%%%%%%%%%%%%%%%%%
gsave
          C4 R3 MBoxShadow NudgeNE LetterBox WhiteFill    %Page coordinates white box
          CapLetter 6 10 moveto (X) TC 1 setlinejoin      %Coordinates, call "X" character path
```

```
        gsave %Remember path
                4 setlinewidth .95  setgray stroke  %Set line width and paint path 5% magenta
        grestore    %Recall path again
        gsave       %Remember path again
        3 setlinewidth .85  setgray stroke  %Set line width and paint path 15% magenta
        grestore    %Recall path again
        gsave       %Remember path again
                2 setlinewidth .75  setgray stroke  %Set line width and paint path 25% magenta
        grestore
        .75  setgray  fill 10 13 moveto (X) White show  %Fill path 25%, move, call "X" and paint white
grestore


%%%%%%%%%   Y  %%%%%%%%%%%%%%%%%
gsave
        C4 R2 MBoxShadow NudgeNE LetterBox WhiteFill    %Page coordinates, white box
grestore


%%%%%%%%%%  Z  %%%%%%%%%%%%%%%%%%

gsave
        C4 R1 MBoxShadow NudgeNE LetterBox .7 setgray fill    %Page coordinates, 30% magenta box
        .7 -.05 0 {setgray  1 1 translate ZLetter } for %Define screen staging and "drift"
        .87 setgray ZLetter      %Fill top "Z" with 13% magenta
grestore


%%%%%%%%%%  MagTitleBlockShadowLetterBox  %%%%%%%%%%%%%%%%%%
gsave
        C2  R5 MagTitleBlockShadow       %Shadow for title block
grestore


%%%%%%%%%%  TitleMagLetterBox  %%%%%%%%%%%%%%%%%%
gsave
        C2  R5 10 10 translate TitleMagBox  %Knock-out for title block
grestore

CenterMarks %Paint registration marks on file

%%%%%%%%%%%%%%%%  Begin Color Marks %%%%%%%%%%%%%%%

C3   -.65 in moveto /Helvetica-Bold findfont 12 SS     %Coordinates, specify font and size
(BLACK) 1 setgray show (CYAN) 1 setgray show     %Paint BLACK and CYAN white
```

```
(MAGENTA) 0 setgray show        %Paint "MAGENTA"  magenta
showpage    %Image the magenta file
restore     %Restore definitions for yellow printer


% Poster (YELLOW)       %Visual reminder of the color printer
Poster Seps  90 Angle        %Set angle to 90° for the yellow printer


%%%%%%%%%%%  PROGRAM  %%%%%%%%%


%%%%%%  BackgroundBox  %%%%%%%%%%%
gsave
        .675 in .3 in translate BackgroundBox .7 setgray fill %Paint background 30% yellow
grestore


%%%%%%%%%%  A  %%%%%%%%%%%%%%%
gsave
        C1  R7 YBoxShadow NudgeNE LetterBox .3 setgray fill
        %Coordinates, Shadow, 70% filled box
        CapLetter 10 13 moveto (A)  White show    %Drop white "A" out of background
grestore


%%%%%%%%%%  B  %%%%%%%%%%%%%%%%%
gsave
        C1 R6 YBoxShadow NudgeNE LetterBox WhiteFill
        %Coordinates, Shadow, white box
grestore


%%%%%%%%%%  C  %%%%%%%%%%%%%%%%%
gsave
        C1 R5 YBoxShadow NudgeNE LetterBox WhiteFill
        %Coordinates, Shadow, white box
grestore


%%%%%%%%%%  D  %%%%%%%%%%%%%%%%%
gsave
        C1 R4 YBoxShadow NudgeNE LetterBox White  fill
        %Coordinates, Shadow, white box
        CapLetter 5 13 moveto (D) .8 setgray show %Move, paint "D" 20% yellow
grestore
```

```
%%%%%%%%%%  E  %%%%%%%%%%%%%%%%%%%
gsave
   C1 R3 YBoxShadow NudgeNE LetterBox .9 setgray  fill
      %Coordinates, paint box 10% yellow
   /ELetter { CapLetter 1.2 setlinewidth 5 7 moveto (E)        %"E" letter definition
gsave WhiteFill  grestore TC stroke } def
   .9 -.05 .1 {setgray ELetter  .5 .5 translate } for  %Define screen staging and "drift"
   0 0 moveto ELetter OutLine  %Coordinates "E" solid yellow  outline
grestore


%%%%%%%%%%  F  %%%%%%%%%%%%%%%%%%
gsave
      C1 R2 YBoxShadow NudgeNE LetterBox WhiteFill    %Page coordinates, white box
grestore


%%%%%%%%%%  G  %%%%%%%%%%%%%%%%%%
gsave
      C1 R1 YBoxShadow NudgeNE LetterBox  %Page coordinates, box routine
      0 setgray fill YGLetterEffect %Solid yellow box, call "G" effect
grestore


%%%%%%%%%%  H  %%%%%%%%%%%%%%%%%%
gsave
      C2 R7 YBoxShadow NudgeNE LetterBox WhiteFill    %Page coordinates, white box
grestore


%%%%%%%%%%  I  %%%%%%%%%%%%%%%%%%
gsave
      C2 R6 YBoxShadow NudgeNE Lette.Box WhiteFill    %Page coordinates, white box
grestore


%%%%%%%%%%  J  %%%%%%%%%%%%%%%%%%
gsave
      C2 R4 YBoxShadow NudgeNE LetterBox 0 setgray fill    %Page coordinates, solid yellow box
      CapLetter 15 13 moveto (J) White show     %Paint "J" white
grestore


%%%%%%%%%%  K  %%%%%%%%%%%%%%%%%%
gsave
      C2 R3 YBoxShadow NudgeNE LetterBox  %Page coordinates, box routine
```

```
        20 0 { exch pop abs 1 exch sub } setscreen        %Specify 20 line, horizontal screen
        .5 setgray fill        %Spec 50% tint (line screen)
        CapLetter 8.5 13 moveto (K) White show     %Paint "K" white
grestore


%%%%%%%%%%   L   %%%%%%%%%%%%%%%%%%
gsave
        C2 R2 YBoxShadow NudgeNE LetterBox WhiteFill     %Page coordinates, white box
        /LLetter  { TRB 32 SS .4 setlinewidth 4 4 moveto (L)  %"L" scaled to 32 point, .6 point outline
        gsave      %Remember these specifications
            WhiteFill     %Paint "L" white
        grestore     %Recall our specifications
        TC   stroke } def  %Outline "L" in solid yellow
        .95 -.1 0 {setgray LLetter  -.1 -.1        %Define screening
        translate  1.1 1.1 scale } for       %Define incremental scaling
        0 0 moveto LLetter  0 setgray stroke        %Coordinates "L" solid yellow outline
grestore


%%%%%%%%%%   M   %%%%%%%%%%%%%%%%%%
gsave
        C2 R1 YBoxShadow NudgeNE LetterBox  %Page coordinates, call box routine
        gsave %Remember this routine
            WhiteFill    %Fill the box with white
        grestore      %Recall our routine
        clip YHorizontalBars   %Use it as a mask for the yellow horizontal bars
   TRB 88 SS 0 13 moveto (m) 0 setgray show       %Call "m" and paint it solid yellow
grestore


%%%%%%%%%%   N   %%%%%%%%%%%%%%%%%%
gsave
        C3 R7 YBoxShadow NudgeNE LetterBox WhiteFill     %Coordinates, white box
        CapLetter 10 13 moveto (N) White show     %Call "N" and paint it white
 -45 6 rmoveto (n) White show %Coordinates, paint "n" white
grestore


%%%%%%%%%%   O   %%%%%%%%%%%%%%%%%%
gsave
        C3 R6 YBoxShadow NudgeNE LetterBox WhiteFill     %Coordinates, white box
grestore
```

```
%%%%%%%%%%   P   %%%%%%%%%%%%%%%%%%
gsave
     C3 R4 YBoxShadow NudgeNE LetterBox .5 setgray  fill
     %Coordinates, 50% yellow box
     CapLetter 15 13 moveto currentpoint translate   %New coordinates
     gsave       %Remember these coordinates
          0 -2 rmoveto  (P) 17 rotate .5 setgray show    %Call "P", rotate,  paint 50% yellow
     grestore     %Restore to original coordinates
     gsave        %Remember these coordinates
     4 0 rmoveto (P)  4 rotate   .2 setgray show      %Call "P", rotate, paint 70% yellow
     grestore     %Recall the coordinates
     4 0 rmoveto (P) -15 rotate  0 setgray show       %Call "P" rotate it, paint it solid yellow
grestore


%%%%%%%%%%   Q   %%%%%%%%%%%%%%%%%%
gsave
     C3 R3 YBoxShadow NudgeNE LetterBox 0 setgray fill     %Page coordinates, paint box yellow
grestore


%%%%%%%%%%   R   %%%%%%%%%%%%%%%%%%
gsave
     C3 R2 YBoxShadow NudgeNE LetterBox .3 setgray  fill
     %Coordinates, paint box 70% yellow
     TRB 120 SS 10 10 moveto (r) TC     %Scale font to 120 pt, call "r"
     gsave %Remember path
          .8 setgray fill   %Fill it with 20% yellow
     grestore     %Recall path
     4 setlinewidth WhiteFill       %Paint 4 pt white outline
     10 9 moveto  (RRR) TC  0 setgray fill     %Coordinates, paint 3 "R"s solid yellow
     10 29 moveto (RRR)  TC  WhiteFill   %Page coordinates, paint 3 "R"s white
     10 49 moveto (RRR)  TC  WhiteFill   %Page coordinates, paint 3 "R"s white
grestore


%%%%%%%%%%   S   %%%%%%%%%%%%%%%%%%
gsave
     C3 R1 YBoxShadow NudgeNE LetterBox  %Page coordinates, call box routine
          10 45 {dup mul exch dup mul add 1 exch sub } setscreen WhiteFill
     WhiteFill        %Fill box with white
     CapLetter 15 13 moveto  %Call capital letter routine, add coordinates
     10 45 {dup mul exch dup mul add 1 exch sub }     %Specify 10 lpi dot screen
```

```
        setscreen   .9 setgray (S) show        %Fill character path with 10% yellow tint
grestore


%%%%%%%%%%   T   %%%%%%%%%%%%%%%%%%
gsave
        C4 R7 YBoxShadow NudgeNE LetterBox WhiteFill      %Page coordinates white box
        CapLetter 0 setlinejoin 12.5 13 moveto (T) TC    %Coordinates, "T" character path
        gsave %Remember character path
            WhiteFill    %Fill path with white
        grestore    %Recall character path
        gsave       %...and remember it again
            clip HalfLetterBox 0 setgray fill   %Use path to filter vertical solid yellow box
        grestore    %Recall character path again
        0 setgray stroke   %Outline it with solid yellow
grestore


%%%%%%%%%%   U   %%%%%%%%%%%%%%%%%%
gsave
        C4 R6 YBoxShadow NudgeNE LetterBox WhiteFill      %Page coordinates, white box
grestore


%%%%%%%%%%   V   %%%%%%%%%%%%%%%%%%
gsave
        C4 R5 YBoxShadow NudgeNE LetterBox WhiteFill      %Page coordinates, white box
grestore


%%%%%%%%%%   W   %%%%%%%%%%%%%%%%%%
gsave
        C4 R4 YBoxShadow NudgeNE LetterBox WhiteFill      %Page coordinates, white box
grestore


%%%%%%%%%%   X   %%%%%%%%%%%%%%%%%%
gsave
        C4 R3 YBoxShadow NudgeNE LetterBox WhiteFill      %Page coordinates white box
        CapLetter 6 10 moveto (X) TC 1 setlinejoin        %Coordinates, call "X" character path
        gsave       %Remember path
            4 setlinewidth .95  setgray stroke        %Set line width and paint path 5% yellow
        grestore    %Recall path again
        gsave       %Remember path again
            3 setlinewidth .85  setgray stroke  %Set line width and paint path 15% yellow
```

```
    grestore      %Recall path again
    gsave         %Remember path again
         2 setlinewidth .75  setgray stroke  %Set line width and paint path 25% yellow
    grestore
    .75  setgray  fill 10 13 moveto (X) White show  %Fill path 25%, move, call "X" and paint white
grestore


%%%%%%%%%%  Y  %%%%%%%%%%%%%%%%%%
gsave
    C4 R2 YBoxShadow NudgeNE LetterBox WhiteFill    %Page coordinates white box
grestore


%%%%%%%%%%  Z  %%%%%%%%%%%%%%%%%
gsave
    C4 R1 MBoxShadow NudgeNE LetterBox .7 setgray fill    %Page coordinates, 30% yellow box
    .7 -.05 0 {setgray  1 1 translate ZLetter } for %Define screen staging and "drift"
    .87 setgray ZLetter     %Fill top "Z" with 13% yellow
grestore


%%%%%  YelTitleBlockShadowLetterBox  %%%%%
gsave
    C2  R5 YelTitleBlockShadow       %Shadow for title block
grestore



%%%%%%%%  TitleYeloLetterBox  %%%%%%%%%%
gsave
    C2  R5 10 10 translate TitleYeloBox %Knock-out for title block
grestore

CenterMarks      %Paint registration marks on file
%%%%%%%  Begin Color Marks %%%%%%%%

C3   -.65 in moveto /Helvetica-Bold findfont 12 SS     %Coordinates, specify font and size
(BLACK) 1 setgray show (CYAN) 1 setgray show      %Paint BLACK, CYAN
(MAGENTA) 1 setgray show      %and MAGENTA white
(YELLOW) 0 setgray show %Paint "YELLOW" yellow


showpage    %Image the yellow file
```

As you can see, this code makes no use of PostScript's color operators. Every bit of color is specified by placing the same image in the same place on each piece of film (each "printer"), and changing the *setgray* for the image on each printer. In essence, it's a manual PostScript separation. This could be automated to some extent by building a set of CMYK color definitions, and calling them as needed, automatically specifying a gray level for a given object on a given printer.

The other method of color separation in PostScript, outlined in Pat Wood's chapter 12, "PostScript Color Separations," is to specify colors using PostScript's color operators, *setrgbcolor* and *sethsbcolor*. Then you run a conversion to turn the HSB/RGB colors into their CMYK counterparts. That raises all the problems of color correction, undercolor removal, etc., discussed in that chapter. I chose to specify everything explicitly for each color, relying on my own knowledge of lithography to specify the angles, percentages, and traps.

The Problems

"Into every life a little rain must fall." This trite little saying can't begin to express the frustrations I encountered when I first output this file to the Linotype. Consider the fact that no one had ever attempted to formulate a PostScript file quite this complex, let alone print it out on an L300. That ought to give you a clue.

If people ever tell you that the Lino is just an overgrown LaserWriter, save yourself a lot of trouble and just shoot them! The only thing those two machines have in common is that they both talk PostScript (albeit different versions). I will list a couple of the most frustrating setbacks in my journey into LinoLand.

Image Rotation. This file will print out on a laser printer in what we lovingly call portrait mode. This means that the short direction of the file will print across the short direction of the paper. This makes pretty good sense. One would tend to assume that this would also be true for the Linotype. But, alas, not so.

This same file, sent unchanged through the Lino, will result in a rotated image that gets cut off by the default clipping region of the "normal" page (someone decided that the default "letter-size" should be considerably less than 8.5 by 11 inches). To overcome this difficulty, a command must be sent to the Lino, prior to the file, to open up the imaging area and rotate the file for the correct orientation. Since we also want the file to be produced as plate-ready negatives, we must put in a couple of lines that will reverse the image from positive to negative, and mirror the image so that we can maintain the proper orientation of the film emulsion to the printing plate. A sample of this command could read as follows:

```
serverdict begin 0 exitserver
statusdict begin
648 828  0 1 setpageparams
/negativeprint true def
end
[ -1 0 0 1 1 1 ] concat
-648 0 translate
```

For us to print something the size of this poster (approximately 10.5 by 14 inches), we had to open up the window even more. See Simon Tuckett's approach in chapter 13 on *Graphic Perspective.* There are some pretty serious limitations to the size of an image, directly related to the output resolution.

Scan Direction. The direction of the scan is directly connected to the rotated image. This is particularly evident when using straight-line halftone screens. The angle specified will appear on the laser printer in its proper orientation, but on the Lino (since the default scan direction is rotated ninety degrees) the screen appears rotated. This means that files may have to be altered before they are output on the Lino.

Time Limitations. One of the most frustrating of all the limitations on this particular file is the limit of how long the Lino will wait to process information before it declares a timeout. When it reaches the magic number of minutes (or seconds) of time waiting to process the code, it will simply spit the file out and quit. To overcome this limitation on files that are complex or effects-intensive, it may be advisable to send another little piece of code ahead of the file that basically makes the Lino act like it took a dozen or so No-Doz' tablets. It's wired! And it will stay very alert and extremely patient until you tell it otherwise or turn it off. The line of code goes like this:

```
serverdict begin 0 exitserver
statusdict begin
```

```
0 setjobtimeout
end
```

The other problems—those having to do with moiré patterns, screen angles, and frequencies, I've already discussed, and they're also covered in Part III. They are perhaps the biggest stumbling block to producing high-quality color separations on the Linotronic.

As the ABCs poster makes clear, though, it is definitely possible to create high-quality color separations on PostScript devices. It may even be possible for software programs to be smart enough to do automatically what I had to do manually way back in 1986. To do so, though, those packages will need to incorporate the knowledge and expertise that lithographers have developed over the course of many years, running many jobs, and (I must admit) making many expensive and educational mistakes.

15 / Graphing and Typesetting With PostScript

Bill Woodruff

In Chapter 2, "PostScript As a Programming Language," we came up with several powerful, if somewhat theoretical, ideas about PostScript. In this chapter we are going to integrate those ideas into real world projects. There are three ideas in particular that apply to the work we'll do here:

1. The *type* command in PostScript returns a potentially executable object

2. PostScript is a very high level language; we can make good use of the freedom we are given to access the mechanism of the interpreter itself

3. We can create complex control structures by redefining the behavior of PostScript's own primitives—either by creating new values associated with them in special dictionaries, or by redefining them in the normal operating context (in userdict)

First we're going to apply these ideas to one very common graphic problem: precisely graphing a numeric data set. Then we'll work on the construction of an embedded-control typesetting program.

Getting Graphic

For our first example, let's assume that we have generated some sets of points that we want to plot on an xy graph, as in Figure 15.1. There may be many points for each overlying plot. There are a number of ways to turn those points into a graph; we'll talk about a few here, but we'll concentrate on using the *token* operator. It's a little-used PostScript operator, but one of the most useful.

315

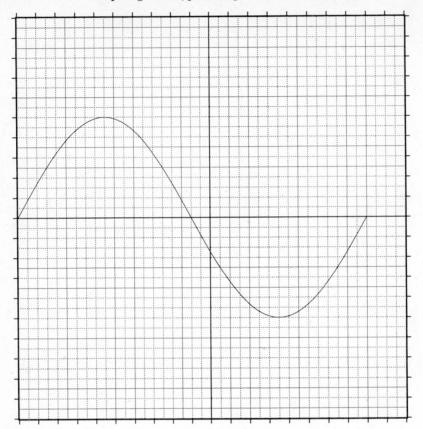

Figure 15.1. This output from the graphing program uses a set of data that produces a sine curve.

Before we get to the *token* operator, though, let's look at some other approaches. Our first sketch is very simple:

```
dogrid        % here you'd create your procedure to
              %set up the background grid
% create abbreviations for primitives
/l /lineto load def
/m /moveto load def
/s /stroke load def


% here's a sample coded string
(100 200 m 200 300 l 210 310 l s 200 300 m 360 300 l s) cvx exec
```

In this example, each *initial* moveto pair is followed by the letter m, which calls *moveto*. Successive legs of the plot line are created with *lineto*, and the final, multi-segment line is stroked. It works, but there are several flaws, which would be compounded if we got into very big plots:

1. Inserting all the m and l and s commands isn't much easier than just writing all the code out directly

2. There's no protection against getting a limitcheck error if we exceed fifteen hundred path elements or so, since stroking only occurs at the end of each plot. There is a benefit in this, however, since lines in the plot will be joined rather than overlapping, possibly creating a better looking graph

A more efficient setup for the string of plotting points looks like this:

```
(! 100 200  200 300  210 310 ! 200 300 360 300)
```

Here one special character, !, tells us the start of a new plot. It's cleaner, but we'd still like some "smart" protection from possible limitcheck errors, while having as many points as possible in a plot, all joined rather than overlapped. How can we avoid having to put in some command after each pair of numbers?

Since we want to have plots of variable length, the use of the "currentfile read" technique to read objects ahead of the interpreter's position pointer in the scanning of the current file is not indicated. This is a dangerous technique if you do not know precisely how many reads you want to do.

We could use *forall* to parse our coded string, but even if we have used *cvx* on the string first, it returns a bunch of character codes, which we would have to scan to find white spaces, etc. The last thing we want to do is recreate the white space handling behavior of the interpreter. Clearly we need a way to munch on a string one object at a time, letting the POSTSCRIPT interpreter do its usual fine job of object construction.

The *token* command is our handle to using the POSTSCRIPT interpreter for our own purposes. Applied to a string, *token* constructs an object—if there is an object there—and returns a true value, the object it created, and the rest of the string. If there is no object left in the string, it returns the value false. Now we can think of a simple loop like this:

```
% a string object is on the stack here
{ token     % apply token
      % if true then do something with object
      % that consume it and leave the rest
      % of the string on the stack
      { doobject }
      % else quit loop (possibly with some final action)
      { exit }
ifelse }
```

This simple loop structure is the foundation for both our graphing program and our embedded-control-code word processor. Note that every time *token* constructs a new object, it leaves true on top of the stack and we enter the doobject clause. As we enter doobject, the object is on top of the stack, the rest of the string below it. When the string is empty, *token* returns false and we quit the loop by using *exit*.

To do our graphing, we can now consider what we will do when we enter doobject:

- Examine the type of the object just created
- If it's the first number of a pair, we'll have to put the number aside in some way for future use
- If we have one number saved, and we have another number, we are going to do either a *moveto* or *lineto*
- If it's not a number (if it's our special character), we execute it. It should cause a *moveto* when we next have two numbers and after that it should cause a *lineto*

Here's how we can design our special plot-delimiter character to be a procedure that flips the definition of another procedure between doing a *moveto* and a *lineto*:

```
/! { /plot { moveto /plot /lineto def } def } def
```

Each time ! is executed, plot is redefined. The first time plot is executed it does a *moveto* and then changes its own definition to do a *lineto*. Note that this is not a recursive structure: plot never calls itself; it does not cause an endless loop.

The case where we encounter our special character ! is simple in that it leaves the string body on the stack with no clean-up for the next pass through the loop. The only messy case is when we get the first number—the x location—of the first point. We need to save it until we get the matching y location and then do a call to plot. The easy, but less-than-elegant way to do this is to put the x value underneath the string and then bring it up when we need it:

```
/doobject {
        dup /! eq                % is it our special character ?
            { exec }             % if true, execute it
            {                    % else: assume it is a number
            count 3 eq                     % if three objects on stack we execute plot
                { 3 -1 roll exch plot } %after getting x,y in right order
                { exch }                   % else, put new number beneath rest of string
            ifelse
        } ifelse
} def
```

While this "meat and potatoes" version works fine (try it!), let's see if we can optimize it. One thing we know is that all numbers in the coded data string are in pairs. Whenever we get one number, rather than the special character, we know we could immediately get another number and call plot. We get the second number by using *token* again. Here is our better mousetrap with the act of forming the pair abstracted into another procedure: aupair. We also want to make the special character user-defined to create more flexibility:

```
/special_ch /! def
/aupair {
        exch  % push x under string
        token % get another number by token
        pop   % discard true
        3 -1 roll exch plot      % plot after putting x,y in right order
} def


/doobject {
        dup special_ch eq % is it our special character?
            { exec }     % if true, execute it
            { aupair }   % else: get an x,y pair and call plot
        ifelse
} def
```

Let's summarize the features of our general graphing module:

1. Within the 64k string size limit of PostScript, a large number of x,y points can be simply mapped. In one single plot you could have more than three thousand pairs, each value with four digits before and four digits after the decimal point

2. Only one special character is needed to delimit the end of one plot and the beginning of another. Only a single white space character (tab; newline, carriage return, space) is needed to separate numbers

3. The user is protected from having to worry about stack overflow from more than five hundred operand stack elements, or from having to write out the plot in a stupidly iterative way

Stroking the Path

Now we can deal with the question of when the path should be stroked. Unfortunately we have no way to measure dynamically the number of path elements active at any point in time (path elements don't affect VM) without using *pathforall* to read through the whole path and count them (time-consuming).

If we don't care that all our segments overlap (we can control line-caps with the *setlinecap* operator), then the solution is clear: stroke immediately after each *lineto*, and modify *lineto* to maintain the currentpoint:

```
/lineto { lineto currentpoint systemdict begin stroke end moveto } def
% or
/lineto { lineto currentpoint stroke moveto } bind def
```

Note that both these definitions make sure the call to *lineto* inside our redefined *lineto* is a call to the original *lineto*, rather than creating an endless loop. The first one makes sure that the call is to the definition of *lineto* in systemdict. The second one uses whatever definition of *lineto* is current at the moment of the new procedure's definition.

Suppose we want as many segments of any one of our plots stroked continuously as possible (but we'll assume we always do a stroke at the end of each plot)? We can set up a limit variable and a counter variable to implement this:

```
/plimit 1400 def
/pcnt 0 def
/pinc { /pcnt dup load 1 add def } def

/lineto {
     systemdict begin lineto end   % do the current line
     pinc  % update pcnt
     pcnt plimit eq {  % is pcnt at the limit ?
          currentpoint stroke moveto   % if true, then stroke,
          /pcnt 0 def % preserving currentpoint, reset pcnt
     } if
} def
```

In the event we arrive at a new plot with the previous plot's segments unstroked, we want to modify the behavior of the special character function:

```
/! { /plot { stroke /pcnt 0 def moveto /plot /lineto def } def } def
```

Here we insert a call to stroke and reset pcnt just before the initial *moveto* of the new plot. This will not cause an error if no path has been created. In the case that we finish the entire loop with the current path unstroked, we will insert a final stroke just before exiting the loop structure. If there is nothing to be stroked, it will do no harm.

Finally, let's map out a template for the graph that will be the background and frame of our plot. Here's what the initial parameters might look like:

```
% GRAPH PARAMETERS
% All distance units in points
% All gray levels in range 0 - 1, where 0 = black, 1 = white
/llx 100 def /lly 100 def     % lower right corner
/urx 500 def /ury 500 def     % upper left corner
/plw .24 def      % set linewidth for plotting lines
/x0 200 def /y0 200 def % where 0,0 is relative to ll corner
/sx? true def /sy? true def   % whether to stroke x and y axes
/ag 0 def /als .72 def  % color and strokewidth of axes
/grid? true def   % whether there is a grid
/gcell 10 def /ggry .5 def /glns .24 def  % cell size, grayscale, and linesize of grid
/xtk? true def /ytk?  true def      % tick marks? Size of ticks
/tsp 20 def /tsize 5 def /tg  .25 def /ts .72 def    % tick spacing, gray, & linesize
```

```
/bord? true def    % whether to do border stroke
/bsg 0 def  /blns 1.2 def     % border stroke gray, linesize

% The procedure init_graph will draw the background grid,
% border, axis lines, etc., based on the above parameters.
/init_graph {
      % DRAW GRAPH BACKGROUND
      /gw urx llx sub def      % compute height and width of grid
      /gh ury lly sub def

      llx lly translate 0 0 moveto  % set grid lower left as 0,0

      grid? {     % do background grid
      gsave
            ggry setgray glns setlinewidth

            % vertical lines of grid
            gw gcell idiv 1 add
                  { currentpoint 0 gh rlineto stroke exch gcell add exch moveto }
            repeat
            0 0 moveto

            % horizontal lines of grid
            gh gcell idiv 1 add
                  { currentpoint gw 0 rlineto stroke gcell add  moveto }
            repeat
      grestore
      } if

      % do x,y axis strokes
      sx? sy? or {
      gsave
            ag setgray als setlinewidth
            sx? { 0 y0 moveto gw 0 rlineto stroke } if
            sy?{ x0 0 moveto 0 gh rlineto stroke } if
      grestore
      } if

      % do ticks
      xtk? ytk? or {
```

```
/tick { gsave rlineto stroke grestore } def
/ticks { gsave 2 exch repeat grestore } def
gsave
        tg setgray ts setlinewidth
        xtk? { % horizontal ticks
                {
                gh tsp idiv 1 add
                        { tsize neg 0 tick currentpoint
                        tsp add moveto }
                repeat
                gw 0 moveto -1 1  scale
                } ticks
        } if

        ytk? {        % vertical ticks
                {
                gw tsp idiv 1 add
                        { 0 tsize neg  tick currentpoint exch
                        tsp add exch moveto }
                repeat
                0 gh moveto 1 -1 scale
                } ticks
        } if
        grestore
} if

bord? {     % whether to do border stroke
        bsg setgray blns setlinewidth

            % we want border to frame plot area
            % so back off half linewidth of border
        blns -2 div dup rmoveto
            % and draw frame gw + blns, gh + blns
        gw blns add gh blns add
        dup 0 exch rlineto
        exch 0 rlineto
        neg 0 exch rlineto
        closepath
        stroke
} if
```

```
% Get Ready To Plot
% set origin to x0,y0
x0 y0 translate 0 0 moveto
plw setlinewidth
} def


/graph {
        {       % begin the loop
                token % apply token
                        % if true then do something with object
                        % that consumes it and leaves the rest
                        % of the string on the stack
                        { doobject }
                        % else quit the loop after a final stroke
                        { stroke exit }
                ifelse
        } loop      % end of the loop
} def


(
! -200 0.0 -196 6.97565 -192 13.9173 -188 20.7912 -184 27.5637 -180 34.202
-176 40.6737  -172 46.9472 -168 52.9919 -164 58.7785 -160 64.2788 -156 69.4658
-152 74.3145 -148 78.8011 -144 82.9038 -140 86.6025 -136 89.8794 -132 92.7184
-128 95.1057 -124 97.0296 -120 98.4808 -116 99.4522 -112 99.9391 -108 99.9391
-104 99.4522 -100 98.4808 -96 97.0296 -92 95.1057 -88 92.7184 -84 89.8794 -80 86.6025
-76 82.9038 -72 78.8011 -68 74.3145 -64 69.4658 -60 64.2788 -56 58.7785 -52 52.9919
-48 46.9472 -44 40.6737 -40 34.202 -36 27.5637 -32 20.7912 -28 13.9173 -24 6.97565
-20 0.0 -16 -6.97565 -12 -13.9173 -8 -20.7912 -4 -27.5637 0 -34.202 4 -40.6737 8 -46.94
12 -52.9919 16 -58.7785 20 -64.2788 24 -69.4658 28 -74.3145 32 -78.8011 36 -82.9038
40 -86.6025 44 -89.8794 48 -92.7184 52 -95.1057 56 -97.0296 60 -98.4808 64 -99.4522
68 -99.9391 72 -99.9391 76 -99.4522 80 -98.4808 84 -97.0296 88 -95.1057 92 -92.7184
96 -89.8794 100 -86.6025 104  -82.9038 108 -78.8011 112 -74.3145 116 -69.4658
120 -64.2788 124 -58.7785 128 -52.9919 132 -46.9472 136 -40.6737 140 -34.202
144 -27.5637 148 -20.7912 152 -13.9173 156 -6.97565 160 0.0
)
graph
showpage
```

PostWord: A PostScript Text Processor

Now that we know how to use the *token* operator in a loop, let's build a text printing program of medium-level complexity. We'll call it PostWord and dedicate it to Bill Bates, whose JustText program was a breakthrough for giving users access to PostScript. You can see some sample output from PostWord in Figure 15.2.

PostWord is meant as a teaching example that demonstrates the general features of the use of buffers, handling of text, printing multiple pages while retaining page structure, and the art of dynamically interpreting a coded structure which may be self-modifying. It shows how suitable PostScript is, as an object-oriented language, for the construction of translators. The real lesson here is the incredible extensibility of PostScript, and how any program can share that extensibility. We are not going to explain every part of the program here (you'll find the complete program in Listing 1), but will focus on some interesting

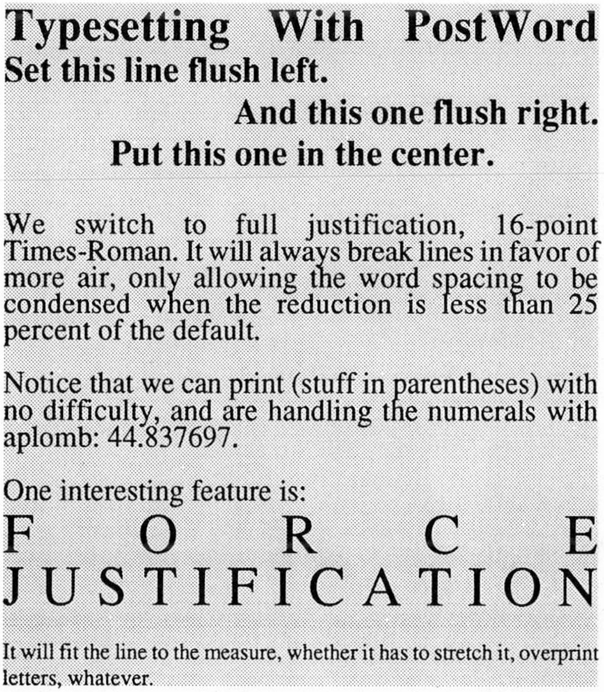

Typesetting   With   PostWord
Set this line flush left.
                              And this one flush right.
          Put this one in the center.

We switch to full justification, 16-point Times-Roman. It will always break lines in favor of more air, only allowing the word spacing to be condensed when the reduction is less than 25 percent of the default.

Notice that we can print (stuff in parentheses) with no difficulty, and are handling the numerals with aplomb: 44.837697.

One interesting feature is:
F   O   R   C   E
JUSTIFICATION
It will fit the line to the measure, whether it has to stretch it, overprint letters, whatever.

Figure 15.2. This output from PostWord demonstrates its various line-breaking and justification powers.

issues in the code, like handling of special characters and full justification. You'll find some of the ideas from my chapter, "POSTSCRIPT as a Programming Language," used here—redefinition of type names for handling parsing objects, for instance, and use of number and string objects as keys in dictionaries.

Listing 1

```
%!PS-ADOBE2.0

% /div {{ div } stopped { buffstr pstack xxxx } if } bind def

/svm vmstatus pop exch pop def
/sut usertime def
% PostWord : AN EMBEDDED CONTROL CODE TEXT PROCESSOR

% copyright 1988, Bill Woodruff
% all rights reserved

%_____

% miscellaneous binding functions
/brd { bind readonly def } bind readonly def
/x { exch def } brd

% position reporting and updating functions

% return x or y current position
/xis { currentpoint pop } brd
/yis { currentpoint exch pop } brd

% global variable holds page x-axis position
/at 0 def

% update position on page x-axis
/xat { /at xis def } brd

%_____

% scratch variables and character definitions
```

```
% for use in transforming numbers, names to strings
/ourscratch 40 string def

% to hold co-ordinate system after 'SETPAGE
/mtx matrix def

/asciispace 32 def
/dot (.) def
/sp ( ) def
/nullsp () def
/fslash (/) def
/cr 1 string dup 0 10 put def
/hcr 1 string dup 0 13 put def


%_____


% low-level printing primitives
        % NOTE : we don't use the PostScript undocumented
        % scratchstring "=string" for a good reason here:
        % it is used internally by the "search" operator
        % if we used "=string" instead of our own string "ourscratch,"
        % the control of decimal places would not work in the
        % routine "realtype" below

/xs { ourscratch cvs } brd
/xpr { xs bpr } brd
/space { sp bpr } brd


%_____


% NEWPAGE PRINT FUNCTIONS

/NEWPAGE {
        % preserve working text string
        /wkstr x
        % preserve current x-axis location
        /oldx xis def
        % label it
        labelpage
        % print the page
```

```
        copypage erasepage
        % restore default page space matrix
        % and current x position
        mtx setmatrix pagebbox
        oldx LEADING neg moveto
        % put working string on the stack, continue
        wkstr
} brd

% do a new page if we are below page bottom
/newpagetest {
        yis neg PH ge { NEWPAGE } if
} brd

%_____

% insert page label
/labelpage {
gsave
        -50 PH neg 10 sub translate 0 0 moveto
        PAGENFONT setfont
        (Page: ) show
        PAGECOUNT =string cvs show
        0 -15 moveto
        (imaging time in seconds: ) show
        /sut dup load
        usertime dup 3 1 roll exch sub
        1000 div =string cvs show def

        0 -30 moveto
        (vm used in bytes: ) show
        /svm dup load
        vmstatus pop exch pop dup 3 1 roll
        exch sub
        =string cvs show def
grestore
} brd

% frame current page
/pagebbox {
```

```
gsave
      0 0 moveto
      PW 0 rlineto
      0 PH neg rlineto
      PW neg 0 rlineto
      closepath
      .95 setgray fill
grestore
} brd


%_____
% PAGE SETUP ROUTINE

/SETPAGE {
      % initialize page count
      /PAGECOUNT 1 def
      % font for page numbers
      /PAGENFONT /Helvetica findfont 10 scalefont def
      % calculate column center for convenience in centering
      /CC PW 2 div def
      % reference copy of PW and left margin x-location in device space
      /REFPW PW def
      /REFPWX PW 0 transform pop def
      % set up the page at upper left
      LM PH BM add translate 0 0 moveto
      % preserve page space matrix for future page resets
      mtx currentmatrix pop
      % frame the page
      pagebbox
      % move down by value of leading
      0 LEADING neg moveto
      % initialize the buffer
      initbuff
      % force justify default is off
      /fj? false def
} brd
%_____


% REDEFINITION OF THE POSTSCRIPT
% "TYPE" FUNCTIONS
```

```
% print out integers as they are
/integertype { xpr } brd

% print reals truncated to number of places
% if variable "dplaces" is defined
/realtype {
      xs /wf x
      currentdict /DPLACES known
      {
            wf dot search
                  { length exch pop exch length
                  dup DPLACES gt
                        {
                        dup DPLACES sub sub add 1 add
                        wf 0 3 -1 roll getinterval
                        }
                        {
                        pop pop wf
                        }
                  ifelse
            } if
      } if
      bpr
} brd

% STRING TYPE: a kludge, but it works
/lpr (\() def
/rpr (\)) def
/stringtype {
      dup length 2 add dup string
      dup 0 lpr putinterval
      dup 3 -1 roll 1 sub rpr putinterval
      dup 1 4 -1 roll putinterval
      bpr
} brd

% IF IT'S A NAME TYPE: print it
% we check for the presence of the
% literal slash and print it if true
/nametype {
```

```
        dup xcheck not { fslash bpr } if  xpr
} brd


% IF IT'S AN ARRAY : TAKE ACTION
/arraytype { exec } brd
%_____


% tabbing must be preceded with a quad left!

% default tab width in points
/tabw 0 def

% set tab width
/tabset { /tabw x } brd

% default tab pointer
/tabp 0 def

% do a tab
/tab { /tabp dup load tabw add dup 0 rmoveto def } brd

% global reset from all tabs
/notabs { /PW REFPW def 0 yis moveto /tabp 0 def /tabw 0 def } brd

% turn off one tab at a time
/taboff { /tabp dup load tabw sub def tabp 0 rmoveto } brd


%_____
% BUFFER MANAGEMENT ROUTINES

% buffer string
/buffstr 400 string def

% initialize buffer
/initbuff {
        % nothing in buffer to begin with
        /buff? false def
        % line at beginning unless we've moved
        /at 0 def
        % start at first place in buffer
```

```
        /bpntr 0 def
        % no space seen so far
        /nspc 0 def
        % set buffstr to all spaces
        0 1 buffstr length 1 sub { buffstr exch asciispace put } for
} brd

% get text from buffer from #0 to supplied value
/getline { buffstr 0 bpntr 1 sub getinterval } brd

% put word into buffer
/putword {
        buffstr bpntr cw
        dup length 2 index add 1 add /bpntr x
        putinterval
} brd

% insert a string into buffer and update pointers
% add 1 so that a space is added by pointer movement
/insertbuff {
        % put word on stack into buffer
        putword
        % something in it now
        /buff? true def
        % one more space seen
        /nspc dup load 1 add def
        % add space width to 'at
        /at dup load cwl add CSW add def
} brd

% use this linebreak if we use both buffer and current word
/usecurrword { insertbuff ql  } def

% use this linebreak if we just use buffer
/usecurrline { ql insertbuff } def

% main buffer evaluation and print routine
/bpr {
        % get current word and its width
        sw /cwl x /cw x
```

```
        % define length of line with current word added
        /at1 at cwl add def

        % define an offset if we are doing full
        % or left justification based
        % on how far the currentpoint is on the x-axis
        /xoff 0 jstyle dup /FULL eq exch /LEFT eq or { xis add } if def

        % see if at + width > PW, taking into
        % account current x position if
        % justification is full or left.
        % forced justification must be off, too
        at1 xoff add PW gt fj? not and
                % true : test for linebreak
                { linebreak? }
                % false : update bufer
                { insertbuff }
        ifelse
} brd


/linebreak? {
        % calculate accurate current line width by subtracting space pad
        /at0 at CSW sub def

        % define two 'fit vectors
        /fit0 PW xoff sub at0 sub def
        /fit1 PW xoff sub at1 sub def
        jstyle /FULL ne  { usecurrline } { fullbreak } ifelse

} brd


/fullbreak {
% we have a current line and a current word.
% The signed difference between the line length and PW
% is in fit0 and fit1

% we want to break the line based on which is closer to PW
% and weight the decision in favor of using the current line (more "air")

% we have to be persuaded by strong evidence that we should
```

```
% contract the line (use current line and current word)

% we calculate change per space for testing and for later use

        % change per space: current line only
        /spc0 fit0 SP mul nspc 1 sub div def

        % change per space if: current line + current word
        /spc1 fit1 SP mul nspc div def

% simple test case: fit0 < absolute value of fit1
% we do the the current line without the current word

% if fit1 is smaller, we examine the ratio of the
% required contraction of a space to the actual
% width of a space: if more than 25% change is
% required, we won't use it

        fit0 fit1 abs le
                spc1 CSW div -.25 le
                or
                % define a flag for later use
                dup /fbrktype x
                { usecurrline } { usecurrword }
        ifelse
} brd



/showtype {
        % do a show only if we're in full justification
        % and we're not within .5 of PW and we are not force justifying

        jstyle /FULL ne fj? or PW xis sub at sub PW .5 mul le or
                {  jshow }
                { getline show }
        ifelse
} brd

% print the buffer contents and re-initialize
% test for lastline conditions and make linebreak decision
```

```
/printbuff {
      buff?
            {
            showtype
            initbuff
            }
      if
} brd


% final page cleanup
/endthepage {
      % added to handle case
      % where full justification is being done
      % and you come to the end of page with stuff in the buffer
      % that has not been justified or printed
      % we need to call linebreak? here if we are doing full justification
      jstyle /FULL eq { linebreak? } { printbuff } ifelse

      labelpage showpage
} brd


%_____
% JUSTIFICATION CONTROL

% define justification styles
      % leave show unmodified so user
      % can always force a normal show
      % without changing justification styles
      % note: this must be followed by a {ql}
      % or the column will be screwed up

% set percentage adjustments to
% space and non-space chars in full justification
/setfull { /SP x /NSP x } brd
% defaults for setfull
.2 .8 setfull

/fullshow {
      % if forced justification is on,
      % use current line, regardless
```

```
fj? {
        % calculate the fit required
        PW at1 sub xis sub
        % handle case of one word only
        nspc 1 sub dup 0 gt
                % there are some spaces to consider
                {
                        % divide the space fit by number of spaces
                        1 index SP mul 1 index div
                }
                % it's a single word to expand
                {
                        0
                } ifelse
        }
        {
        fbrktype
                { fit0 nspc 1 sub spc0 }
                { fit1 nspc spc1 }
        ifelse
        }
ifelse

/perspace x
/nspaces x
/fit x

/nonspaces bpntr 1 sub nspaces sub def

% each non-space changes by total fit less space fit
/pernonspace fit perspace nspaces mul sub nonspaces div def

% adjust each space character change by 'pernonspace
% factor to get proper space change
% only if there are spaces
perspace nspaces 0 ne { pernonspace sub } if 0 32

% every character adjust
pernonspace
% a kludge that works for doing one word only
```

```
        nspaces 0 eq { dup nonspaces 1 sub  div add } if
        0

        % show the adjusted current line
        getline awidthshow
} brd

/gshow { getline show } brd
/sw { dup stringwidth pop } brd
/rm0 { 0 rmoveto show } brd
/LEFT { gshow } brd
/RIGHT { getline sw neg rm0 } brd
/CENTER { getline sw -2 div rm0 } brd
/FULL /fullshow load def
/jshow { jstyle load exec } brd

% force justify line at next quad left
/fj { /fj? true def } brd

/just {
        % print and clear out buffer, as needed
        % using old value of 'jstyle
        buff? { ql } if

        % define new jstyle
        /jstyle x

        % when we change justification style
        % do a margin setup
        getxoff currentpoint exch pop moveto
}  brd

% QUAD LEFT ROUTINES
% when a quad left occurs:
% take action based on justification style
% we'll exploit the fact that the style names
% have different lengths and get an index
% into an array that has the right point to move to

% if we are writing to a buffer, and something is in the buffer,
```

```
% then we have to print the current line first

/getxoff { [ O PW CC ] jstyle length 4 sub get tabp add } brd

/ql {
        % have we just done a forced justify?
        % if so, reset fj
        printbuff
        fj? { /fj? false def } if
        getxoff yis LEADING sub moveto
        % test for needing to start a new page
        newpagetest
} brd


%_____
% FONT CHANGE PRIMITIVE
% find and scale a font by name
% keep track of current space width
/font { findfont exch scalefont setfont /CSW sp sw exch pop def } brd


%_____
% THE MAIN EVALUATION LOOP
/PostWord {
        {
                token
                        { dup type exec }
                        { endthepage exit }
                ifelse
        } loop
} brd


%_____
% START OF OUR TEXT STRING
(
% you can use comments and unlimited carriage returns or white
% space in your text string
% a comment line must be terminated with a carriage return

% you can define variables and functions inside or
% outside your text string
```

```
% set truncation of floating point numbers
% to two places after the decimal point
{ /DPLACES 2 def }

% create a function to return inches
{ /inch { 72 mul } def }

% set page width and height, left margin, bottom margin
{
/PH 5 inch def
/PW 4.5 inch def
/LM 2 inch def
/BM 1 inch def
}

% set initial leading
{ /LEADING 20 def }

% the page initialization procedure sets a currentpoint
{ SETPAGE }

% let's define a macro
{
     /hd#0 {
            % select and scale font
            24 /Times-Bold font
            % set new justification style and leading
            /FULL just
            /LEADING 22 def
     } def
}

% activate head, turn on forced justification
{ hd#0 fj }

Typesetting With PostWord{ ql }

% let's define a paragraph indent
% relative to the current leading value
{ /INDENT { LEADING 3 div 0 rmoveto } def }
```

```
% define paragraph start routines
% note that we need to do a quad left to
% flush the buffer if there's anything in it

{  /PARAl { /LEFT just ql  } def }

{ /PARAr { /RIGHT just ql } def }

{  /PARAc { /CENTER just ql } def }

{ /PARAf { /FULL just ql   } def }

% we can execute PostScript directly
% here we reduce the hd#0 font to .8
% of its current size, or 11.2 points
{ currentfont .8 scalefont setfont }
{ /LEFT just }
Set this line flush left.{ql}
{ /RIGHT just}
And this one flush right.{ql}
{ /CENTER just}
Put this one in the center.{ql}
{ /FULL just 12 /Times-Roman font /LEADING 14 def }
{16 /Times-Roman font}
{ PARAf} We switch to full justification, 16-point Times-Roman. It will
always break lines in favor of more air, only allowing the word spacing
to be condensed when the reduction is less than 25 percent of the default.
{ PARAf }Notice that we can print (stuff in parentheses) with no difficulty,
and are handling the numerals with aplomb: 44.837697.{ql}
{ PARAl }
One interesting feature is:
{PARAf fj 30 /Times-Roman font}
F O R C E
{PARAf fj 30 /Times-Roman font}
J U S T I F I C A T I O N
{PARAf}
{12 /Times-Roman font}
It will fit the line to the measure, whether it has to stretch it,
overprint letters, whatever.{ql}
)
```

```
%_____
% END OF THE TEXT STRING
```

```
PostWord
```

In our previous example we worked our way through a string whose only inhabitants were either numbers or a single escape character that triggered a *moveto* action. In PostWord, we want to recognize and act on the following:

1. PostScript-style comments: lines starting with % and ending with a carriage return. These will cause no action to be taken; just as in PostScript, they are for internal documentation

2. Any arbitrary sequence of direct PostScript commands. We'll execute them immediately as we find them

3. Any arbitrary sequence of commands defined inside other sequences within the text itself (macros). We'll execute these immediately

4. Commands or sequences defined external to the text block, but defined to allow the user to change justification style, etc. These are executed, too

5. A single soft escape character that will handle the printing of special characters, perhaps adding or subtracting space as needed. In other words, we want to be able to use this program without doing a remapping of the fonts we are using to handle the Macintosh encoding vector (see chapter 8 on font encoding)

6. Everything else will be treated as text to be printed in a current font and in a current justification style

For this example we will redefine the type-names returned by the *type* operator to handle type-specific actions we want to take. A very neat property of applying *token* to a string is that it will construct only number, name, and procedure objects. Example:

```
([1 2 3]) token pop              ({  1 2 3}) token pop

returns                          returns

[                                {1 2 3}
(1 2 3])                         ()
```

This example shows that when the *token* command is applied to an array object in a string, it returns the "[" object (its type is nametype). The example on the right, where a procedure object is in the string, returns a ready-to-execute procedure object. This is very convenient indeed, since it saves us writing a complex routine to print an array object. It also means we don't have to worry about defining such type-names as booleantype, etc. Let's take a look at the main loop, which is entered with the text object to be evaluated and printed on the stack:

```
% The main evaluation loop

/PostWord {
     {
          token
                { dup type exec }
                { finalpage exit }
          ifelse
     } loop
} bind readonly def
```

If we come to a procedure object, we can execute it immediately:

```
/arraytype /exec load def
```

Some short routines will handle number to string conversion:

```
/ourscratch 40 string def
/xs { ourscratch cvs } bind readonly def
/xpr { xs bpr } bind readonly def
```

An integer number can be simply converted to a string and shown:

```
/integertype { xpr } bind readonly def
```

If you look at the code for realtype that handles floating-point numbers, you'll see a routine that, based on the value of a variable named DPLACES, cuts off the printing of numbers after the decimal point, and you'll find some information about why we shouldn't use PostScript's undocumented scratch string =string. When token constructs a number object, the limits of the PostScript implementation will apply. Thus you may see round-off in the final printed number.

A commented line (begins with % and ends with carriage return) will be ignored by the operator, so you can put in any number of comments.

What we will print appears as nametype objects, and can be made into strings. If the nametype object doesn't have the executable attribute (returned by the function xcheck), then we know we are looking at a name that starts with a slash, a PostScript literal name, and we could take steps to process that, but that's getting very fancy.

SPECIAL CHARACTERS

The handling of special characters is done through recognizing a user-defined escape character and calling a procedure, specialchar. If the escape character alone has occurred, then a space is added to the current line position; else it is assumed that there is one other character after the escape character which is to be printed.

```
% If it's a name type, convert to string and
% check for escape character in 0th. position of converted name
% call routine to handle special char or just print it
/escape (·) def
/nametype {
        ourscratch cvs dup 0 1 getinterval escape eq
            { specialchar } { bpr }
        ifelse
} bind readonly def
```

Our dictionary of special characters uses the characters themselves as keys; their values are the Adobe codes that will print the right characters. For some of the codes we will also define them as procedures that will be used to handle the elimination of automatic spacing for each name object that is printed. Study this code a moment to make sure you understand it. For example, do you see how the character (") becomes a key in escapedict whose value is 170, and the number 170 becomes a key whose value is the procedure object { nextback }? This is object-oriented programming!

```
/escapedict dup 16 dict def load begin
        ([) 91 def
        (]) 93  def
        ({) 123  def
        (}) 125  def
```

```
(") 170 dup /nextback load def def
(") 186 dup /thisback load def def
(`) 96 dup /nextback load def  def
(´) 39 dup /thisback load def def
```
end

We can test to see if the character is known in escapedict, and if it is, we can do a *get* with the character itself to find the key. Note the call to codetochar, a standard fixture in handling text. Wouldn't it have been nice to have a built-in primitive to convert the code back to a string?

```
% utilities for character code to string conversion
/scratch1 1 string def
/codetochar { scratch1 dup 0 4 -1 roll put } bind readonly def

% enter with special character on stack
/handlechar {
        % is character known in escapedict ?
        % if so, get it, convert it, and send off for printing
        escapedict exch 2 copy known
                { get handlecode } { pop pop }
        ifelse
} bind readonly def
```

The procedure handlecode gets the code on the stack and looks to see if it's known in escapedict. If it is, the procedure object is executed. You can examine how the procedures work to make sure that a space is not inserted before or after the printing of the special character.

Take a moment and think about what we have just done: with a small number of lines of code and a few commands defined, we have a structure that will go through a supplied string systematically and allow embedding of comments, and execution of complex procedures of any length having either global or specific side-effects. Note that we may need a routine to tidy up when we are through in case we haven't printed out all our data cookies (we'll call it finalpage).

GOING TO TYPE

So now let's set some type! PostWord will have the following features:

1. A generic command to force a line break (quad left). You will call it like this: { ql }

2. Your choice of left, right, center, and full justification. Line spacing (leading) is controlled by a single global variable, LEADING.

    A force-justify command { fj } will override controls until the next { ql }. In full justification, this will force the line to fit the current page width. In other justification styles, this will allow the line to go outside the page boundaries.

    Text will be written to a buffer for all justification styles so that, even in left justification, we can always look for a best fit given a current line and a current word which may or may not be added to the line.

    There will be some fine tuning controls for full justification which are user-modifiable and which determine how much the spaces in a line are changed compared to how much non-spaces are changed. You can learn from this code (see fullshow) how to calculate values for *awidthshow* that isolate the effect of changing spaces from changing all characters' letterspacing. Justification can be changed by a command like: { /CENTER just }

3. The ability to print multiple pages, preserving the page setup for all pages.

4. A simple way to activate a font by passing in a font-name and a point size. Example:

```
{ 12 /Helvetica font }
```

5. A simple tabbing facility built-in with a command to set the tab width (*tabset*), to create a tab (*tab*), to undo a tab (*untab*), and to clear all tabs (*notabs*).

Of course, you'll have the ability to create your own macros, or put in any PostScript you like, to be executed. Here's an example of a running head macro defined in the text block itself:

```
% let's define a macro
{ /rh#0
    {
    % select and scale font
        24 /Times-Bold font
    % set new justification style and leading
```

```
                  /CENTER just
                  /LEADING 22 def
          } def
}
% activate it and print something
{ rh#0 }
GETTING CENTERED NOW !
{ ql }
{ /LEFT just }
{ currentfont .5 scalefont setfont }
Printing with left justification, what printers call right-rag.
{ ql }
```

Note the last command above: it takes the currentfont, 24-point Times Bold, and scales it to 12-point—in "pure" PostScript.

LINE WIDTH AND LINE BREAKS

Now we can focus on how, in general, we build up text in the buffer, decide when to break the lines, and how we calculate where to show the current line.

A routine initializes the buffer (initbuff) by setting a 400-character string to contain only spaces. This will save us the task of inserting a space each time we put a word in the buffer. A pointer (bpntr) is set to the beginning of the buffer, and another pointer (at) is set to where on the current page x-axis we are located. This is so that in full and left justification only we can maintain user-supplied tabbing or indentation.

As we read in each word, we test to see if the current x-axis position (in at) plus the stringwidth of the newly read word is greater than the width of the column (PW). If this is true, we know we have to do a linebreak. Else we can insert the current word into the buffer and update the buffer pointer (so it points to end of the current word plus a space) and keep going.

```
% main buffer evaluation and print routine
/bpr {
        % get current word and its width
        sw /cwl x /cw x

        % define length of line with current word added
```

```
/at1 at cwl add def

% define an offset if we are doing full or left justification based
% on how far the currentpoint is on the x-axis
/xoff 0 jstyle dup /FULL eq exch /LEFT eq or { xis add } if  def

% see if at + width > PW taking into account current x position if
% justification is full or left
% forced justification must be off, too
at1 xoff add PW gt  fj? not  and
        % true: test for linebreak
        { linebreak?  }
        % false: update bufer
        { insertbuff }
    ifelse
} brd
```

We measure the current line by taking its stringwidth less one space's stringwidth (since it's padded with one space):

```
% calculate accurate current line width by subtracting space pad
/at0 at CSW sub def
```

There are two options in breaking the line:

```
% use this linebreak if we use both buffer and current word
/usecurrword { insertbuff ql  } def
% use this linebreak if we just use buffer
/usecurrline  { ql insertbuff } def
```

LINE-BREAK DECISIONS

While exactly how to break a line, particularly in full justification, is a subject for a long monograph, we'll use a quick-and-dirty method. For each possible line, we calculate the net change involved in being justified to the target line length less any x-axis offset:

```
/fit0 PW xoff sub at0 sub def
/fit1 PW xoff sub at1 sub def
```

Except in full justification, we always use the current line so all printing falls inside the page bounding box; we have a special line-breaking routine for full justificaiton:

```
jstyle /FULL ne { usecurrline } { fullbreak } ifelse
```

In full justification, we are always biased toward using the current line and expanding it. We calculate change per space required by the two possible breaks. We will use the longer line only if the width of a space shrinks less than one-eighth of its own size. You can re-define the values of SP (must be between 0 and 1, and sum of SP and NSP must equal 1) and SPACESHRINK to create different full justification constraints.

```
/fullbreak {
    % change per space:  current line
    /spc0 fit0 SP mul nspc 1 sub div def

    % change per space if:  current line + current word
    /spc1 fit1 SP mul nspc div def

    fit0 fit1 abs le
        spc1 abs CSW div SPACESHRINK lt
        or
        % define a flag for later use
        dup /fbrktype x
        { usecurrline } { usecurrword }
    ifelse
} bind readonly def
```

Printing is done by a call to ql to initiate printing. To actually break the line, we get the line, trim a space off it, and call the jshow operator that handles justifying the line. We make double use of the jstyle variable: it keeps track of what the style is, and its contents (one of /RIGHT, /LEFT, /FULL, /CENTER) are procedure names that carry out the act of setting the line start.

To calculate how space and non-spaces change as we expand or contract the current line to fit the page width (PW) to achieve full justification requires some effort. The *awidthshow* operator lets us specify one change for all characters and another change for a specified character. We've already created all the variables we need to use in the fullbreak procedure, and we know which ones to use because we set a flag, fbrktype.

There is some complex business at the start of fullshow to handle the case where forced justification is in effect and the parameters of line width and fit and space adjustment must be calculated. In any event these parameters get defined:

```
/fit exch def
/nspaces x
```

We need to recalculate how much spaces and non-spaces must change:

```
% uncorrected space change factor
/perspace fit SP mul nspaces div def
```

```
% each non-space changes by:
/perchar fit NSP mul
      % divide by number of non-spaces
      bpntr 1 sub nspaces sub div
def
```

The problem now is that we can't isolate the effect of changing the non-space characters from the spaces. So we subtract the perchar change from the perspace change to get a corrected space change factor. Now we have our arguments for awidthshow, and can call it:

```
% use corrected space change factor
perspace perchar sub 0 32
% every character adjust
perchar 0
% show the adjusted current line
getline
awidthshow
```

PostWord can print pages with moderate density of commands at around thirty to forty-five seconds per page. This is not fast in the world of PostScript printing. On the other hand, we have incredible flexibility to turn PostWord into our own specialty text processing system by defining macros. These can be defined outside the text block itself to speed up processing time.

Obvious extensions to PostWord would include hyphenation and kerning, though we could do a form of kerning (loosely defined) by altering the page width and using forced justification. If we do that, we have to be careful to restore the old page width when done. By increasing the complexity of the main parsing loop, we could grab a line at a time by doing a search for a hard or soft carriage return; we could then examine the line for the presence of special characters and print it very quickly if there were no commands in it. But that's meat for a longer lesson than we have time for here.

If you've had the thought in reading this chapter that PostWord really constitutes another language implemented in POSTSCRIPT, you are right. The essence of POSTSCRIPT is its incredible extensibility, and any symbol system grafted onto it shares that extensibility.

16 / The Evolution of a Complex Geometric Logo

Tony Smith

In the early days (mid-1985), we all just wrote PostScript code that made interesting images appear on a printed page. Positive feedback at its best. But when one or two of those images started to be used more and more frequently, then we had to come to terms with some of the practical questions as to what makes the best PostScript.

This is the story of one such image, a geometric solid in which I had a long-standing interest and which was quickly adapted as the logo for PICA Pty Ltd, the new company that Joe Selvaggi and I had just set up to pursue some business interests relating to the Apple Macintosh. Unsatisfied with the traditional definition of regular Euclidian solids, which limited that class to the five with regular polygons for faces, and bored with its seemingly artificial extension into stellated variants, I had long before pursued extensions to the inversion relationship between the dodecahedron (twelve-faced) and the icosahedron (twenty-faced) to produce a highly symmetric solid with 120 congruent (albeit irregular) triangular faces. I have since discovered sketches suggestive of this figure in the works of R. Buckminster Fuller and others, but have still not seen any formal name applied to it in the literature. So it soon got to be referred to as simply the "picahedron" (see Figure 16.1).

It took a long weekend and suggestions from a couple of colleagues whose vector algebra was a little less rusty than mine to produce the first satisfactory image of a picahedron viewed and lit from points far away, with the viewing point restricted to an extension of one of the picahedron's axes of symmetry and with the lighting direction arbitrarily perpendicular to one of the faces in the upper right quadrant of the visible hemisphere. While I had originally used a Microsoft BASIC program to produce a wire frame image on screen, considering that the most interactive way of proving most of the logic needed to construct the image, it seemed only natural at the time to use the general-purpose

351

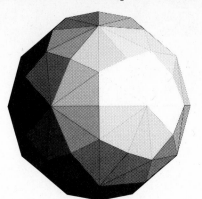

Figure 16.1. The results of
the early picahedron-
generating program.

programming capabilities of the PostScript language to compute the
apparent positions and illumination levels of the sixty visible faces in
preparation for printing the desired image.

Once we started using the original picahedron PostScript on every
letter and document produced by our growing company, it quickly
became obvious that it was too slow. The solution was to go back to
the original BASIC program and let it calculate the positions and gray
levels of the sixty triangles and output them as a very boring-looking
PostScript program consisting of many numbers computed to six decimal places and a short routine for actually imaging the triangles. While
it may not be pretty, the new picahedron PostScript program is an
order of magnitude faster, causing less delay in printing the first page
of a letter than usually comes from caching the letter's new font-style-
size combinations.

That discovery led us to a fundamental understanding as to how
calculations relating to an image to be printed should be shared between a PostScript-generating program and the PostScript it generates. And it is that understanding, rather than the idiosyncratic nature
of the picahedron image itself, which justifies the picahedron's place
as my most instructive PostScript project.

Since the speed-up, I have had two occasions to further generalize
the underlying programs. On the first occasion, I extracted the five
Euclidian solids plus the truncated dodecahedron/icosahedron whose
vertices are subsets of the vertices of the picahedron for scattering with
variable lighting as the background of a poster. On the second, the goal
was to freely rotate the picahedron and its derivative solids in three
dimensions to soften the harsh symmetry of the view used in our logo.

As both these extensions move a bit more of the computation back into the PostScript, they are used only when those special effects are really needed. In the meantime we have also taken the fast PostScript version and built a special logo font and, later, an EPS file so we could use the logo more easily with a wide range of Macintosh applications.

Overutilizing the Generality of PostScript

The Picahedron has 120 faces, 180 edges, and 62 vertices. While the faces are all the same size, there are three different edge lengths and three different types of vertex: thirty at the "quad" junctions of four faces which together appear to form a diamond; twenty at the "hex" junctions of six faces which appear to form a triangle; and twelve at the "dec" junctions of ten faces which appear to form a pentagon. The "hex" points correspond to the faces of an icosahedron or the vertices of its inverse dodecahedron, while the "dec" points correspond to the faces of that dodecahedron (and the vertices of the icosahedron).

These vertex positions were thus calculable from the geometry of the figure, and then utilized by the drawing routines for individual faces. The method of calculating the three-dimensional coordinates of the 62 vertices from geometric principles is beyond the scope of this article. The actual vertex coordinates for a picahedron centered at (0,0,0) in Euclidean space with unit external radius and symmetric orientation are enumerated by the first executable sections of the BASIC and PostScript programs shown (listings 1 and 2).

However, it proved impractical to try to enumerate these vertices in any kind of arrangement from which those that belonged to each face would be directly obvious. In fact, the quickest method of identifying the individual faces turned out to be working systematically through the quad junctions, for each of which the BASIC or PostScript program searches through the hex and the dec junctions looking for the two that are at the correct (minimum) three-dimensional edge distances from the diamond junction. Each such set of points found then directly identifies the four faces that make up the that particular diamond surrounding that quad junction.

Listing 1

```
% The original PostScript to generate the Picahedron logo
% Needs translate, scale, setlinewidth and setmiterlimit
```

```
% as desired
350 350 translate
50 50 scale
0.02 setlinewidth
2 setmiterlimit

/TripleSign {  % Reflect points on three axes of symmetry
    /s0 1 def /s1 1 def /s2 1 def
    7 {
        /s0 s0 neg def
        s0 0 gt {
            /s1 s1 neg def
            s1 0 gt {
                /s2 s2 neg def
            } if
        } if
        2 index s0 mul
        2 index s1 mul
        2 index s2 mul
        6 3 roll
    } repeat
} def

/DoubleSign % Reflect points on two axes of symmetry
    { /s0 1 def /s2 1 def
    3 { /s0 s0 neg def
        s0 0 gt
            { /s2 s2 neg def
        } if
        2 index s0 mul
        0
        2 index s2 mul
        6 3 roll
    } repeat
  } def

/CycPerm {      % Rotate points around two axes of symmetry
    { counttomark -3 roll
    1 index 1 index 4 index
    1 index 1 index 4 index
```

```
        } repeat
} def


/ShortSide {      % Store first or second adjacent point coordinates
      found 0 eq
            { 2 index /x1 exch def
            1 index /y1 exch def
            0 index /z1 exch def
            /found 1 def }

            { 2 index /x2 exch def
            1 index /y2 exch def
            0 index /z2 exch def }
      ifelse
} def


/LongSide {      % Store first or second adjacent point coordinates
      found 0 eq
            { 2 index /x3 exch def
            1 index /y3 exch def
            0 index /z3 exch def
            /found 1 def }

            { 2 index /x4 exch def
            1 index /y4 exch def
            0 index /z4 exch def }
      ifelse
} def


/Orthog {      % Determine vector perpendicular to face
      /xa x0 xi sub def /xb x0 xj sub def
      /ya y0 yi sub def /yb y0 yj sub def
      /za z0 zi sub def /zb z0 zj sub def
      /xp ya zb mul za yb mul sub def
      /yp za xb mul xa zb mul sub def
      /zp xa yb mul ya xb mul sub def
      zp 0 lt {/xp xp neg def /yp yp neg def /zp zp neg def} if
} def


/Triangle % Determine light level of and draw forward facing face
```

```
{ /zj exch def /yj exch def /xj exch def
/zi exch def /yi exch def /xi exch def
z0 zi zj add add 0 ge
        { Orthog
        /xs xp pn div def /ys yp pn div def /zs zp pn div def
        x0 y0 moveto xi yi lineto xj yj lineto closepath
        /angcos xr xs mul yr ys mul zr zs mul add add def
        angcos
        dup 0 lt {pop 0} if
        dup gsave setgray fill grestore
        2 exp setgray stroke
        } if
} def


% Calculate the basic coordinate values
/low 0.0001 def
5 sqrt 1 sub 2 div dup
/a exch 1 atan def
/b exch 2 exp 1 atan def
/alth a 2 div sin 2 mul 2 exp def
/blth b 2 div sin 2 mul 2 exp def
/s a sin def /c a cos def
/q 5 5 sqrt sub 8 div sqrt def
/r 1 3 div sqrt def


% Determine arbitrary lighting direction
/x0 r def /y0 r def /z0 r def
/xi s def /yi 0 def /zi c def
/xj q s mul def /yj q c mul def /zj q s c add mul def
Orthog
/pn xp 2 exp yp 2 exp zp 2 exp add add sqrt def
/xr xp pn div def /yr yp pn div def /zr zp pn div def


% Build up tables of points by reflection and rotation
[0 0 1 0 0 -1
q s mul q c mul q s c add mul
TripleSign
10 CycPerm]
/quadpts exch def
[r r r
```

```
TripleSign
[b cos 0 b sin
DoubleSign
4 CycPerm
] aload pop]
/hexpts exch def
[s 0 c
DoubleSign
4 CycPerm]
/decpts exch def

% For each 'quad' point calculate and print its four triangles
quadpts aload pop
30 {
        /z0 exch def /y0 exch def /x0 exch def
        hexpts aload pop
        /found 0 def
        20 {
                2 index x0 sub 2 exp
                2 index y0 sub 2 exp
                2 index z0 sub 2 exp
                add add blth sub abs low lt {ShortSide} if
                pop pop pop
        } repeat
        decpts aload pop
        /found 0 def
        12 {
                2 index x0 sub 2 exp
                2 index y0 sub 2 exp
                2 index z0 sub 2 exp
                add add alth sub abs low lt {LongSide} if
                pop pop pop
        } repeat
        x1 y1 z1 x3 y3 z3 Triangle
        x3 y3 z3 x2 y2 z2 Triangle
        x2 y2 z2 x4 y4 z4 Triangle
        x4 y4 z4 x1 y1 z1 Triangle
} repeat
```

One of the major controversies in the study of evolution, be it the evolution of organisms or of ideas, is whether evolution occurs gradually or in bursts. The development of computer programs is often considered to be a contemporary model of evolutionary processes, and the evolution of the Picahedron program certainly shows a few major bursts, with intervening periods containing just a few minor adaptations.

The version shown in Listing 1 actually predates use of the picahedron as a logo, and the first minor adaptations that were made provided parameterization of position and the introduction of some very device-dependent screen functions that improved the differentiation between the many grays of the logo, first for the LaserWriter with its large single dot size problem, and later for the dataproducts LZR-2665 with the very different performance of its write-white mechanism.

Achieving Practical Efficiency

Eventually our use of the picahedron spread from occasional advertisements to regular correspondence and even whole sheets to be cut up into business cards. The lengthy print times became more and more unacceptable. It was obvious that the uncomfortably long print times were due almost entirely to that fact that all of the PostScript had to be interpreted every time the logo was printed. Rather than just constructing the image, the interpreter had to recalculate the positions and lighting levels of the faces every time. And when it seemed to take not a lot longer to image an 11.7-inch diameter version on a Linotronic than to image a logo-sized version on a LaserWriter, some kind of reevaluation could no longer be avoided.

So I went back to the original Microsoft BASIC program that I had used to draw a wire frame version of the picahedron on a Macintosh screen and added a bit of extra code to calculate the lighting level of the faces and to store those coordinates and intensities in a text file. This file could then be incorporated in a much simplified PostScript program. Whereas I originally had to rewrite my wire frame code from BASIC to PostScript, this time I had to start with the calculation of vectors perpendicular (orthogonal) to the three-dimensional picahedron faces. From them I derived the lighting intensities of each face in the PostScript in which it had been developed, and turned it all back into BASIC programming code.

As can be seen from a comparison of the original (calculating) PostScript program (Listing 1) and the early (PostScript-generating) BASIC program (Listing 2), fundamentally the same calculations are carried out either way. The differing fundamental syntax, data structuring, and subroutine/function forms of the two languages, however, lead to very different general appearances.

From before the time that I revised the BASIC program until very recently, all our PostScript development work was done in JustText, and so it was only necessary to take the numerical results from the BASIC program and attach them to the PostScript Triangle and PicaLogo routines using JustText's text editor, then save it as a PostScript file suitable for inclusion in other documents by JustText's PostScript file *include* command. However, it was only a simple step to aesthetically complete the BASIC program by having it output the Triangle and PicaLogo routines automatically, producing a complete PostScript file in a single pass. An early version of such a program is shown in Listing 2.

Needless to say, the fact that we were using JustText for all our document production in that era had considerable influence on how this task was tackled. Also, the ability of JustText to edit any text file—including Microsoft BASIC program code—made it easy to get proven PostScript back into a BASIC program, which could then reliably generate the same PostScript.

Listing 2

```
REM: An early Basic program to generate complete Picahedron PostScript

DIM a(61,2),x(29,3),t(59,6),s(59)

REM: Calculate the basic coordinate values
low=.000001
z=(SQR(5)-1)/2:a=ATN(z):b=ATN(z^2)
e=(2*SIN(a/2))^2:f=(2*SIN(b/2))^2
s=SIN(a):c=COS(a):q=SQR((5-SQR(5))/8)
r=SQR(1/3)

REM: Determine arbitrary lighting direction
xa=r-s:xb=r-q*s 'Determine vector perpendicular to face
ya=r-0:yb=r-q*c
za=r-c:zb=r-q*(s+c)
xr=ya*zb-za*yb
```

```
yr=za*xb-xa*zb
zr=xa*yb-ya*xb
IF zr<0 THEN xr=-xr:yr=-yr:zr=-zr
pn2=xr^2+yr^2+zr^2


REM: Build up tables of points by reflection and rotation
a(0,2)=1:a(3,2)=-1
a(6,0)=q*s:a(6,1)=q*c:a(6,2)=q*(s+c)
s0=1:s1=1:s2=1 'Reflect points on three axes of symmetry
FOR i=9 TO 29 STEP 3
     s2=-s2:IF s2>0 THEN s1=-s1:IF s1>0 THEN s0=-s0
     a(i,0)=s0*a(6,0):a(i,1)=s1*a(6,1):a(i,2)=s2*a(6,2)
NEXT i
FOR i=0 TO 29 STEP 3 'Rotate points around two axes of symmetry
     a(i+1,0)=a(i,1):a(i+1,1)=a(i,2):a(i+1,2)=a(i,0)
     a(i+2,0)=a(i,2):a(i+2,1)=a(i,0):a(i+2,2)=a(i,1)
NEXT i
a(30,0)=r:a(30,1)=r:a(30,2)=r
s0=-1:s1=-1:s2=-1 'Reflect points on three axes of symmetry
FOR i=30 TO 37
     s2=-s2:IF s2>0 THEN s1=-s1:IF s1>0 THEN s0=-s0
     a(i,0)=s0*a(30,0):a(i,1)=s1*a(30,1):a(i,2)=s2*a(30,2)
NEXT i
a(38,0)=COS(b):a(38,2)=SIN(b)
a(50,0)=s:a(50,2)=c
s0=-1:s2=-1:i0=38 'Reflect points on and rotate points around two axes
FOR i=38 TO 61 STEP 3
     IF i>49 THEN i0=50
     s2=-s2:IF s2>0 THEN s0=-s0
     a(i,0)=s0*a(i0,0):a(i,2)=s2*a(i0,2)
     a(i+1,1)=a(i,2):a(i+1,2)=a(i,0)
     a(i+2,0)=a(i,2):a(i+2,1)=a(i,0)
NEXT i


REM: For each 'quad' point calculate and print its four triangles
FOR i=0 TO 29
     FOR j=30 TO 49 'Store first or second adjacent point coordinates
          d=(a(i,0)-a(j,0))^2+(a(i,1)-a(j,1))^2+(a(i,2)-a(j,2))^2
               IF ABS(d-f)<low THEN IF x(i,0)=0 THEN x(i,0)=j ELSE x(i,1)=j
          NEXT j
```

```
    FOR j=50 TO 61 'Store first or second adjacent point coordinates
        d=(a(i,0)-a(j,0))^2+(a(i,1)-a(j,1))^2+(a(i,2)-a(j,2))^2
            IF ABS(d-e)<low THEN IF x(i,2)=0 THEN x(i,2)=j ELSE x(i,3)=j
    NEXT j
    p=x(i,0):q=x(i,1):r=x(i,2):s=x(i,3)
    g=i:h=p:GOSUB L:h=q:GOSUB L:h=r:GOSUB L:h=s:GOSUB L
    g=p:h=r:GOSUB L:h=s:GOSUB L:g=q:h=r:GOSUB L:h=s:GOSUB L
    u=i:v=p:w=r:GOSUB T:w=s:GOSUB T:v=q:GOSUB T:w=r:GOSUB T
NEXT i

REM: Produce PostScript file of definitions and data
OPEN FILES$(0,"PS of Logo") FOR OUTPUT AS #1
PRINT #1,"%!PS-Adobe-1.0"
PRINT #1,"/Triangle"
PRINT #1,"  { /angcos exch def"
PRINT #1,"    moveto lineto lineto closepath"
PRINT #1,"    angcos 0 lt {/angcos 0 def} if"
PRINT #1,"    angcos setgray"
PRINT #1,"    gsave fill grestore"
PRINT #1,"    angcos 2 exp setgray"
PRINT #1,"    stroke"
PRINT #1,"  } def"
PRINT #1,""
PRINT #1,"/PicaLogo"
PRINT #1,"  { gsave"
PRINT #1,"    /diam exch def"
PRINT #1,"    translate"
PRINT #1,"    diam dup scale"
PRINT #1,"    0.4 diam div setlinewidth"
PRINT #1,"    2 setmiterlimit"
PRINT #1,"    currentscreen 3 2 roll pop 60 3 1 roll setscreen"
PRINT #1,""

FOR i=0 TO t-1:s(i)=i:NEXT i
FOR i=0 TO t-1
    l=s(t-1)
    FOR j=t-2 TO i STEP -1
        IF t(l,6)<t(s(j),6) THEN s(j+1)=s(j) ELSE s(j+1)=l:l=s(j)
    NEXT j
    s(i)=l
```

```
      PRINT #1,USING "###.######";t(1,0);t(1,1);t(1,2);t(1,3);t(1,4);t(1,5);t(1,6)
NEXT i

PRINT #1,""
PRINT #1,"    60 {Triangle} repeat"
PRINT #1,"    grestore"
PRINT #1,"  } def"
PRINT #1,""
PRINT #1,"315 378 180 PicaLogo"
PRINT #1,"showpage"
CLOSE #1
END


L: 'Display wire wrap version on screen
x0=140+120*a(g,0):y0=140+120*a(g,1)
x1=140+120*a(h,0):y1=140+120*a(h,1)
LINE (x0,y0)-(x1,y1)
RETURN


T: 'Determine light level of forward facing face
IF a(u,2)+a(v,2)+a(w,2)<0 THEN RETURN
t(t,0)=a(u,0):t(t,1)=a(u,1)
t(t,2)=a(v,0):t(t,3)=a(v,1)
t(t,4)=a(w,0):t(t,5)=a(w,1)
xa=a(u,0)-a(v,0):xb=a(u,0)-a(w,0) 'Determine vector perpendicular to face
ya=a(u,1)-a(v,1):yb=a(u,1)-a(w,1)
za=a(u,2)-a(v,2):zb=a(u,2)-a(w,2)
xp=ya*zb-za*yb
yp=za*xb-xa*zb
zp=xa*yb-ya*xb
IF zp<0 THEN xp=-xp:yp=-yp:zp=-zp
t(t,6)=(xr*xp+yr*yp+zr*zp)/pn2
t=t+1
RETURN
```

You can see the POSTSCRIPT output from this BASIC program in
Listing 3. This time the very advent of automatic POSTSCRIPT code
generation enabled us to make another small adaptation. On early
versions of the logo the order of drawing faces was totally arbitrary
and, because the logo looks better with very thin edges that are slightly

darker than the adjacent faces, there was no control over which of the two drawings of an edge occurred most recently. The overall result, while much better than no edges at all, left some unevenness in that area.

With all the overhead calculations being done once and once only by a BASIC program, however, it was practical to add the one option that had always been considered just too extravagant even to try to run in POSTSCRIPT—the sorting of the faces in order from darkest to lightest, so that edge color would always be dependent on the lighter of two adjacent faces (see Figure 16.2). While this resulted in a significantly smoother appearance for the logo, that method of improvement is not compatible with the later evolutionary leaps into generalized lighting directions, derivative solids, and free rotation.

Listing 3

```
%!PS-Adobe-1.0
%%Title: PICA Pty Ltd Logo
%%Creator: Tony Smith et al
%%RevisionDate: 27 April 1986
/LogoDict 99 dict def
LogoDict begin


/Faces [
    [  0.000000   0.000000   0.000000   0.356822   0.525731   0.000000 ]
.

.     % More faces here
```

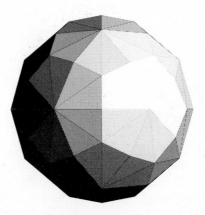

Figure 16.2. The results of the later picahedron-generating program.

```
    [  0.500000   0.809017   0.577350   0.577350   0.000000   0.850651  ]
    [  0.500000   0.809017   0.577350   0.577350   0.850651   0.525731  ]
.
.
    % More faces here
.
.
    [ -0.309017 -0.500000   0.000000 -0.356822   0.000000 -0.850651  ]
] def

/Triangle {
    /angcos exch def
    /face.ix exch def
    Faces face.ix get aload pop
    moveto lineto lineto closepath
    angcos 0 lt {/angcos 0 def} if
    angcos setgray
    gsave fill grestore
    angcos dup mul setgray
    stroke
} def
end

/PicaLogo {
    LogoDict begin
    gsave
        /diam exch def
        translate
        diam dup scale
        0.4 diam div setlinewidth
        2 setmiterlimit

        % Sorted table of lighting levels with index to faces
        42 -0.588291
        11 -0.488748
        54 -0.467349
        41 -0.380101
        53 -0.373321
        10 -0.321989
        31 -0.290183
        9 -0.187822
```

43	-0.187258
38	-0.110769
28	-0.020932
37	-0.010874
8	0.010874
40	0.020932
55	0.042331
27	0.042331
56	0.052738
30	0.052738
52	0.136359
26	0.136359
57	0.161385
29	0.321989
45	0.353447
24	0.373321
59	0.380101
33	0.393327
39	0.393327
34	0.399195
5	0.399195
25	0.467348
58	0.488748
49	0.493222
36	0.493222
44	0.514621
2	0.514621
7	0.588291
50	0.597890
4	0.597890
18	0.613881
46	0.613881
19	0.622916
1	0.622916
6	0.755050
47	0.775055
22	0.775055
14	0.794149
32	0.807938
35	0.813806

```
                      48   0.813806
                       3   0.820586
                      17   0.836576
                      21   0.845611
                      16   0.845611
                      13   0.855211
                      51   0.918474
                      23   0.928880
                       0   0.928880
                      15   0.938938
                      20   0.999436
                      12   1.000000

                      60  {Triangle} repeat
             grestore
             end
   } def
```

Implications for the Document Structuring Conventions

Conventional wisdom states that PostScript is almost always to be automatically generated by a printer driver–like function of application programs written in other languages. Direct PostScript programming, by this wisdom, is really only useful for developing graphic effects that can eventually be called up via a naturalistic interface. As such, the Picahedron PostScript shown in Listing 3 certainly qualifies. It also complies with Adobe's PostScript Document Structuring Conventions; it is suitable for inclusion in document prologues or even procedure sets, activated by the execution a simple x y r PicaLogo sequence in a document script.

However, it seems to me that strict differentiation into prologue and script seriously weakens the potential of PostScript to be used for the generation of desirable artistic effects. The Document Structuring Conventions assert that a given application (or driver such as Laser Prep) will use a prologue that is an appropriate set of procedure definitions, while individual documents produced by such an application are made up of calls to those procedures. This leaves no scope for an individual document to create its own procedures used only within that document, even though that is the normal method of operation for the people who work directly with POSTSCRIPT to discover new visual effects.

Incidentally, it must be understood that the use of a BASIC program to generate POSTSCRIPT bears no relation to the Document Structuring Conventions' concept of an application producing a standard prologue. In contrast, a complying application might simply copy the prologue from an associated resource file and interactively determine, say, the position and size of one or more renditions of the logo to produce a script consisting only of those calls. The individual "document" would be a list of positions and sizes. I actually did something like that with a promotional poster, which scattered celestial fields of picahedrons and derivative solids (see below). The script consisted almost entirely of position and size entries for selected polyhedra.

This issue came to a head as a result of discussions on Jim Von Ehr's early ideas for his Masterpiece program (which ultimately formed the basis of Aldus's FreeHand). Jim suggested that he would provide a drawing platform for an open-ended library of special effects developed by others, and I had a look at the kind of facilities that would be needed (3D rotation controls, etc.) to enable my polyhedra to be included in such a library. The kind of growth that such a library would produce would quickly make impractical the retention of all such procedures in a constant application prologue. (It is an interesting aside that it was Jim who originally conceived the need for an encapsulated POSTSCRIPT file format, which necessarily complies fully with the Document Structuring Conventions.)

An even more general problem comes up with the repetitive use of (possibly transformed) complex compound objects. A POSTSCRIPT programmer instinctively creates the code for a generalized version of such an object, defines it as a procedure, then calls that procedure repeatedly. While Adobe Illustrator's method of repeating the individual objects without any generality may interpret slightly faster than the much more compact form that can be produced by hand, the large size of files can run into printer limitations. The experimental POSTSCRIPT and Plastic $10 banknote produced to commemorate Australia's bicentenary ran into serious capacity problems on a Linotronic 300 partially because it enumerated every line, even when there was a substantial amount of repetition and regular variation.

Getting the PostScript into wysiwyg Applications

As the desktop publishing revolution started to roll, we were increasingly faced with requirements to put other people's logos in a form suitable for use by MacDraw, MacWrite, and other wysiwyg applications. Fortunately Altsys's Fontographer proved a suitable tool for creating logo fonts, which often contained only a single character, representing the logo with a single key stroke. As Fontographer provides an option to save the raw PostScript (without font structures) of characters and logos, it was a simple matter to generate PostScript files suitable for use by JustText documents.

It was not until tackling the rampant lion logo (Figure 16.3) of our local (Australian Rules) football club that we ran into a device-dependent limitation that forced us to look inside the Fontographer-generated PostScript and develop a comprehensive understanding of PostScript's font mechanism. On that occasion, stack capacity limits forced us to break the lion image up into half a dozen procedures. We formed the complete image by executing those procedures in turn.

However, the various grays of the picahedron demanded that we further break down Fontographer's encoding method and build the Pica Logo font almost from scratch. The one thing that had to be retained was Fontographer's link between the Macintosh screen font and the printer font, which involved naming and other conventions that are beyond the scope of this chapter. One simple rule of thumb was to scan in a previously printed version of the logo and do a sufficiently good job with Fontographer to provide an adequate screen representation, then open up the printer font so constructed in JustText

Figure 16.3. This image had to be split up into several separate paths in order to print without exceeding PostScript points-per-path limitation.

and replace most of Fontographer's PostScript with the code I have shown above for the picahedron logo.

As PostScript's font caching mechanism cannot be used with variable gray levels, that had to be turned off. This avoided any concern about choking the printer with the misleadingly large size we used for most logo characters (enabling the preset font sizes of MacWrite and MacDraw to give useful sized logo images). Amusingly, Apple Laser Prep's default method for italicizing printer fonts has enabled us to produce "italic" versions of the picahedron and other logos.

Then along came EPSF support embodied in the new generation of PostScript-exploiting drawing and page layout applications. Quickly it made our logo work virtually redundant, although the lessons learn earlier again proved useful—at least as something to be improved upon. Now instead of using a rough approximation of the logo for our screen image, we have chosen a black circle of correct size, with cross hairs for accurate positioning, and some instructions displayed in reverse type across the black circle so it can be used by an expanding staff with various skill levels.

We used Adobe Illustrator to create that screen "representation" and a raw EPS file, and again we used JustText to replace most of the PostScript, including the Illustrator prologue but excluding the essential EPSF document structuring comments. To maintain the link between the EPSF text and its associated PICT resource, it was easiest just to remember always to *save* changes and never *save as*.

But Illustrator can also be used to start with "complying" PostScript only and produce its own very accurate PICT representation for saving as Macintosh EPSF. Having pre-dated Illustrator by a long way, our Picahedron PostScript certainly does not comply. However, we have several methods open to us for producing complying code.

Of course we could go back to the BASIC program which generated our original PostScript and modify it to generate Illustrator format. But JustText's Feedback window also offered an unexpectedly simple alternative. It was just a matter of taking the Picahedron PostScript and replacing the Triangle routine, which outputs triangle images to the printer, with an alternate version, which sends Illustrator format PostScript text to the default output "file." You can see the new version in Listing 4. The output goes straight into the JustText Feedback window, where it can be further edited and merged into an empty Illustrator document.

Listing 4

```
% Variation to PICA Logo program to generate Illustrator format data

/Triangle {
      /angcos exch def
      /face.ix exch def
      angcos 0 lt {/angcos 0 def} if
      angcos dup mul = (G\n) print % stroke
      angcos = (g\n) print % fill
      Faces face.ix get aload pop 5 index 5 index
      xyr transform exch = = (m\n) print % moveto
      3 {xyr transform exch = = (l\n) print} repeat % lineto
      (b\n) print
} def
end

/PicaLogo {
      LogoDict begin
      /r exch def
      /y exch def
      /x exch def
      /xyr [r 0 0 r x y] def
      (u\n) print % group all faces in one object
      (0.4 w\n) print % linewidth
      (2 M\n) print % miterlimit
      (0 i\n) print
      (0 J\n) print
      (0 j\n) print
      ([]0 d\n) print % dash

% Sorted table of lighting levels with index to faces (see Listing 3.)

      60 {Triangle} repeat
      (U\n) print % ungroup
      end
} def

297 -297 144 PicaLogo
```

The complete Illustrator-format PostScript document can then be opened by Illustrator itself, then saved as Macintosh EPSF. Using ResEdit, the PICT part of the Macintosh EPSF file can be copied to the Clipboard or Scrapbook for subsequent pasting into any PICT-supporting Macintosh program.

Generalization, or Who Needs 3-D PostScript?

Because the picahedron vertices contain the vertices for several other regular and semi-regular solids, when we wanted to do a poster design to demonstrate the larger paper size capabilities of the dataproducts LZR-2665, we finally found an excuse to extend our BASIC program to identify the faces of those various solids.

Basic geometry shows that the dec points form the vertices of an icosahedron, the hex points a dodecahedron, and the quad points a truncated figure intermediate between those two. What is less obvious is that the quad points also form the vertices of five octahedra and the hex points the vertices of five cubes. In the latter case, each of the twenty hex points belongs to two different cubes. Students of solid geometry may already have noted that the vertices of any cube are also the vertices of two regular tetrahedra.

The procedure for identifying which vertices actually define faces of the various solids again started with finding those pairs of vertices that were the correct distance apart to be edges. But from there it got a bit harder. For the triangular faces, it was a case of finding sets of three points in which all three pairs therof were the correct length. For the square and pentagonal faces of some of the solids, it was necessary to add a coplanar test for potential candidates for the fourth and fifth sides. Fortunately the mathematics for coplanar testing is closely related to that for determining lighting intensity, so some of the hard work had already been done.

We actually used another BASIC program to simulate the semi-random placement of clusters of those solids in space. That program generated parts of the poster script, consisting of a series of calls to a more generalized solid drawing function in the poster prologue, including allowing 90-degree rotation of a random selection of the solids.

To demonstrate the then-exceptional blackness of the LZR-2665 output, the poster comprised lighter gray solids on a black background. However, the obvious wish to print long runs of the poster, with its twenty-minute imaging time on this fifteen-page-per-minute printer quickly showed up one other limitation: the toner flow rate was insufficient to maintain a black image for much more than five copies at a time.

Ever since POSTSCRIPT first appeared, there has been a conventional wisdom that its two-dimensional imaging model would eventually have to be superceded by a three-dimensional one. Therefore, we kept working with these images of solids in the one highly symmetric orientation for which we felt comfortable with the mathematics. But now with all these classical geometric figures computed in a form from which they could easily be rendered, and with ever-increasing comfort with POSTSCRIPT's coordinate transformation system, I started to get the feeling that 3-D might not be so hard after all.

So I sat down and had a go. The first step was obviously to simplify the vertex-positioning and face-selecting BASIC program so that it no longer ignored the previously hidden points on the back side of the picahedron, because arbitrary rotation would usually shift some of them to the visible hemisphere. I also had to output all three spatial coordinates of each vertex as POSTSCRIPT.

Doing 3-D rotations turned out to be simply a matter of doing 2-D rotations in each of the orthogonal coordinate planes of 3-D space. To render a solid it was thus necessary only to do a 3-D rotation on the solid's orthogonal vector to test whether it was forward facing, and if it was, to do 3-D rotations on each of its vertices in turn while constructing a path around the face. The POSTSCRIPT code in Listing 5 does all that for each face, and also determines its lighting level.

Listing 5

```
% 3-D rotation and its calling routine for Picahedron and derivatives

% x y z TurnXYZ x' y' z'
% This routine rotates the supplied 3-D coordinates by ax degrees
% around the x axis, ay around the y, and az around the z.
/TurnXYZ {
        ax matrix rotate transform 3 -1 roll
        ay matrix rotate transform 3 -1 roll
        az matrix rotate transform 3 -1 roll
} def


% DrawFace is called for each forward-facing face of a particular solid.
```

```
% The "face" array contains the orthogonal vector to the face and the
% indexes into the Vertex array of the vertices which define that face.
% px py pz is the lighting vector, psize and size are the pre-calculated
% squares of the lengths of the lighting and face-orthogonal vectors.
/DrawFace {
Vertex face 3 get get aload pop TurnXYZ pop moveto
     4 1 face length 1 sub {
          Vertex face 3 -1 roll get get aload pop TurnXYZ pop lineto
     } for
     closepath
     /angcos
          x px mul y py mul z pz mul add add size psize mul sqrt div
     def
     angcos
     dup 0 lt {pop 0} if
     dup gsave setgray fill grestore
     2 exp setgray stroke
     /n n 1 add def
} def


% FindFace is called for each face of a particular solid.
/FindFace {
     /face exch def
     face 0 get face 1 get face 2 get TurnXYZ
     /z exch def /y exch def /x exch def
     z lim gt { DrawFace } if
} def
```

I certainly do not consider that the story should finish there. We are currently working under Sun's NeWS, with multi-colored lighting from multiple light sources. It will not take much more work to calculate the vertices of the solid that is the inverse of the picahedron, and from that the truncated cube-octahedron and possibly other solids. Further down the track we might even get into stellation, whereby each face of a solid becomes the base of a pyramid. The ultimate objective is the incorporation of these solids in an interactive drawing tool in such a way that it might even be possible to break them apart as well as varying parameters such as size, rotation, lighting, and stellation.

Index

Colophon

Lance Hildy created the cover design for *Real World PostScript*, using Adobe Illustrator 88 on a Macintosh II with a 19-inch SuperMac Trinitron Display. Color proofs and film and other assistance were provided by Typesetting Service Corporation of Providence, Rhode Island.

The contributing authors created text art in PostScript and generated the art as positives on laser printers and Linotronic 300 equipment. Film for four-color separations and halftone negatives were produced on the L300.

Following design specifications by David Ford, the book was composed using typefaces in the Trump family. The authors provided manuscript for text and program listings in Microsoft Word in Macintosh format. The disks were sent to Impressions, Inc., of Madison, Wisconsin, where they were read into an MS-DOS Wyse with Xchange conversion software. The data was then read to a Penta MV7800 front end system where it was composed and paginated. The text was set direct to pages, with space left for art, on an Autologic APS μ5. Text and art were then combined traditionally with manual pasteup.

Real World PostScript was printed on 50-pound Amherst stock by The Alpine Press. The four-color insert and cover were printed by New England Book Components. The book was bound at The Alpine Press.

Disk to Accompany

Real World PostScript®

Edited by Stephen F. Roth

The programs listed on *Real World POSTSCRIPT* are available on one 3¹/₂" Macintosh® disk or one 5¹/₄" IBM® PC disk.

Equipment you will need:

Hardware: Macintosh 512K enhanced, Macintosh Plus, Macintosh SE, or Macintosh II; 2 disk drives or one disk drive and a hard disk;

     IBM Personal Computer, or 100% IBM PC compatible; at least 256K, DOS 2.0 or higher.

Available by mail only. Use the postage-paid card below.

Please send the following disk(s) to accompany *Real World POSTSCRIPT*, edited by Stepen F. Roth, at $19.95 each.

Quantity: _____Macintosh version   _____IBM version
      (3 ¹/₂" disk)   (5 ¹/₄" disk)
      ISBN 0-201-19638-7   ISBN 0-201-19636-0

_____Check enclosed (include your state sales tax; Addison-Wesley will pay postage and handling)

_____Charge to my Visa card #_____Exp. date:_____

_____Charge to my MasterCard #_____Exp. date:_____
            Four digits above your name:_____

_____Charge to my American Express #_____Exp. date:_____

YOUR SIGNATURE:_____

Name:_____ Title:_____

Company (if applicable):_____

Address:_____

City:_____ State:_____ Zip:_____

BUSINESS REPLY CARD
FIRST CLASS   PERMIT NO. 11   READING, MA.

Postage Will Be Paid By Addressee

ADDISON-WESLEY
PUBLISHING COMPANY, INC.
Order Department
Reading, Massachusetts U.S.A. 01867-9984